Shaping Texts: From Essay and Narrative to Memoir

Lucy Calkins and Alexandra Marron

Photography by Peter Cunningham

HEINEMANN ◆ Portsmouth, NH

This book is dedicated to Dad, my greatest advisor, for believing in me all along.
—*Ali*

This book is dedicated to my father, Evan Calkins, with thanks for finding among family papers 24 book-length memoirs dating back to 1800 and for editing and celebrating these in ways that help us see the storyline that binds together generations. —*Lucy*

DEDICATED TO TEACHERS™

firsthand
An imprint of Heinemann
361 Hanover Street
Portsmouth, NH 03801–3912
www.heinemann.com

Offices and agents throughout the world

© 2013 by Lucy Calkins and Alexandra Marron

All rights reserved. No part of this book may be reproduced in any form or by any electronic or mechanical means, including information storage and retrieval systems, without permission in writing from the publisher, except by a reviewer, who may quote brief passages in a review, with the exception of reproducible pages, which are identified by the *Units of Study in Opinion, Information, and Narrative Writing* copyright line and can be photocopied for classroom use only.

"Dedicated to Teachers" is a trademark of Greenwood Publishing Group, Inc.

The authors and publisher wish to thank those who have generously given permission to reprint borrowed material:

"Everything Will Be Okay" from *When I Was Your Age* by James Howe. Text copyright © 2001 by James Howe. Reprinted by permission of Writers House LLC, acting as agent for the author.

From *Journey* by Patricia MacLachlan, copyright © 1991 by Patricia MacLachlan. Used by permission of Yearling, an imprint of Random House Children's Books, a division of Random House, Inc. Any third party use of this material, outside of this publication, is prohibited. Interested parties must apply directly to Random House, Inc. for permission.

"Laughter" from *The House on Mango Street*. Copyrights 1984 by Sandra Cisneros. Published by Vintage Books, a division of Random House, Inc., and in hardcover by Alfred A. Knopf in 1994. By permission of Susan Bergholz Literary Services, New York, NY and Lamy, NM and by permission of Bloomsbury Publishing Plc. All rights reserved.

"Mama Sewing" from *Childtimes: A Three-Generation Memoir*. Copyright 1979 by Eloise Greenfield and Lessie Jones Little. Thomas Y. Crowell/HarperCollins. Used by permission of HarperCollins Publishers and the author.

Excerpts from "Eleven" from *Woman Hollering Creek*. Copyright © 1991 by Sandra Cisneros. Published by Vintage Books, a division of Random House Inc., and originally in hardcover by Random House Inc. By permission of Susan Bergholz Literary Services, New York, NY and Lamy, NM and by permission of Bloomsbury Publishing Plc. All rights reserved.

Excerpts from *What You Know First* by Patricia MacLachlan. Text copyright © 1995 by Patricia MacLachlan. Used by permission of HarperCollins Publishers.

Excerpts from "Bike" from *Summer Life by Gary Soto*. © University Press of New England, Lebanon, NH. Reprinted with permission.

Cataloging-in-Publication data is on file with the Library of Congress.

ISBN-13: 978-0-325-04742-3
ISBN-10: 0-325-04742-1

Production: Elizabeth Valway, David Stirling, and Abigail Heim
Cover and interior designs: Jenny Jensen Greenleaf
Series includes photographs by Peter Cunningham, Nadine Baldasare, and Elizabeth Dunford
Composition: Publishers' Design and Production Services, Inc.
Manufacturing: Steve Bernier

Printed in the United States of America on acid-free paper
17 16 15 14 13 ML 3 4 5

Acknowledgments

THE FIRST UNITS OF STUDY for Teaching Writing, Grades 3–5 series, *Memoir: The Art of Writing Well* was always a special book, a stand-out. We've brought it back and reimagined it so that it fits into the pace, the pressures, and the principles that are important in today's schools.

We're grateful to all who helped with the original book and to all who helped us reclaim that book and make it just right for today. First, the original book. Thanks go to two people, especially, who each made invaluable contributions. The first is Kathy Doyle, fifth-grade teacher extraordinaire, who opened her classroom and joined the endeavor of teaching her students to engage in the most ambitious writing project of their lives. The work that Kathy's students produced was a big part of the former volume, and we've kept a good portion of it in this volume. The second person who made invaluable contributions to the first volume is Mary Chiarella, another extraordinary teacher and a former staff developer at the Project. Mary coauthored *Memoir*. We are honored to know that some of her ideas and words are still present in this book, and we thank her for that contribution. You, our readers, will be the wiser because you are standing on her shoulders.

This new volume benefits especially from a deep knowledge of essay writing, of the Common Core State Standards, Webb's theories on depths of knowledge, and Grant Wiggins' work on teaching for transfer. It benefits, too, from John Hattie's research on the importance of clear goals and feedback and Danielson's emphasis on teaching as inquiry and data-based teaching. We've had learning partners in this work, and we especially thank Audra Robb, director of performance assessment at the Teachers College Reading and Writing Project, Mary Ehrenworth, coauthor of *Pathways to the Common Core,* Janet Steinberg, data analyst at the Project, Katherine Bomer, former TCRWP staff member and author of *Writing a Life,* and Kelly Boland, coauthor of *Boxes and Bullets: Personal and Persuasive Essays.*

The class described in this unit is a composite class, with children and partnerships of children gleaned from classrooms in very different contexts, then put together here. We wrote the units this way to bring you both a wide array of wonderful, quirky, various children and also to illustrate for you the predictable (and unpredictable) situations and responses this unit has created in classrooms across the nation and world.

—Lucy and Ali

Contents

Acknowledgments • iii

Welcome to the Unit • vi

BEND I Generating Ideas about Our Lives and Finding Depth in the Moments We Choose

1. What Makes a Memoir? • 2

In this session, you'll guide students through an inquiry in which they will study the qualities of memoir. You'll invite children to notice not only the specific elements of memoir, but the ways in which the genre draws heavily on what they already know about writing personal essays, persuasive essays, and personal narratives.

2. Interpreting the Comings and Goings of Life • 11

In this session, you'll teach students that writers usually have issues or themes that surface in their writing again and again. You'll invite children to uncover these by rereading their notebooks, looking for connections, and asking, "What's this really about?"

3. Writing Small about Big Topics • 19

In this session, you'll teach students that writers often shift between abstract ideas and concrete specifics, between themes and stories, between big meanings and small moments.

4. Reading Literature to Inspire Writing • 28

In this session, you'll teach students another strategy writers use to write with depth: letting literature influence their own writing.

5. Choosing a Seed Idea • 37

In this session, you'll remind students of ways they've chosen seed ideas—or the material that will become seed ideas—during previous cycles through the writing process. You'll help students draw on and improvise off from these strategies to devise a process that works for them.

6. Expecting Depth from Your Writing • 47

In this session, you'll teach students that writers of memoir dive deep into their topics by studying how other authors write with depth.

BEND II Structuring, Drafting, and Revising a Memoir

7. Studying and Planning Structures • 58

In this session, you'll teach students that writers study published texts to get ideas for ways to structure their own texts. You'll demonstrate how to study the structure of a text in order to help students learn how to do this.

8. The Inspiration to Draft • 67

In this session, you'll teach students some ways that writers inspire themselves to write better than ever as a way to support drafting.

9. Becoming Your Own Teacher • 77

In this session, you could teach students that writers confer with themselves as they revise. You'll teach students a few questions to ask to assess themselves, plan their goals, and choose their paths to those goals.

10. Revising the Narrative Portion of a Memoir • 81

In this session, you'll teach students to remember that if their memoir contains narratives, those stories need to carry meaning.

11. Editing for Voice • 91

In this session, you could remind students that editing is something that writers do as they write, drawing on all they've learned in previous units and writing in a way that allows their voice to come through.

BEND III   A Second Memoir

12. Seeing Again, with New Lenses: Interpreting Your Own Story • 96

In this session, you'll teach students to study themselves as they would characters in a book, uncovering ideas and theories that can lead to new memoir ideas.

13. Flash-Drafting • 104

In this session, you could teach students that writers often draft their second memoirs in one sitting, conjuring an image of how the piece will be structured and then writing quickly to capture their ideas.

14. Revising the Expository Portions of a Memoir • 108

In this session, you'll teach students that when writers write about ideas, just as when they write about events, it is important to find or create a structure that allows them to say what they want to say.

15. Reconsidering the Finer Points • 118

In this session, you'll teach students that the best details are the truest.

16. Rereading Your Draft and Drawing on All You Know to Revise • 127

In this session, you'll teach students ways that writers reread their writing intently, to learn from it how they need to revise.

17. Metaphors Can Convey Big Ideas • 139

In this session, you'll teach students that writers take a tiny detail from their lives—often something that could be very ordinary—and let that one detail represent the whole big message of their writing.

18. Editing to Match Sound to Meaning • 147

In this session, you'll teach students to listen to their writing carefully, then to choose words, structures, and punctuation that help them to convey the content, mood, tone, and feelings of the piece.

19. An Author's Final Celebration: Placing Our Writing in the Company of Others • 155

In this session, students will read aloud their memoir to their friends and family.

Welcome to the Unit

THERE ARE PEOPLE OUT THERE in the world today who scoff at schools providing time for students to reflect on their own lives. One influential spokesperson for the Common Core State Standards (CCSS) is even going around the country saying, "Kids need to learn this: no one cares about your life anyway. No one gives a s*** about your life." Others convey the same message differently—by suggesting that all the writing that students do in fifth grade should be writing about the teacher's assigned topic, and those topics should all be based on the social studies curriculum.

We believe the Common Core standards offer an incredibly important challenge, and we want to move heaven and earth to help teachers and kids meet these high standards. But here's the thing. The Common Core standards define the end goal; they detail what kids should be able to do. They leave decisions about curriculum squarely in the hands of the professionals. And for reasons we detail here, we think that there are few units that could be more important to your young writers than this one. The Common Core is not, after all, a curriculum. It is a set of benchmarks for academic skills. When students compose, they apply those skills not as an end goal in themselves, but *in the service* of enlightenment and expression. Learning to tell their own stories with grace and power will empower your students, because, in fact, many people will care about their lives if they know how to make their lives meaningful.

Fifth grade is a time of transitions. Your students are on the cusp of becoming teenagers. They are moving into whole new worlds, and with those new worlds come new pressures, new angst. In the blink of an eye, your students will be making life-defining decisions about what they will and will not do—what they will and will not be—in the face of peer pressure.

The evidence suggests that many young people aren't well prepared for the pressures that will be coming their way. Although the CCSS spotlight the need to prepare students academically for what lies ahead, the truth is that it's not just academics that derail young people today. All too often, middle school students suffer from anxiety, confusion, depression, anger, and a lack of purpose—and that, in the face of adolescent peer pressures, can be a toxic cocktail.

Time and again, we have found that something profound happens when you give young people an opportunity to work deeply and closely together to help each other author memoirs. Time and again, we've seen this unit become a defining force in the lives of fifth-graders. You'll see that this unit gives your students a chance to define themselves, a chance to author life stories that they can take with them as they leave the safety of childhood and head out into the world. It will not only be those life stories that matter; it will also be the ability to write them that matters. That is, a big part of being a healthy, happy, and fulfilled person is being able to imbue your life with meaning, to see significance in your own comings and goings. When the Common Core suggests that students should be able to discern the central ideas and themes in a text, that can also mean the texts of their lives. In this unit, you'll teach students to analyze that text, to find new meanings.

It won't be long, after all, before the last day of fifth grade comes. The kids will help you pack up the class, take down the charts. Then you'll sit in the bare room, waiting for the buses to be called. "Bus 19, 23," the call will come. "Bus 12." Soon there will be just one child left, and soon he, too, will shoulder his backpack and head for the door. For a moment, he'll linger in the door. "Bye," he'll say. "Have a good summer."

"You too," you'll say, brightly. And then, once the doorway is empty, you'll say to no one, really, "Have a good life." And for a few minutes before you join the throng of teachers celebrating the last day of school, you'll sit in the now quiet room, in the afternoon sunlight, and think, "What have I given them?" "Will it make a lasting difference?"

It changes you, watching your child, your students, head off into the rest of their lives. It makes you remember that our job, really and truly, is to put ourselves out of a job. We really and truly are educating young people for a time when we are not there. To us, this unit is all about giving young people the life skills they need to construct lives of significance or meaning. We are convinced that this matters.

The unit also matches the one to follow—The *Research-Based Argument Essay*—in its level of sheer academic challenge. It asks students to strive toward the Common Core aims of discerning meaning, conveying events and experiences precisely, and logically linking opinions and evidence. This genre brings together the art of memoir and the art of personal essay. Read memoirs by Barbara Kingsolver, Joan Didion, and David Sedaris, and you'll see the blending of ideas and vignettes that lead the writer and reader on a compelling journey of introspection and insight. Memoir also demands innovative structure, because the writer moves from storytelling to explication. It's a challenging genre, one that some might say is overly ambitious for eleven-year-olds. If your students have been in these units of study, though, they've been composing narratives and opinion pieces for six years. We think this challenge will be just right for them.

To imagine what memoir asks of the writer, imagine that you were asked to construct a text that says to the world, "This is who I am." Imagine that you collected, in your notebook or on your laptop, entries about the moments that define you and reflections on those moments as well. Imagine you wrestled to find the themes that weave in and out of your life. Now picture that we said to you, "Use all you know about constructing essays and stories to figure out the kind of text that you need to write." Imagine we said to you, "No one is going to tell you if this will be an essay or a story or something in between. That's part of your job, as the writer."

This unit doesn't begin with a preset structure into which students pour their content. The unit begins, instead, with a charge: author a memoir. Make a text that says, "This is who I am." You'll need to teach with as much intensity and power as you can muster. Teach students to look back on all they have learned, to draw from it all. Teach them to use form in the service of meaning. And teach, above all else, that yes, indeed, your life matters. It is, after all, all that we have.

OVERVIEW OF THE UNIT

Your emphasis during the first part of the unit will be on helping students to write a lot, to work productively and cycle through the writing process with independence and a sense of repertoire. Then you will spend a fair amount of time helping children to meld the learning they have done in both opinion and narrative writing, drawing on each as required by the memoir they decide to write. We believe the best way to do this is to shepherd them through two cycles of writing within this unit. Whirling them along will make them less apt to feel paralyzed, wondering "*How* do you want me to revise?" "What should I do next?" You will probably channel them to do only a couple days' worth of revising and editing on their first piece of writing before you get them started on a second piece, and then they will revise, edit, and publish that second, stronger piece of writing. The CCSS expect students to write with this kind of volume, writing "routinely over extended time frames (time for research, reflection, and revision) and shorter time frames (a single sitting or a day or two)." As teachers, we understand that one of the most effective ways to get children to write long and to write meaningfully is to allow them the time and freedom to write about what they know a lot about and are passionate about—knowledge from their lived experience.

In the first bend of this unit, you will teach children to use their notebooks to research their lives, collecting both entries and idea-based writing. That is, they will learn that writers write both "big" and "small," writing about large ideas or theories and then zooming in to write about one time when that idea was true. Students will be familiar with this sort of work from the fourth-grade unit *Boxes and Bullets*, and we recommend pulling out charts and mentor texts from that unit to support this one. After a bit of collecting and pondering, children will be ready to select one of these entries as a "seed idea."

You may want to think a bit about how you will frame this work as intensive research. The Common Core emphasizes research, particularly text-based research. We do think that the ability to research from print is important—hence the units of study on literary essay, information writing, and research-based argument essays. In the world, however, there are other forms of research. Think of scientists, historians, and journalists. Sometimes they research through experimentation in a lab or by accessing data sets or through collecting in field studies. Sometimes they research by reading what others have written. And sometimes they research from experience—as journalists and writers such as Chris Hedges and Anna Quindlen do. We think it's important to instill a research stance in children. The beginning of this unit, therefore, aims to help students develop a research stance so that they don't merely collect entries and ideas; they research and reflect on their own experiences.

Bend II continues research, this time into memoir structures, exposing children to the variety of forms a memoir can take (narrative with reflection, essay-like structure, list-like structure) and then ushering students to choose the form that best suits the idea they want to put forth. After a day of rehearsal and then of flash-drafting, students will spend a bit of time revising their first drafts. This revision work will focus on ways to strengthen both the expository and the narrative portions of their writing. If you've taught opinion and narrative already in your units of study, this is a time to expect students to apply what they know. Grant Wiggins often talks about how children (and adults) may apply skills easily when the situation makes it clear exactly what skills are called for (such as drilling for soccer) (Wiggins, "What is Transfer?" *Authentic Education*, March 27, 2010). But when the situation calls for flexibility and decision making (the scrimmage), sometimes children falter in knowing which skills to apply. Memoir is the scrimmage. Writers have to make meaningful decisions about what moves they want to make, especially including how they want to structure their pieces and how they will call on their prior knowledge as writers. All those Common Core skills you taught children—how to focus a piece around a clear opinion or central idea and support it, how to convey experience and event with precise detail that evokes the inner meaning—all those skills will be needed now, in writing that has that it's-all-happening-at-once feeling of a scrimmage. Because in memoir, it does all happen at once. The move from idea to storytelling is often rapid; the storytelling itself must be quick, to the point, and clearly evidence the central idea.

One tool that will help enormously with this work will be the student checklists, because those will increase students' efficacy and ability to self-assess. You'll want both the Opinion/Argument Writing Checklist and the Narrative Writing Checklist on hand, because memoir bridges those types of writing. (You'll also invite students to meld these and adapt them into their own checklist!) It's one of those moments when the elegant schema of the Common Core, which helps us focus on particular types of writing, doesn't exactly match how writing always works in the world. That's okay. It's good for children to learn to be innovative.

In Bend III, children will briefly return to their notebooks to research their lives again and collect new ideas and moments, then quickly choose a new seed for a second memoir. Some children will choose an entirely different topic, while others will choose to try the same topic (say, what it means when a brother leaves for middle school), this time writing using different evidence or a different structure. The important thing will be that after working on the first piece of writing, you'll ask students to transfer all they have learned through that work to their second piece of writing. You will want to be sure they revise this text in very significant ways, embarking on more ambitious, large-scale revisions. You'll undoubtedly call on Common Core close reading skills, setting students to rereading mentor texts and comparing and contrasting these with their own to analyze writing craft that they can try in their own pieces. In these second pieces, you'll be able to focus more on the Common Core reading standards 4-6, which invite students to consider language, symbolism, structural choices, and perspective. Remember that this work is not just reading work: one reason your students should be more powerful writers is because what they've noticed in texts as readers, they consider applying to their own writing.

ASSESSMENT

If one of your major goals is teaching your students to write with independence and stamina, the next goal is for students' writing to become dramatically better across the unit. To hold yourself and your students to this goal, it is critically important that you start the year by devoting a day to an on-demand writing assessment. You can make this on-demand writing feel celebratory. Give your students a chance to show off what they know about writing. The prompt we recommend, put here and in the *Writing Pathways: Performance Assessments and Learning Progressions, K–5* book is as follows:

> "Think of a topic or issue that you know and care about, an issue around which you have strong feelings. Tomorrow, you will have forty-five minutes to write an opinion or argument text in which you will write your opinion or claim and tell reasons why you feel that way. When you do this, draw on everything you know about essays, persuasive letters, and reviews. If you

want to find and use information from a book or another outside source, you may bring that with you tomorrow. Please keep in mind that you'll have forty-five minutes to complete this, so you will need to plan, draft, revise, and edit in one sitting."

You might be asking, "Why would I ask children to write about an opinion in this on-demand task when I am asking children to write memoir in the unit?" and that is a valid question. Our reason is this: because memoir draws on both narrative and opinion writing skills, you will want to have a strong sense of each. The year's first unit, *Narrative Craft*, likely left you with a great deal of data concerning your students' ability to craft a solid, focused narrative. Therefore, take this opportunity to assess their expository writing abilities so you'll have data on both skill sets—and you'll also see patterns in what students do in terms of beginnings and endings, focus and elaboration. Ultimately, however, the choice is yours.

We recommend hanging a chart with the following reminders to help children along.

In your writing, make sure you:

- Write an introduction
- State your opinion or claim
- Give reasons and evidence
- Organize your writing
- Acknowledge counterclaims
- Use transition words
- Write a conclusion

During the writing time, be sure you do not coach into what they are doing. You want to see what they do in a hands-off situation, and frankly, you will want to be in a position to show great growth from this starting point. That means you'll want to find out what children's starting points are, so you can extend their skills.

The next day, you may decide to admire publicly how much the children know by bringing in a chart on which you collect some of the qualities of good writing that you saw most students were able to put into action. If many of them enter the unit already knowing the importance of moves such as including quotations or including reasons and evidence for their opinions, then you can celebrate this and expect it from now on. You may want to give children an opportunity to show their on-demand piece to a partner, pointing out what they did as writers.

The job is not just to give this on-demand assessment, but also to take seriously the challenge of making sure that as the unit unfolds, the students' work gets progressively better. In this unit, you'll give students the opportunity to study examples of what they are aiming to create. Children will engage in close reading of complex mentor texts to learn more about memoir craft, annotating and noting the qualities they want to replicate. As they set goals, you'll want to make sure students have plenty of time to work toward them with repeated practice and feedback. An important part of that feedback will come from the children themselves. You can expect that at the start of writing time, students will reread their writing and ask, "What's the work I'm going to do next?" We suggest they create personal assignments, where they record the strategy or goal they are working on, before writing. And certainly, you'll want to give them ample time to study the very criteria that you use to assess them. To this end, we provide checklists for the students and rubrics for you, both based on the learning progressions found in the *Writing Pathways* book. All of these align to the Common Core State Standards for opinion and narrative writing.

GETTING READY

Some of the lessons will be *explicit*, taught in minilessons and conferences, and some of the lessons will be *implicit*, gleaned as children study texts that sound like the ones they will be writing. Even just one dearly loved and closely studied text can infuse a writing workshop with new energy and lots of opportunities for implicit learning. You will want to read a few focused memoirs aloud and to pull your students close to study one or two with tremendous detail. You'll want to be sure the mentor texts you use in this unit are ones that represent an array of structures. That is to say, you'll want at least one memoir that is essay-like (we recommend *Quietly Struggling* by Kelly Boland Hohne, available on the CD-ROM) as well as a few memoirs that incorporate both storytelling and exposition. A few of our favorites of that kind are:

"Last Kiss," from Ralph Fletcher's memoir, *Marshfield Dreams*

"Mr. Entwhistle," from Jean Little's memoir *Little by Little*

"Everything Will Be Okay" by James Howe and other stories from Amy Erlich's *When I Was Your Age: Original Stories about Growing Up*

"Eleven," by Sandra Cisneros, from *Women Hollering Creek*

Generating Ideas about Our Lives and Finding Depth in the Moments We Choose

BEND I

Session 1

What Makes a Memoir?

IN THIS SESSION, you'll guide students through an inquiry in which they will study the qualities of memoir. You'll invite children to notice not only the specific elements of memoir, but the ways in which the genre draws heavily on what they already know about writing personal essays, persuasive essays, and personal narratives.

GETTING READY

- ✓ The opening portion of "Eleven," by Sandra Cisneros, on chart paper (see Teaching and Active Engagement)
- ✓ Copy of the full text of "Eleven," in the meeting area
- ✓ Students need their writing notebooks
- ✓ Small folders of texts at each table, with a few samples of memoir (See Getting Ready in the front matter of this book for suggestions. We recommend including "Quietly Struggling" by Kelly Boland Hohne as an example of an essay-like memoir.)
- ✓ Chart paper and markers at each table (see Link)
- ✓ "Strategies for Generating Essay Entries" chart from the fourth grade *Boxes and Bullets: Personal and Persuasive Essays* unit (see Mid-Workshop Teaching)
- ✓ "Strategies for Generating Personal Narrative Writing" from the first unit in this series, *Narrative Writing* (see Mid-Workshop Teaching)
- ✓ Completed charts and folders of texts in the meeting area, at the end of the session (see Share)
- ✓ Chart entitled "What We Notice about Memoir" to be compiled during the share

COMMON CORE STATE STANDARDS: W.5.1, W.5.3, W.5.4, W.5.5, W.5.10, RL.5.2, RL.5.9, RL.5.10, SL.5.1, SL.5.3, L.5.1, L.5.2, L.5.3

IT IS IMPORTANT FOR YOU TO HEAD into this unit feeling clear about why the unit matters, so if you have not read the front matter to this book, take a minute to do so. Then, let's get to work.

As you approach the unit, your first question will probably be, "How is this similar to and different from personal narrative?" That's a very good question, but actually you should also be asking, "How is this similar to and different from personal essay?" Memoir is a hybrid kind of writing, including elements of both personal narrative and personal essay. That is, about half the texts that students write will feel somewhat like narratives, and the other half of the texts that students write will feel more like essays. But the truth is that most of them will contain sections and features of each genre. The texts that your students study in this first session illuminate this. Both "Eleven" and "Quietly Struggling" can be called essays, but "Eleven" does not match what the students think of as an essay. There is no explicit thesis, or topic sentences, and there is a large portion of "Eleven" that is a personal narrative. If this is complicated to you, it will be all the more complicated to your students—and that's okay.

Your students are growing old enough to wrestle with complexity—with complex text levels, with complex text structures, with complex intellectual and emotional work. That will be the nature of this unit. Specifically, and most of all, you will be asking youngsters to think about really complicated questions such as "What matters most to me? What kind of person am I? What is one of the big things I want to say about the whole of my life?"

With that, you will teach your youngsters that it often happens that the form in which a person writes a message is not preset, nor does it adhere to rules. Writers think, "What do I want to say, and how can I best say it?" As part of that, writers choose from among a variety of text structures, and they cobble together text structures to create their very own design. This lesson introduces students to this intellectual work. The goal is to give them an overall sense of the kind of thing they will begin to write so they can begin collecting entries with some sense of the larger enterprise.

MINILESSON

What Makes a Memoir?

CONNECTION

◆ COACHING

Create a drumroll to build excitement for the upcoming unit.

How many of you are nine years old?" Some kids so indicated. "Ten?" Others so indicated. I'm asking because many of you have just turned (or are soon turning) two digits. If you were Australian Aborigines, you'd be leaving soon on your walkabout. Do you know what that is?"

Adam said, "It is kind of like what the Native American did when you went into the woods alone for a bunch of days, and when they came back they were given a new name after a beast like the tiger, or something like that?"

I nodded. "It's what people call a *rite of passage*. It's a way to mark the shift from being a child to being an adolescent. In the Aborigine culture, the young person goes into the wilderness alone for six months. And they retrace the path of their history (including the paths of their ancestors) as a way to make the path forward. I'm telling you this because I was thinking, for our next unit of study, that it would be good for you to each head off on walkabout."

The kids knew I was teasing. "I'm joking, but I do think that it is important that we have a unit of study that marks the fact that you are going from being young kids to being teenagers. In the blink of an eye, you'll be in middle school.

"In high school, there is some writing that kids do that helps them look back on the olden days and look forward to the next chapter in their lives—and I thought even though you are going from elementary school to middle school, not from high school to college, that our next unit should be that kind of writing. The high school kids call it writing college essays, but really, they are also writing memoir. You will write pieces that say, 'This is who I am.'

"This will probably be the most challenging unit you have ever experienced. One of the hardest things about this unit is that I can't tell you, 'This is how a memoir goes.'

"Some memoirs are essays, some are poems, some are stories—and most are what people call a *hybrid*—a combination. And you will have to figure out what shape your writing might take.

A week from now, you'll have a notebook full of entries out of which you will make your memoir."

In the front matter to this unit, we tried to convey to you why this unit matters. It is equally important to rally kids' *investment. You'll want to make the unit sound more adult and more challenging than anything your students have experienced thus far— and it is. You'll also want to display utter confidence in the fact that they're going to love the unit. Trust us—they will. When John Goodlad interviewed kids (in his book* A Place Called School, 2004) *to learn what they cared most about in school, the universal answer was "friends." People want to share life stories, to bring the moments and themes that define us into conversations.*

❖ **Name the teaching point.**

Today, I want to teach you that when you start a big writing project, it helps to take time to read over work that is the sort of thing you plan to make. It's a bit like looking at the picture on the cover of a jigsaw puzzle before setting to work making that puzzle. It helps to think especially about how all the parts fit together into the whole."

TEACHING AND ACTIVE ENGAGEMENT

Recruit students to reread a familiar memoir with you, noticing the way it combines story and reflection—narrative and essay.

"So, we need to look at a finished memoir, something you know well." I revealed the excerpt from "Eleven" that the class had studied earlier during the personal narrative unit. "This time, you'll see that I have included a section in addition to the red sweater story we studied earlier." I pointed to a sheet of chart paper that contained the opening to "Eleven"—a section that the kids may not have read (or at least focused on) before.

"I'm going to read the start of this, and will you join me in thinking about whether there are different parts of this memoir?" I put a copy of the text on the overhead and said, "Read along with me as I study this text. Feel free to jot down what you are noticing in your notebooks. I'll do some annotating up here as well."

I began to read aloud, making sure that my voice accentuated that there is an abrupt change once the story about Mrs. Price and the red sweater begins.

> *What they don't understand about birthdays and what they never tell you is that when you're eleven, you're also ten, and nine, and eight, and seven, and six, and five, and four, and three, and two and one. And when you wake up on your eleventh birthday you expect to feel eleven, but you don't. You open your eyes and everything's just like yesterday, only it's today. And you don't feel eleven at all. You feel like you're still ten. And you are underneath the year that makes you eleven.*
>
> *Like some days you might say something stupid, and that's the part of you that's still ten. Or maybe some days you might need to sit on your mama's lap because you're scared, and that's the part of you that's five. And maybe one day when you're all grown up maybe you will need to cry like if you're three, and that's okay. That's what I tell Mama when she's sad and needs to cry. Maybe she's feeling three.*
>
> *Because the way you grow old is kind of like an onion or like the rings inside a tree trunk or like my little wooden dolls that fit one inside the other, each year inside the next one. That's how being eleven years old is.*
>
> *You don't feel eleven. Not right away. It takes a few days, weeks even, sometimes even months before you say Eleven when they ask you. And you don't feel smart eleven, not until you're almost twelve. That's the way it is.*
>
> *Only today I wish I didn't have only eleven years rattling inside me like pennies in a tin Band-Aid box. Today I wish I was one hundred and two instead of eleven because if I was one hundred and two I'd have*

You may squirm at the idea of revisiting "Eleven," feeling that it is old news. But when learning to write by studying finished work, familiarity matters. When Hemingway was asked, "How do you learn to write?" he answered, "Read Anna Karenina, *read* Anna Karenina, *read* Anna Karenina."

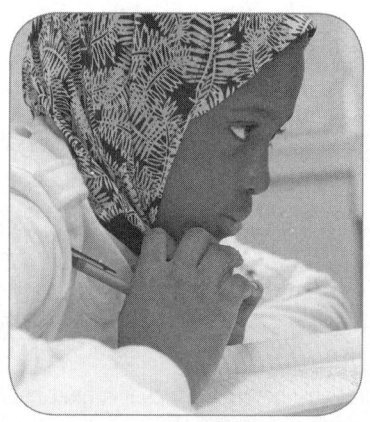

known what to say when Mrs. Price put the red sweater on my desk. I wouldn't know how to tell her it wasn't mine instead of just sitting there with that look on my face and nothing coming out of my mouth.

"Whose is this?" Mrs. Price says . . .

"Even before I finish reading, can you sense that there are different kinds of writing in here?" I asked. "Turn and talk."

After children talked a bit, I reconvened the class. "I'm hearing many of you say that 'Eleven' has almost a tiny essay on being eleven up front, and then a long personal narrative."

Debrief.

"So, do you see that a memoir might be both personal narrative and essay, combined? What makes the entire text of 'Eleven' a memoir is (in part) the fact that Sandra Cisneros does not just tell stories, but she also writes about ideas. She tells the story of the red sweater, but she also writes ideas about how this makes a statement about herself."

LINK

Send children off to spend the workshop time reading memoirs and thinking about the different pieces that fit together to make a memoir, and about how memoirs differ from each other.

"There are many ways that memoirs can go, and I've put copies of 'Eleven' and a few other memoirs on your tables for you to study and think about. As you study these samples, you will probably notice that every memoir contains some storytelling and then some writing about ideas and opinions. For the first twenty minutes of today's workshop, will you read a memoir from the folder on your table—it might be 'Eleven' you reread, or another text—and talk with each other about this question: How does this memoir go? How do memoirs tend to go?" After children were settled at their tables and had begun reading, I delivered large sheets of paper to each cluster of children. "When you speak with the other children at your table about how memoirs go, use this chart paper to jot down your observations so we can discuss them as a class later."

This is where the abrupt change starts. Let your voice show that the text has changed.

This is a brief, simple minilesson. The instruction during later portions of today's session add complexity.

Texts like these will all go into a basket of memoir texts. Over the next few days, you and your children will add other texts to this basket. Be sure that it is prominently displayed and that you bear in mind that throughout the writing workshop, it is always wise for children to take time from writing in order to immerse themselves in reading the sort-of-text they hope to write.

CONFERRING AND SMALL-GROUP WORK

Noticing the Similarities and Differences in Memoir Structure

AS STUDENTS HEADED TO THEIR TABLES, I knew they would be reading not only "Eleven" but also an essay, "Quietly Struggling," written by our colleague, Kelly Boland Hohne. I'd put that essay into their folders and now convened a fairly large group of children who had read the text. Because it is an essay, I wanted to make sure that I helped children talk about this structure so that it was in the forefront of their minds as they embarked on the unit.

"Writers, I think you'll find that this is a very different kind of memoir. Most of you have already read up to where I have put a mark in the text. If you haven't, do this now. And will you think about the component parts? As you read it, will you ask: How does this memoir go? How is it like and unlike 'Eleven'?" As they finished reading this memoir essay, I went off to make sure other writers were settled and working. This is what they read.

Quietly Struggling

I've always struggled with putting myself out in the world. When I was little, my mom would go to parent-teacher conferences, and every year she would come home with the same comment from my teachers: "Kelly is very quiet." My mom would ask me if I could make a goal to speak up once a day in class, and I would try, but I didn't always succeed. Even today, there are times that I am not outgoing. It is hard for me to be outgoing for many reasons. It can be hard for me to be outgoing because observing helps me to feel more comfortable, I need time to organize my ideas before speaking up or acting, and I don't want to look foolish.

The first reason why it can be hard for me to be outgoing is because observing helps me to feel more comfortable. In middle school, when I went to dances, I stood back before going out on the dance floor. Other kids just dove right onto the middle of the floor and starting moving to the music, but I couldn't do that. Even if I am on vacation, I like to take some time to watch before I jump in and start doing things. Like the time I went on a cruise. The minute I got onboard, I was surrounded by people. There were people asking questions and carrying suitcases and blocking hallways and crowding into the elevators. I stood back and found a seat by a window and gave myself time to watch. It was hard for me to be outgoing and just jump into the middle of the action. Observing makes me feel more comfortable.

When I came back, a few students had started to talk to each other quietly. "I hear some of you whispering to each other, already thinking what you can add to your chart after reading this memoir. Will you annotate the text while we wait for everyone to catch up? Underline key lines. Make marginal notes."

The children jotted quietly for a minute, underlining and noting techniques in the margins of the text. "What have you uncovered?" I asked after a bit.

As you listen in to your students, you can be forming ideas about who to call on later to guide the lesson along and keep it as tight and focused as possible. Alternatively, you don't have to call on the students, but can simply sum up what they said.

Dakhari began. "I think that this looks almost just like an essay. So maybe some memoirs can look more like essays than stories."

I pushed for more specifics, asking the children to turn and talk about what, exactly, made this piece seem essay-like. They agreed that the text had many obvious essay components, like an introduction, a conclusion, and body paragraphs with reasons and examples. Wanting to clarify the difference between this text and "Eleven," and to make a few other points of my own, I called for the children's attention.

"So what I hear you saying is that 'Quietly Struggling' is an essay-like memoir because it has the typical things we'd expect from an essay—like an introduction and reasons and examples. 'Quietly Struggling,' is organized like an essay and has little, tiny stories inside of it. On the other hand, 'Eleven' has a bunch of essay-like writing on the top and then a big, important, drawn-out narrative. Both of these are ways that memoir can be structured."

I helped children add what we'd noticed to their charts and then left them to compare what they'd charted with other new texts from the baskets on their tables.

After leading this one small group, I checked on other children who'd been making their own charts of the characteristics of memoir writing, and then decided I needed to move children from reading to writing. I convened their attention for the Mid-Workshop Teaching.

MID-WORKSHOP TEACHING **Collecting Stories from Life**

"There are many things you've noticed about how memoir goes, and you'll have a chance to share some of what you noticed during today's share. But before today's workshop is over, I want to ensure that you have a bit of time to collect stories from *your own* life. No matter what structure a memoir takes, I'm sure you've noticed that each and every one has a single thing in common: it is a piece of writing that is about something that is significant to the writer. The red sweater event, the struggle to speak up, growing up—these are topics and themes of importance to the memoir writers we've studied today. If you are like me, I'm sure that all this *reading* about significant, life-changing moments has begun to spark ideas for *writing* about your own life.

"I've hung up some charts from past units, so we can remind ourselves of all we know about collecting writing for personal essay *and* for personal narratives. Some of you will find these charts helpful as you turn to collecting your own entries. Others of you are already brimming with ideas and will be eager to get those on the page. Either way, write at least one entry by the end of the workshop."

Strategies for Generating Essay Entries

- We take a subject (a person, place, or object) that matters to us and list ideas related to that subject. Then we take one of those ideas and write about it.
- We observe and then write, "The thought I have about this is . . ."
- We let writing spark new thoughts, and we take those sparks and write new entries about them.
- We reread our earlier writing and ask questions about those earlier entries.

Strategies for Generating Personal Narrative Writing

- Think of a **person** who matters to you, list Small Moment stories connected to him/her, and write one.
- Think of **first times, last times,** or **times you realized something,** list stories you could tell about each, and write one.
- Think about a **place** that matters, list small moments that occurred in that place, and write one.
- Think of a **strong feeling**. List stories of particular times you felt it and write one.
- **Live differently** because you are a writer. Notice small moments, and capture them in entries.
- **Read the words another author has written** and allow them to spark your own story ideas.

SHARE

Compiling Ideas about Memoir

Ask children to pause in their own writing and join you in the meeting area, bringing along their charts and observations about memoir.

"Writers, I know you're in the midst of your first entry, but I'm going to need to stop you. Will each of you find the group you worked with today and choose an item or two from your chart that seems especially important to share? If your writing has given you new ideas about how memoirs tend to go, add those to your list, too." As children talked, I began a class chart entitled "What We Notice about Memoir."

"Will each of you turn to your group and decide on one or two items from your list that seem important?" As children did this, I revealed a chart entitled "What We Notice about Memoir."

I called the students back together. "Let's see if we can combine our charts and make one big class chart of what we've noticed. Jill, will you start us off?"

Jill began, "We noticed what we were saying in the minilesson, that memoir has a little bit of story but also sometimes seems like an essay."

"Hmm, thumbs up if you noticed the same." Nearly the entire class signaled that they had, indeed, noticed this too. "Let's try to be really specific about the *ways* authors can combine ideas and story. Right now, take a look at 'Eleven.' What did Sandra Cisneros do, specifically?"

I gave the children a moment to talk, then interrupted, "So, what I hear most of you saying is that Cisneros begins by writing about her ideas, like an essay, and then she tells a story that shows what she is trying to prove." I wrote on our chart:

Now, and during the independent work time, you'll want to gather some intel on what children are noticing. This will help you to choose wisely when asking children to share their ideas for the class chart.

> **What We Notice about Memoir**
> - The writer has an idea to share and might begin by explaining this idea to the reader (the way an essayist would explain a claim).
> - The writer might use a personal narrative to <u>show</u> how his or her idea is true.

When compiling a class list, don't be afraid to "restate" or "reshape" some of the answers your children provide. They are novices, and it is likely that their observations about memoir will be under-developed. By reframing these observations into clean, concise language, you help each child (and the class as a whole) to develop their ideas and form a shared language.

"Many of you studied 'Quietly Struggling' now. How is this different? What does this lead us to add to our chart? . . ." Again, I gave the children a moment to talk and then called for their attention.

Ali chimed in. "It's written like an essay. It has an introduction, body paragraphs, and a conclusion."

"Ahh," I said, "so what you are saying is that some memoirists might write their ideas more like an essay, with big patches of idea-based writing and tiny, little life stories to support their idea." Again, I added a bullet to our chart.

This is an instance when you want to call on children who say something close to what we've said here. If you let children talk in pairs first, you can overhear their conversation and call on children whose responses will help the class. If you haven't heard the responses you want, there will be times when you resort to saying, "I heard several of you saying . . ." and then say what you wish you'd heard.

> - Some memoirs might look more like stories, with patches of idea-based writing around a big story (like "Eleven"). Other memoirs look more like essays, with a lot of ideas and just a few, small stories (like "Quietly Struggling").

Recap what children have learned and the big message you hope to leave them with.

"I think you've gotten a feeling for how memoir combines story and opinion. You might first tell a story and then suggest that it helps you realize an idea, an insight, which you then share with your reader. Or you might discuss an idea and then illustrate that idea with one or more stories from your life. There are a lot of possibilities. In the end, I think we all agree that most memoirs have *both* idea-based writing and storytelling, and that they say something important about the writer. You'll want to keep this in mind as you collect writing for the memoir you'll be writing in this unit."

> **What We Notice about Memoir**
> - The writer has an idea to share and might begin by explaining this idea to the reader (the way an essayist would explain a claim).
> - The writer might use a personal narrative to show how his or her idea is true.
> - Some memoirs might look more like stories, with patches of idea-based writing around a big story (like "Eleven"). Other memoirs look more like essays, with a lot of ideas and just a few, small stories (like "Quietly Struggling").

FIG. 1–1

Recap what children have learned and the big message you hope to leave them with.

"I think you've gotten a feeling for how memoir combines story and opinion. You might tell a story that's an example of some issue or idea you want to think about. Or you might want to explain an idea, something you learned, and then show the reader how you learned that. There are a lot of possibilities, and I think you already have some idea of how this kind of writing tells the reader a lot about what you believe in and care about. In the end, though, I think we all agree that most memoirs have *both* idea-based writing and storytelling and that they say something important about the writer. You'll want to keep that in mind as you collect writing for this memoir, now and tonight and in the future!"

SESSION 1 HOMEWORK

STUDYING PUBLISHED MEMOIR AND THEN REVISING YOUR OWN ENTRY

In school you studied several memoirs by thinking about their component parts. You tended to find that memoirs contain stories and ideas—and that they don't always fall into the predictable structures you studied earlier this year.

Tonight, study another memoir from the folder at your table. Continue to notice the shape and the parts of the memoir. Then make a diagram or plan for how the entry you wrote today could be shaped—for a new shape, a new design—and try rewriting that entry based on that design.

Session 2

Interpreting the Comings and Goings of Life

IN YESTERDAY'S WORKSHOP, you strove to give young writers a sense of the genre of memoir—by channeling them to study examples you highlighted about the way this unit will draw on what they know about opinion and narrative writing, and you ushered them to have a go in their notebooks. Today you will want to help students turn to their own lives and begin to uncover the themes, topics, and ideas that sit beneath the surface. I've come to believe that it can be very powerful for a young person to pause, to reread all that she has written, and to think, "What are the topics and territories that I revisit often in my writing and thinking?" This involves interpretation, a skill that we often think of as part of reading, but that is actually also essential in writing.

This session invites students to reread their past entries, reconsider their lives, and locate the topics that feel intense and close to their minds and hearts. In a speech at Teachers College, Patricia MacLachlan author of *Journey* (1993) and *What You Know First* (1998), explained that she always keeps a bag of prairie dirt near her as she writes because it reminds her of her childhood home. She said she believes that every book she has ever written is really about a child's longing for home. That writing territory is the one she returns to again and again.

When I heard her say that all of her books are about a child's longing for home, I was puzzled. I thought to myself, "*Journey* is not about a boy's journey toward home. It is the story of a boy who lives with his grandfather and tries to reconstruct his life in the absence of his mother." But as I started to think about it, I realized that really *Journey* is all about that boy coming to feel that he's at home when he is with his sister and his grandparents. Then I thought about *What You Know First*, and again my first thought was that this is not about a child's longing for home. I thought, "It is about moving." But then I remembered the ending.

> What you know first stays with you, my Papa says. But just in case I forget I will take a twig of the cottonwood tree. I will take a little bag of prairie dirt. I cannot take the sky.

IN THIS SESSION, you'll teach students that writers usually have issues or themes that surface in their writing again and again. You'll invite children to uncover these by rereading their notebooks, looking for connections, and asking, "What's this really about?"

GETTING READY

- ✓ Prominently displayed basket containing exemplar memoirs of various kinds (might include *Been to Yesterdays: Poems of a Life* by Lee Hopkins (1999); *When I Was Your Age: Original Stories about Growing Up* by Amy Ehrlich (2001); *What You Know First*, and *The Relatives Came* by Cynthia Rylant (1993))
- ✓ Student notebooks brought to the meeting area (see Active Engagement)
- ✓ Your own writer's notebook, filled with entries (see Teaching)
- ✓ Chart paper and marker (see Mid-workshop Teaching)

COMMON CORE STATE STANDARDS: W.5.4, W.5.10, RL.5.2, RL.5.10, SL.5.1, L.5.1, L.5.2, L.5.3

This initial puzzlement—how does this particular bit of writing connect to a recurring topic that is meaningful to the writer?—is the puzzlement we invite children to work through in this session. Then, of course, we channel each of them to think, "What are my recurring topics, my own personal writing territories? What is this one bit of writing that I've already written *really* even about for me?"

"This session invites students to reread their past entries, reconsider their lives, and locate the topics that feel intense and close to their minds and hearts."

As you invite children to identify some recurring themes by looking through their own past writing, you can expect that they will begin by listing large, and perhaps somewhat clichéd, topics as their recurring topics or writing territories. As they list topics like loving their moms and soccer, you'll be wise to remember two things. First, as John Updike wrote, "Writing and rewriting are a constant search for what one is saying." It takes most of us a lifetime to figure out what it is we really want to say about ourselves or about the world. It's no wonder that your children are still at the level of clichés. Then too, you'll want to honor the seeing your students *do* do. By lending an ear and believing that a topic is important, you help writers coax the meaning out of these topics, inch by inch, line by line.

MINILESSON

Interpreting the Comings and Goings of Life

CONNECTION

Tell students that a writer once told you that most of us have a few topics we revisit repeatedly, and explain that this has been true for your writing.

"Don Murray, a Pulitzer Prize–winning writing teacher, once came to work with my colleagues and me on our writing. We all gathered around him, and he began. 'As writers,' he said, 'most of us have just three topics that we continually revisit. Even when we think we are writing about new topics, we are really, deep down, revisiting one of those three topics.' Then Murray said, 'List your own three topics.'

"I was flabbergasted. I thought about all the writing that I do in my life. How could he suggest that I really only write about *three* subjects? I quickly peeked back into the entries in my writer's notebook. To my astonishment, one after another after another somehow related back to the same topics—topics like my father, or the teaching of reading and writing.

"Since then, I have found that other great writers agree that most of us, as writers, have just a few topics that we continually revisit. F. Scott Fitzgerald, for example, says this: 'Mostly we writers repeat ourselves—that's the truth. We have two or three great moving experiences in our lives—experiences so great and moving that it doesn't seem at the time that anyone has been caught up and pounded and dazzled and astonished and beaten and broken and rescued and illuminated and humbled in just that way ever before.' F. Scott Fitzgerald suggests that as writers, we continually return to those experiences to mine them. We mine those moments for big ideas, for themes."

Explain that memoir writers reread entries, memories, jottings to grow big ideas.

"Naomi Nye, one of my favorite authors, says, 'My notebooks are filled with beginnings, images, dreamy meanderings, single lines overheard at health clubs, airports, or in the last sweet chunk of sleep before waking. They come from everywhere.' Then she adds something that is critical to this unit. 'I trust these entries can take me somewhere else. Every few pages of the notebook, lines start growing into something larger than themselves.'

"I think Naomi is telling us that when she writes, as when she reads, she expects to grow big ideas. She interprets."

◆ COACHING

As you begin this work with your children, you will find that some students will start by simply listing subjects that recur: my dad, my brother, bullying. Others will analyze their life stories through more interpretative lenses, pulling out themes like "life is full of ups and downs" or "sometimes you just have to keep fighting." As the unit progresses, your teaching will quickly lift children from simply naming topics to interpreting ideas.

This is a much longer connection than usual. You should become accustomed to noticing when this is so, and to scanning the minilesson, thinking, "What could I delete if it seems like too much for my kids?" This bit is dispensable.

❖ **Name your teaching point.**

"Today, I want to teach you that writers don't just chronicle their life, record their lives. Writers interpret. When analyzing their life stories, writers ask, 'What are the big ideas here?' and then they look for themes and issues that appear again and again in their entries and memories."

TEACHING

Explain that writers reread their writing, looking for topics or patterns that underlie many of their entries.

"Help me think about whether some of my entries address one topic on the surface, and another, more significant theme or issue deep down. In a minute you will be thinking about this with your own entries, too."

"Like you, I've only written two entries so far in this unit, so I'm going to look back to entries from the start of the year—and you can do that, too. I flipped through entries I'd gathered at the start of the year and began skimming one. "Do you remember this entry about my Civil War play? It tells about the time I got a part as Sarah Lincoln and the kids said I could wear my usual dress because it looked antique enough. I didn't say anything because all I wanted was to be liked by one of the other girls in the cast. So Hmm . . . What's that entry really about, I wonder? What's the theme, the deeper meaning, of it …?" I let my eyes glance over the page and mused, "Its not really about being in a play, because the main thing I was thinking, worrying about was being popular. That's it! It's about wanting to be popular."

Then I paused and looked up at the children. "Do you see the way I'm not just recalling what happened in the moment, but looking a bit deeper and asking, 'What deeper theme or issue might this address?' I am going to annotate the entry by writing a little entry about the ideas I'm starting to have. Remember, memoir shifts between stories and ideas." I picked up my pen and began jotting in my notebook. "This shows my struggle to fit in. I felt tugged in different directions. On the one hand, I wanted to be friends with kids like Eliza. But also, I just wanted to be myself. Wait!" I stopped writing abruptly and began leafing through my notebook, visibly having made a discovery. "I'm *just* realizing that this theme, about wanting to be accepted, connects to *another* entry I wrote about the time I teased the new girl, Elena. She hadn't done anything wrong and was perfectly nice to me, but I teased her because I knew it would make the other girls look up to me. This might be a much bigger issue than I realized. Wanting to fit in made me act all sorts of different ways when I was younger. I'll have quite a bit to say about this. Wanting to fit in, to find my place in the world, seems to be a topic I come back to in several entries."

Then, shifting from my role as a writer to my role as a teacher, I said, "As I read on, I'll do the same with other entries. As I uncover more ideas and themes, I'll ask myself if the theme has to do with just that one entry, or if it is something I come back to again and again."

When you read during the reading workshop, you collect Post-its filled with jottings and thoughts about what you are reading. The important thing is that when you read over these tiny jots, you find bigger ideas. You make interpretations. You say, "The big idea I'm growing here is . . ."

You will see that the role of demonstration is small yet purposeful in this minilesson. I do not think kids need to spend a lot of time today watching me reread entries. So I opt for only a small bit of demonstration and a larger bit of time rallying children to the unit as a whole. Still, during the demonstration, I am active and strategic enough that kids can see me doing work that they can emulate. For example, I show them that I push past an easy, surface-level answer to a longer, more thoughtful entry. I show them that I look for patterns, immediately recalling other life moments that fit with my insight. A demonstration can't be effective unless we enact replicable activities.

"So writers, I'm hoping you noticed what I did just now. I went back to my notebook entries, expecting to see more. I interpreted, asking 'What are the big ideas here?' As a result of this, I found a pattern—a theme that threads through much of my writing.

ACTIVE ENGAGEMENT

Ask writers to reread their notebooks, looking for underlying issues or themes and to write about what they find.

"Writers, would you reread from your notebook now, perhaps returning to an entry you wrote at the very start of this year? As you read it, think to yourself, 'What deeper meaning might this address?' Then, annotate the entry."

As the children worked, I coached in with reminders and supports. "Celia is doing something really smart. She's starting off by looking at one entry, jotting a bit about what it is *really* about, and then moving to another. I'm sure she'll find some patterns in no time." A moment later, "If you are stuck, look for a topic that weaves through a lot of your writing. Maybe you always write about soccer, or your dad, or times with your sister. When you find a topic that repeats, ask, 'What makes this so important? What do I really want to say about my dad or soccer or my sister?'"

LINK

Remind writers that in this unit, each child will be expected to compose her own writing process. Remind them that today they will invent ways to find their themes and issues in their lives.

You'll reread your entries like you reread your Post-its—you'll collect as you read. You'll ask, 'What are some bigger themes or issues here? And 'Do any of my entries fit together?' Annotate your entries. Write marginal notes. When you find a bigger theme or issue, then you can take that idea and write entries to explore it.

"So, writers, today you'll do two kinds of work. Your job will be to think about the topics that matter a great deal to you, themes that you tend to return to, issues you want to write about in your memoir. You'll be collecting ideas and entries for your draft for several days. As writers do, you can draw on any strategy for generating writing that you've learned this year or other years," I said, gesturing to charts gathered across the year, "or you can invent new strategies to help yourself write. Among other strategies for generating writing, you may want to reread previous entries, asking yourself that question that Don Murray asked my colleagues and me: 'What do I write about again and again, sometimes without even realizing it? What are my main writing territories?' and then write a bit about what makes them important.

"I can't wait to admire the choices you make and the work you do today."

Money Shortages

I think about money a lot. Sometimes I worry if we have enough to pay the bills. I start to feel bad that my parents are getting me stuff that's less important than paying bills. Whenever my dad comes home, one of the very first things he says is, "Did we get that check today?" and my mom always says no. It gets me worried and makes me feel that we need more money. Whenever I ask my mom if we *do* need more money, she always says that we don't. But I have a feeling that she's just saying that so I won't be worried anymore.

FIG. 2–1 Jose identifies a repeating issue in his entries and writes to explore it.

There are many methods we use to help children become independent and resourceful writers, and we can't underestimate the power of our words in supporting (or undermining) this effort. Peter Johnston, in Choice Words: How Our Language Affects Children's Learning *(2004), talks about the importance of using language that invites students to act with agency and independence. By telling children that I look forward to admiring the choices they make as writers, I suggest that they are expected* to make fruitful choices.

CONFERRING AND SMALL-GROUP WORK

Listening Intently to Support Reflection

YOU AND YOUR COLLEAGUES WILL WANT TO ANTICIPATE THE SORT OF WORK your students will be apt to produce today, and to rehearse how you will respond to that work. Because I've taught this unit of study so many times and have watched other teachers teach it well, I can almost promise you that the work your children do today will be disappointing. Gone will be all the detail and fluency you've come to expect in their writing; instead, children will often annotate their entries in ways that feel cliché. You might find things like 'Baseball is the best!' and 'I love camp' written beside the students' entries, and sigh at the thought that this is the deepest work they can produce. I've realized, though, that if I did the work that this session asks writers to do, the annotations I would create would not be all that different than those you will see around your classroom. I'd note the struggle to fit in, the importance of my family, and perhaps even the fact that writing is the best! But, in fact, for me, every word on my list would brim with poignancy. It's important to believe that your children's do, as well.

The goal for today, then, will not involve helping writers *write* well, but will instead involve helping them *reflect* well. Your first job will be to affirm the importance of each child's entries, letting each youngster see universal themes in the comings and goings of his or her life.

As you confer today, remember this: It can be an extraordinarily powerful thing to have someone listen and say, "What you're onto is really huge." When someone listens like that, really taking in the significance of what you've only gestured toward, you find yourself saying more than you knew you had to say. Although your goal for this unit will be to help children become more interpretive, more at home writing about ideas, another goal is for them to write with honesty and precision. It is therefore important that we, as teachers, begin this unit with an enormous spirit of receptivity and empathy.

MID-WORKSHOP TEACHING
Collecting Entries Related to a Theme

"Writers, can I have your eyes and your attention? You have been fast at work, writing entries in which you grow ideas about your ideas. I'm noticing that many of you have found two, three, and even four themes or issues that thread through your life. I'm going to ask that you switch gears now. So far as memoirists, you have been going from 'small' to 'big,' looking at *small* moments from your life to uncover *big* themes and issues. As writers, though, you can also go from 'big' to 'small.' Let me show you what I mean.

"I can take a 'big' theme or issue in my life—let's say the struggle to fit in—and put it at the top of a blank page of notebook paper." I modeled doing this on chart paper, jotting 'The Struggle to Fit In' at the top of the chart paper. "Then, I can try to think 'small' and ask myself 'What small moments from my life fit with this big theme or issue?'"

I began to think, jotting a few small moments ideas in bullets below my issue.

The Struggle to Fit In
- The time Eliza made fun of my dress and said it was antique-looking
- The time I made fun of Elena to impress the other girls in my class
- The time my entire class took a field trip to my house to see my pet monkey, which I had pretended to have, but didn't

> "Now I can choose one of these story ideas and write an entry, knowing that I want to write it in a way that shows what the entry is *really* about. When I finish one entry, I can begin again and write about a second small moment that illustrates my big theme.
>
> "Right now, will you take one theme or issue you've found and write it at the top of a blank page in your notebook? Then, think small and list out some moments that fit with that theme. When you are ready, you can write those entries."

I will never forget the time Maya read me an entry about the day her friend came over to play. The two girls raced up to Maya's bedroom, planning to play bride with Maya's dolls. They'd chosen the flower girls and the ushers. All of a sudden, they opened the bedroom door, and there in front of them they found all Maya's dolls and teddy bears hanging helplessly from nooses. Hearing this entry, I gasped in utter horror. How awful, how devastating!

Of course, I could have responded differently. These were dolls and teddy bears hanging from nooses, not pets or children. The event was not *really* one of life's worst tragedies. But in the life of this one child, that moment brims with pathos. Teaching writing is all about that gasp. We read a student's entry, we gasp, and we say, "That's so huge." And all of a sudden, tears glisten in the writer's eyes and she says, "I know."

As teachers of writing, you need to be people who gasp and wince and weep and cheer in response to the heartbreak and the happiness that children bring into the writing workshop. Ultimately, a child will only be able to write well about his own life if that child can re-experience it. You need to listen deeply and to be profoundly moved by children's life themes so that children can do the same. The most important work you can do today will be to listen, to acknowledge the gigantic significance of children's entries, themes, and issues.

SHARE

Assigning Oneself Work and Recording Self-Assignments

Celebrate the choices students have made. Ask them to record self-assignments beside their entries.

"Writers, can I stop you? I want to remind you that in the writing workshop and at home, writers don't just write; writers reread, writers study mentors, writers revise. And, more than that, writers plan for the work they'll do. You'll often need to pause, taking a moment to plan before you go off to write. Take a moment now and jot down the work you plan to do next. For example, before you read your writer's notebook and wrote about the topics that threaded through your entries, you could have written, 'Reread notebook, look for themes that underlie many topics, and then write about them' as your self-assignment. That would have been a wise self-assessment because usually when we write long, we find ourselves generating ideas we never knew we had.

"Right now, would you look back on the work you did today, and then think forward, writing a self-assignment for the work you'll do next?"

Ask children to share their work with a partner, especially noticing the strategies each chose to use today.

"Will you share the work you did today with your partner, then share what your next steps will be? Help your partner to reflect on how writing went today, and make sure that you each set goals that will help you develop your themes and issues in both big and small ways."

◆ COACHING

> Rewrite the same scene I wrote today with dialogue and details that show more about my relationship with my dad.

FIG. 2–2 Takuma plans to revise an entry to bring out more details related to his theme.

SESSION 2 HOMEWORK

EXPLORING PATTERNS IN OUR LIVES

As you looked through your notebook today, reflecting on the writing territories you are most drawn to, many of you began to see patterns. These patterns are no coincidence! When you return to a subject again and again, it is generally because you have something big to say about it. Tonight, take one of these patterns you noticed and write to discover what it is you really want to say. You might get started by asking yourself, "What is it I really want to say about this theme or issue?" or "This is important to me because . . ." Push yourself to write at least two pages.

Session 3

Writing Small about Big Topics

NEW YORK CITY'S RECENT DEVASTATION FROM HURRICANE SANDY reminds me of the first time I saw the pictures from a devastated New Orleans after Hurricane Katrina. I remember the faces of people left behind to cope with the floods; an old woman, clinging to a rooftop as the water rose around her. I remember Ivory, who had been a garbage collector and now sat on a cot in the Convention Center, listing on a little sheet of paper all he'd left behind. Somehow Ivory found solace in simply writing the words of what he had lost: my radio, my picture of Agnes, the rocking chair. For many of us, the particular details captured in those New Orleans photographs conveyed gigantic truths about America today. In the faces of those people who were left behind, big ideas became poignantly real to us: the gap between rich and poor became real; the unfairness of it all became real. When I think about the impact that those specific images and stories from New Orleans had on me and on so many others, I am reminded that big truths are carried through specific images and stories.

Over and over, you have helped writers learn that when they write they use tiny particulars to convey big ideas. First graders, even, have learned that writers don't write about "big watermelon ideas" but instead, they write "tiny seed stories." They learned that instead of writing about "I love my grandma, "they write about the morning when Grandma braided their hair.

Now, years later, you will continue to remind children that writers write with tiny, significant details. But as children become older and their understanding of good writing matures, concepts that were once hard-and-fast must now become more flexible, and ideas that were once one-dimensional must now become more complex. By now, it is important for children to learn that, in fact, writers do write about big ideas, but that they use tiny stories to represent those ideas. A writer might tell the story of her grandma braiding her hair to convey a truth that is too big for ordinary words—the fact that yes, indeed, she loves her grandmother very much.

IN THIS SESSION, you'll teach students that writers often shift between abstract ideas and concrete specifics, between themes and stories, between big meanings and small moments.

GETTING READY

- ✓ Exemplar piece of writing that uses a small moment to convey a larger Life Topic (see Teaching)

- ✓ An excerpt from Jean Little's memoir (see Acitve Engagement) or any other memoir that exemplifies the ways in which writing small can support big topics. Have this excerpt on chart paper or the overhead for students to see.

- ✓ "Ways to Bring Out the Big Ideas in a Story" chart (see Mid-Workshop Teaching)

COMMON CORE STATE STANDARDS: W.5.3, W.5.4, RL.5.2, RL.5.10, SL.5.1, L.5.1, L.5.2, L.5.3

MINILESSON

Writing Small about Big Topics

CONNECTION

Celebrate that children have reread their notebooks, finding themes and issues that feel huge and significant.

"Yesterday many of you read over your writer's notebooks; you reread entries about falling off your scooter and buying a sweater that matches your mother's and standing in a hospital room beside your grandmother and getting your puppy from the dog pound. Like you, I also reread my writer's notebook yesterday; it was powerful, turning through the pages, turning past all those parts of my life. Although there were many topics that threaded through my entries, I found that like Don Murray suggested, under all that variety, there actually were a few themes or issues that I came back to again and again. Lots of my entries told about my struggles to fit in, for example. Can you give me a thumbs up if the same thing happened to you?" Many students signaled yes.

Remind students that in earlier grades, they may have learned that writers do not write about big watermelon topics, but instead about small, seed stories. Invite students to wrestle with the fact that their themes and issues resemble the once 'forbidden' watermelon topics.

"But you know what? These could also be called *watermelon topics*. The term doesn't do these topics justice, of course, but do you agree that these topics—fitting in, being pressured by parents, being a child of divorce—resemble those watermelon topics that you learned years ago to avoid?

"How many of you remember that when you were younger, you learned that writers don't write about big watermelon topics, but instead write little seed stories? Kids in the younger grades practice telling the difference. Their teachers might say a topic such as 'Spending time with my grandmother,' and the little kids use gestures to show whether that is a big watermelon idea," I showed the gesture, using outstretched hands to measure an imaginary watermelon, "or a teeny tiny seed story." I again gestured, showing that such an idea could fit between pinched fingers. "So what's up? Am I now telling you that writers write about watermelon topics (and I made the gesture) after all?"

❧ **Name your teaching point. Specifically, tell children that the bigger the topic, the smaller one will need to write.**

"This is what I want to teach you today. A poet named Richard Price said it well. He said, 'The bigger the meaning, the smaller you write.'"

◆ COACHING

When you compose your own units of study, you will find that one day's minilesson often leads almost inevitably to the next day's minilesson. Yesterday's teaching definitely set the stage for today's minilesson.

Piaget has said that growth involves disequilibrium, and more specifically, both assimilating and accommodating. As children learn more, some of their new learning will lead them to revise previous learning. When a child learns to read, a teacher will teach that child to point under each word as she reads it. As the child grows older, the same teacher will tell a child to stop pointing under each word. Similarly, the teacher of writing might first suggest that writers do not write about big topics but instead focus on small specifics. That's an over simplification and this unit brings students toward complexity.

TEACHING

Suggest that writers need to write with topics that are both big and small. Share a text in which the writer has used tiny details to convey a Life Topic.

"Earlier, when I told you that writers do not write with big watermelon ideas but with little tiny seed stories, I was oversimplifying the truth. Because the truth is that sometimes writers *start with* a gigantic theme or issue or topic. And on the other hand, sometimes writers *start with* a teeny glimpse of life, with a little sliver of experience (as we did earlier this year). But either way, in the end, good literature needs both big meaning and tiny details.

"Earlier this year, you started with tiny moments and asked, 'What is this story really about?' and revised to find the deeper meanings in those tiny moments. Now many of you have begun this unit of study instead with deeper meanings, and that is okay too, as long as you remember, 'The bigger the meaning, the smaller you write.'

"My brother Geoff is the sports columnist for the *Commercial Appeal*, Memphis's newspaper. Usually he writes about sports topics: Mike Tyson coming to town, Shani Davis's gold medal. But one year, Geoff decided that for his January-first column he would break his pattern and write about the memory of a time our mother invented games to distract him while in the hospital waiting room—and the larger themes he finds in those memories. As I read, notice the ways Geoff, starts writing about memories but shifts to writing about ideas, about life lessons. He is interpreting his life, just like you interpret books.

> *The games I remember most from my childhood aren't Little League or hoops. Instead, the game I remember most was penny pitching. This was usually played in hospital waiting rooms. I grew up with leukemia and spent a lot of time in hospital waiting rooms. To pass the time, my mother would take off her shoe, push it onto the middle of the rug, and we'd take turns pitching pennies into her shoe.*
>
> *Now when people ask me what it was like, growing up with leukemia, I do not tell them about the scabs around my mouth or the IV lines. Instead I tell them that what I remember most is the thrill of the perfect arc and the soft thud as the penny landed squarely in my Mum's shoe.*
>
> *I am writing this column not because this has anything to do with Memphis or sports, but because I do not want another year to go by without saying thanks. My mother took a potentially scary time and made it sweet.*
>
> *And isn't that the lesson of September 11? Whatever it is we have been meaning to do—we need to do it, and do it now. Write that letter. Go for that job. Make that phone call. Not because at any moment, a plane might come out of the heavens and reduce our world to smithereens, but because we are still here on this fragile spinning earth, and never has that seemed so precious.*

"Talk to the person beside you. What do you notice about how Geoff wrote both small and big?" I gave the children a minute to talk and then called them back together, sharing some of what I'd heard. "What most of you noticed was that Geoff wrote about small moments—penny pitching—and a big theme."

Roy Peter Clark often discusses "the ladder of abstraction" when talking about the graphics of good writing. Popularized by S.I. Hayakawa in his 1939 book Language in Action, *the "ladder of abstraction" reminds writers that it is important to write both "big" and "small," and to move between these two as you write. You'll want to help students understand the power of writing big, from the top of the ladder (about concepts, ideas, and themes) but also small, at the bottom of the ladder (providing specific details and examples to exemplify the ideas they hope to express).*

Whenever you are about to read a text aloud in a minilesson, pause to be sure you have set students up to listen with whatever lens you want them to bring to the text. If you aren't able to display an enlarged version of the text, they won't be able to reread it with the lens you hope they eventually bring to the text. So set them up to listen with that lens in mind. Here, I ask them to listen for the mix of ideas and story, generalization and specific.

Quickly shift to your own writing, giving children one more opportunity to understand the difference between writing big and small.

"Yesterday I found an issue that often emerges in my writing—the difficulty of fitting in. I've also asked, 'What are some moments from my life that show that issue and I've begun to collect other related stories. I will also see if there is another theme or issue that is equally compelling to me and collect entries around that.

I flipped through my writer's notebook. The episode in which the kids laughed at my dress, calling it antique enough to be in a Civil War play, relates to my struggles to fit in. I could also write the story of when my dad embarrassed me at the basketball game, climbing up the bleachers to sit with me and my friends. I'll be writing Small Moment stories in my notebook that relate to the big themes and issues in my life."

Debrief.

"Writers, hopefully you are beginning to see how wise Richard Price's words are. When we want to share big ideas with a reader, it is often effective to do that by writing small stories. You can do this by naming the big thought you hope to show and then thinking of one or two small moments that will show that thought to your reader. Then, just like when you write personal narratives, you can write the true story of those moments."

ACTIVE ENGAGEMENT

"It was fun for me to make this minilesson. To make it, I needed to think about a time when someone wrote about a big thought, but wrote small to show its truth. It doesn't seem fair for me to have all the fun! I'm going to read you a bit of a famous writer's memoir, and will you think about what her idea is, her theme, and notice how her story and her theme fit together?" Then I said, "This is from the memoir *Little by Little* by Jean Little," and revealed the excerpt on chart paper.

"Early in the book," I explained, "Jean sets out to climb a tree, and her neighbor Marilyn restrains her from doing so, saying, 'You have bad eyes.'"

> "I do not have Bad Eyes," I told her defiantly. "If your mother said that, she's wrong. My mother never said so and my mother is a doctor so she'd know. My father is a doctor, too, and he never said so, either. They both said I can climb any tree I like." (1987, p. 3)

I gave the students a bit more context. "Marilyn, however, is persistent. She continues to taunt Jean, 'You do so have bad eyes!' until Jean runs into the house to her mother.

> "What is it, Jean?" she asked in a quiet, calming voice.

> "Marilyn says her mother says I have bad eyes," I burst out, my words sputtering in their rush to get said. "She said I can't climb the tree because it's dangerous if you have bad eyes. I don't have them, do I? I can climb trees, can't I?"

Be purposeful in your choice of texts. That is, you'll want to make sure you choose texts where children can do this work with some ease. For partnerships that might struggle, consider giving them an easier text with a more obvious structure.

Mother did not hesitate. I can still hear the words that set my world turning on its axis again.

"You do have bad eyes," she said, "but you go right ahead and climb the tree." (p. 4)

Channel students to discuss the ways Jean Little's "small," anecdotal writing supports her larger message.

Then I said, "Turn and talk. What is the theme? How does the story support this theme? I moved around the meeting area, coaching in as children worked and sharing what they noticed.

LINK

Send children off to write with generalizations and particulars. Tell them ways that they can use strategies they've learned across the year to generate writing that is both gigantic and tiny.

"So today, if you have been writing *small*, ask yourself, 'What's the big theme or issue here?' And if you have been writing about a big theme or issue, please pause to think, 'What small stories are inside here?'

"Remember, writers, that so far this year you have learned a handful of strategies for generating writing. Some of those strategies help you generate Small Moment stories, and some help you generate big ideas, but by now, you have learned that writers can begin with either one of these—big ideas or small moments—as long as they write their way toward the other!

On this day, you might consider asking children to add to the collection of memoirs, seeking out their own mentors for the work they are doing. You might say, "Writers, I have an idea. If any of you know of other memoirs that we could study, would you be willing to bring them in? This way, we can start a basket with an even larger collection of memoirs and study texts that resemble those we will be writing." If you haven't already exposed your students to the following, I highly recommend them as alternate mentors: "Alone" by Jacqueline Woodson; "Statue," "Eating the World," and "Last Kiss" by Ralph Fletcher; "Regrets" by Richard Margolis; "Everything Will Be Okay" by James Howe; and "Mr. Entwhistle" by Jean Little.

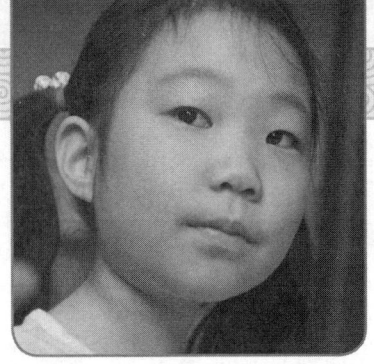

CONFERRING AND SMALL-GROUP WORK

Settling Down to Write Well

TODAY YOU WILL DEFINITELY WANT TO HELP YOUR CHILDREN RECALL what they learned earlier in the year about writing powerful narratives. It is important that children write well. Magical writing is contagious. It is possible that your efforts to help students shift between writing about abstract ideas and writing particular stories will lead them to forego writing the focused, detailed Small Moment stories that you've emphasized all along, channeling them instead toward texts that are neither idea-based texts nor detailed stories, but something in between. Often these "in-between texts" are voiceless, generic, dull. Your goal is for your students to write rather like "Eleven." You hope portions of their texts will be idea-based and portions will be poignant, detailed narratives. That is, you hope portions will address ideas as Cisneros did when she compared growing old to being like an onion, and you hope portions will be like the red sweater vignette.

If children are no longer writing focused small moments, it is urgent for you to confer with them to remind them to do this. Your hope is that within today's workshop, many of your children will write detailed, true, Small Moment stories about events that are charged with emotional significance for them—events related to the themes and issues they have chosen to explore. If this happens, the unit will be off to a strong start. The children who are well launched will be able to sustain themselves and help you bring the others along.

MID-WORKSHOP TEACHING Angling Your Stories to Bring Forth Themes

"In the personal essay unit and in the personal narrative unit, too, you learned to angle the way you tell the story of a small moment so that your writing answers the question, 'What's this really about?' This is more important now than ever. You are not writing about an episode in your life just to tell a good story about something true that happened. Instead, you are writing about playing catch with your dad to illustrate that your dad pushes you to be your best self. You are writing about burying your dog to write that times of loss make a person think about what matters. As you write the story of an episode from your life, then, you need to forward the meaning you are trying to communicate.

"So right now, writers, will you write the theme or issue that your entry is addressing? Write this at the top of the paper." They did this.

"Now, here's the challenge. Over the years, you have learned ways to bring out the big ideas, theme, or issue in your Small Moment stories. Can you and the people at your table try to recall and collect ways you've learned to bring out the big ideas, the themes, in a story? How did you help readers know what a story is *really* talking about?" Soon a chart was under way.

> Ways to Bring Out the Big Ideas in a Story
>
> - Make sure your story starts and ends in a way that shows the big ideas/themes
> - Stretch out the part of the story that illustrates the big idea/theme
>   - Use dialogue, internal thinking, and details to pop out this part

To accomplish this, you'll need to be ready to do some intense conferring. Aim to help children who are writing with big ideas ground those in focused narratives, and to help children who are writing with focused narratives mine them for big ideas.

Trust that any child's vignette relates to a theme or issue of great importance, remembering that often a draft of writing is like an iceberg: beneath the bit that shows, there's a tremendous part that doesn't show. Confirm the significance of the child's topic (even if you are doing so on faith only). Say, "I can tell you are onto something that's important for you," and act as if it is absolutely clear to you that this topic has depths that merit exploration. Then, help the writer shift between writing the story of a moment and exploring the big themes of that moment.

If the child has written about ideas, you'll probably want to remark on this. "What I notice is that you are writing about ideas. "Explain that this is special. Many kids will choose to first capture little moments, and only later reach for the ideas that fit with those moments. You are special, because as a writer you seem to be especially at home writing about ideas." You'll want to be more specific, too. For example, when I read Rie's idea-based entry, I congratulated her on writing with honesty and precision about ideas. To highlight what she *did* do, I juxtaposed it with the commonplace. "You didn't write in general about ideas. You reached for exactly true, specific words to convey your feelings." Here is Rie's entry (Figure 3–1).

After supporting what Rie had done, I challenged her to shift between writing ideas and writing stories. A repertoire of questions can help writers make this shift. For example, a writer might ask, "How can I show this idea by telling the story of one time in my life?" If a writer is most at home in the land of idea-based essay-like entries, she may need to be reminded that to capture a story on the page, it helps to make a movie in one's mind, to go to the start of the episode and record it, to write step by step, not rushing over details. Here is the small moment Rie wrote about the idea addressed in the entry cited earlier (Figure 3–2).

Meanwhile, if a child is writing highly-focused narratives, then after naming again what you see that child doing, you'll want to convey your absolute trust that the small moments contain big meanings.

> I sometimes have a hard time being myself. I try to be like other people. It sometimes feels like everybody else does everything right, and I just mess up everything. So I'm always looking to see what other people do. All I want is to be like other people, and this makes me feel really bad. When I think about this, I realize that I should be happy to be myself rather than being like someone else.
>
> Rie

FIG. 3–1   Rie explores themes and issues.

> "Up, up, down. Up, up, down..." my ballet teacher shouted out to the class. Oh, I wish this was over, I thought.
> "Rie!" Her voice called over the music right to me. "Your knee isn't straight!" I looked down at my knee. This is all I can do. I don't have a skinny American knee.
> She came over to me and pushed my knee down like she was making a dough flat. Why do you have to do this to me? I screamed out in my head. I looked at the girl next to me. Her knee was back and flat. Oh if she's like that, why can't be like that? As I stood there, my mother's voice came into my head. She said, "Be yourself, Rie. You're not Kathy or Paula or Helene..."

FIG. 3–2   Rie was reminded to make a movie in her mind.

SESSION 3: WRITING SMALL ABOUT BIG TOPICS

SHARE

Trust that There's Treasure

If you notice a problem, point it out, and propose a solution. In this case, tell children to be aware that the desire to write about something important can lure them to give up on great possibilities.

"Writers, I need your full attention." I waited. For some of you, the effort to write about big themes and issues has made you insecure. It's as if you are a kid looking for treasure. You know it is somewhere, so you run around with a shovel, digging just a little here and then just a little there. You never get to really digging deep because you are frantically worrying that first this place and then that place won't, in the end, hold any treasure.

"In order to write well, you need to trust that there are huge meanings and themes and issues in almost any moment. A writer I know once said, 'There is an illusion that writers live more significant lives than the rest of us. The truth is that writers are just more in the habit of finding the significance that is there.' Right now, reread the work you've written and ask yourself, 'Am I giving up on stories too fast?'" I left some silence. "Tell your partner what you think," I said.

Children talked and eventually I said, "Trust that the themes of your life are there, hidden in almost any entry. You can write in ways that surface those big ideas."

FIG. 3–3 Judah decided that she was hopping from one moment to another and went back to write the first moment in more detail.

SESSION 3 HOMEWORK

COMPLEX TEXTS CONTAIN MORE THAN ONE CENTRAL IDEA

In our writing workshop, all of us have become skilled at looking at an entry and thinking, "What do I really want to say?" or asking, "What's my big idea about this?" and then using details to support the one idea we decide to advance. *However*, most of the time in life, we do not have just one big idea or one big feeling about a subject. Usually our ideas and feelings are more complicated than that. Many of the things that I love are also things that trouble me. In *Hey World! Here I Am!* (1990) many of the notebook entries that Jean Little has included are about the friendship between Kate and Emily. Jean shows different sides to Kate and Emily's friendship. In "Maybe a Fight," Jean Little shows that friendships aren't always peachy.

> "Emily Blair," I said, struggling with my conflicting emotions, "are you trying to pick a fight with me?"
> "I wasn't, but I *will* if that's what you're after," she growled.

But in the very next notebook entry, "Not Enough Emilys," Kate writes as if Emily is the only person in the world who really understands her.

> There are not enough Emilys in the world.
> What I mean is . . . Emily is the kind of person
> Everybody needs to have sometimes.

Tonight, will you take an entry about a theme, issue, or idea that matters to you, an entry in which you write with details and also show a big idea? Perhaps it's an entry about loving your family's homeland in Missouri or about grieving over your big brother's upcoming departure. Write another entry, and this time, write in a way that is the opposite of what you wrote earlier! Writing from opposite sides of an idea will help you think about your ideas with more depth.

Session 4

Reading Literature to Inspire Writing

IN THIS SESSION, you'll teach students another strategy writers use to write with depth: letting literature influence their own writing.

GETTING READY

- ✔ Evocative published text, such as the chapter "Alone" from Jacqueline Woodson's *From the Notebooks of Melanin Sun* (1995) (see Teaching)

- ✔ Example of your own writing inspired by the text above (see Teaching)

- ✔ Passage from a text children know well, one that is either a memoir or that has a memoir-like quality, such as *Journey* by Patricia MacLachlan (1993) (see Active Engagement)

- ✔ Example of student writing after reading the text above (see Active Engagement)

- ✔ Example of student writing that layers different strategies from published texts (see Mid-Workshop Teaching)

- ✔ Four pre-chosen student authors to read their writing in small groups (see Share)

COMMON CORE STATE STANDARDS: W.5.3, W.5.4, W.5.5, W.5.10, RL.5.2, RL.5.10, SL.5.1, L.5.1, L.5.2, L.5.3

ADRIAN PEETOOM, A CANADIAN LITERACY LEADER, once told me, "If I could say just one thing to teachers of writing, I would tell them this. Trust the books. Trust the books and get out of their way." It is true that the authors who write the books we love can become coteachers, helping us teach students to write. Authors teach not only by demonstrating craftsmanship, but also by inspiring writers to write about the themes and issues of their lives. Author Cynthia Rylant has often written about the significance of reading authentic literature to children. She writes, "Read to them. Read with the same feeling in your throat as when you first see the ocean after driving hours and hours to get there. Close the final page of the book with the same reverence you feel when you kiss your sleeping child at night. Be quiet. Don't talk the experience to death. Shut up and let those kids feel and think. Teach your children to be moved and you will be preparing them to move others."

Great literature can call us all from our hiding places. When we write in the wake of a great story, it is as if those stories have called out, "All-y, all-y, in free! Come out, come out, wherever you are!"

I'm thinking of Andrew, a fifth-grader. During fourth grade he'd written an entry about his camp. In the piece, he wrote about fishing a pair of dirty underpants from the camp's pond. It was a silly piece, written to evoke guffaws from his peers. Then, in fifth grade, Andrew's teacher, Kathy Doyle, created a trusting community where it was okay for Andrew and the others in his class to address tough issues. Kathy did this especially by using literature as an ice ax, as Kafka has said it can be, to break the frozen sea within us.

From the safety of this new community, Andrew looked back at the piece he'd written the preceding year. "The truth is, camp was nothing like I wrote in this entry," he said. "When I wrote it, in fourth grade, there was a school-Andrew and a home-Andrew. Back then, I acted completely different in school than I really am." Andrew returned to the topic of summer camp, and this time, he wrote about how, on the last day of camp, he'd struggled to keep from weeping when he paused to say good-bye to the goats and to the gravel driveway. His memoir ends:

We took pictures until finally Soren joked, "Now it looks like we're all peeling onions!" Driving away, we stopped to say goodbye to the goats who had been with us the whole time. We drove up the gravel driveway, still crying. I thought the magic was gone. At the end of the gravel driveway, just before the paved road began, we stopped to pick flowers and to wave one last goodbye to the goats and to the gravel driveway.

In the car, I knew one thing. I could never truly explain what happened at camp. I couldn't explain the magic. I'd try to explain, to tell my parents what it had been like, how we'd felt, but I would never really explain and secretly, I didn't mind. These were my friends, these were my memories.

"It is true that the authors who write the books we love can become coteachers, helping us teach students to write."

Today, you will help children to bring the themes and issues of their lives into their writing by using literature to evoke those themes, and by teaching writers that readers turn to literature for inspiration.

MINILESSON

Reading Literature to Inspire Writing

CONNECTION

Tell students that literature can be evocative, leading writers to the themes and issues of their lives.

"A writer named Kafka once wrote, 'Literature can be an ice axe to break the frozen sea within us.' It's true for me that sometimes I've been busy, busy, busy, running from one thing to another and then I pick up a novel and read a bit. The book makes me pause and reflect and remember. It makes me think of the stories and themes of my own life."

♣ **Name your teaching point.**

"Today, I want to teach you that when writers want to write powerfully, one strategy they use is to read (or listen to) literature and then write. Reading literature can help writers write their own literature. Writers write 'off from' the texts."

TEACHING

Tell students that reading can be a way to push themselves in their writing. Show an example of a text you read and wrote off from.

"As a writer, I often start with a text that I know will be powerful for me. It is often a text I already know. Then I simply read the text, taking in the words and the images. Then, when the text is done, I let it sink in. I might reread it a little. Then, when I feel in the middle of that text, I write. I don't write *about* the text, and I don't write more of the text, I write *off from* the text.

"Let me show you what I mean. I recently reread my favorite chapter from Jacqueline Woodson's *Notebooks of Melanin Sun*, titled 'Alone.' Let me read just a little bit of it to you, and then I'll read what I wrote off of this chapter."

> Alone
> Some days I wear alone like a coat, like a hood draping from my head that first warm day of Spring, like socks bunching up inside my sneakers. Like that.
>
> Alone is how I walk some days, with my hands shoved deep in my pockets, with my head down, walking against the day, into it then out again.

◆ COACHING

To teach this concept, you have two choices. You can demonstrate this, or you can show an example. If you decide to demonstrate, then you will actually do the work in front of the class. That is, you'll actually read a text and then pick up a marker pen and freewrite on the white board as the children watch. You'll probably want to choose to read a poem if you are going to demonstrate because time will be an issue. If you do this, be sure you write fast, without worrying about your wording, without censoring yourself. You will see that in this instance, I decide not to demonstrate, but instead to show the writing I did at a different time.

I love this text. I love the images of everyday ordinary things and routines that characterize the feeling "alone" so precisely. I love that I get a pit in my stomach—the same one kids get, though it's been years since I felt alone in these ways. You'll want to make sure you choose a text that evokes equally strong emotions in you, so that your writing can be as authentic and powerful as possible.

Alone is the taste in my mouth some mornings, like morning breath, like hunger. It's lumpy oatmeal for breakfast when Mama doesn't have time to cook and I still don't know how much oatmeal and water and milk will make it all right.

"This is what I wrote, and you'll notice that I didn't write *about* Woodson's text or even about the same topic. I just let the words of her writing roll over me and I wrote whatever was in my mind. I wrote practically without thinking, all in a rush, very quickly."

> Some days I feel as if stress has seeped into every nook and cranny of our classrooms. It's there, on teachers' faces, when we try to nudge more and more into the day, when we read the practice tests with a sinking feeling, when we glance up at the clock, the calendar, and realize time is passing.
>
> Stress is what we feel as we approach the meeting area: what did I forget? What must I cover? Will my students understand the heart of today's lesson?
>
> Stress presses in to our minds and bodies, making our hearts beat quickly, our skin get damp, our heads pound. Stress clings to us like a great, dark shadow that won't leave our side.

Debrief, pointing out that you didn't write about the text or even about the subject in the text.

"Do you notice that I didn't write *about* Jacqueline's text, or even about the same topic? I just let the words of her writing roll over me, and I wrote whatever was in my mind. I wrote practically without thinking, all in a rush, very quickly."

ACTIVE ENGAGEMENT

Set children up to try this. Read a text aloud and then join them in writing off from that text.

"Let's try. I will read aloud a passage from our read-aloud book. This is a passage that I know you heard earlier. I will read it aloud, and then in the silence after I finish reading, would you pick up your pen and write *off from* the story I read? Don't write *about* the story. Write *off from* it." Then, opening Patricia MacLachlan's novel, *Journey*, to pages 11–13, I reminded children that Grandma has just brought a bowl of soup and a photo album to her grandson, Journey, and they are looking through the pictures together.

> *In the picture the girl who was my mama sat behind a table, her face in her hands, looking far off in the distance. All around her were people laughing, talking. Lancie, Mama's sister, made a face at the camera. Uncle Minor, his hair all sun bleached, was caught by the camera taking a handful of cookies. In the background a dog leaped into the air to grab a ball, his ears floating out as if uplifted and held there by the wind. But my mother looked silent and unhearing.*

Be careful to give children all the directions for the entire activity before you begin to read so that once you finish reading, you will not need to reiterate directions. You will not want instructional words to break the spell of the story, to separate the text from their writing off from that text.

Journey is a demanding book and has been one of our most important touchstone texts. Consider also Paulsen's The Monument, *too. Like* Journey, *that book has a great deal to teach writers. Of course, if your children do not know* Journey, *you'll choose another excerpt to read aloud at this moment.*

"It's a nice picture," I said. "Except for Mama. It must have been the camera," I said after a moment.

Grandma sighed and took my hand.

"No, it wasn't the camera, Journey. It was your mama. Your mama always wished to be somewhere else."

"Well, now she is," I said.

After a while Grandma got up and left the room. I sat there for a long time, staring at Mama's picture, as if I could will her to turn and talk to the person next to her . . . The expression on Mama's face was one I knew. One I remembered.

Somewhere else. I am very little, five or six, and in overalls and new yellow rubber boots. I follow Mama across the meadow. It has rained and everything is washed and shiny, the sky clear. As I walk my feet make squashing sounds, and when I try to catch up with Mama I fall into the brook. I am not afraid, but when I look up Mama has walked away. Arms pick me up, someone else's arms. Someone else takes off my boots and pours out the water. My grandfather. I am angry. It's not my grandfather I want. It is Mama. But Mama is far ahead, and she doesn't look back. She is somewhere else.

The silence after I finished reading was palpable. Students looked up at me, as if to ask, "What do you want us to do now?" but I didn't want instructions to come between the literature and their writing. I simply picked up my pen, and began writing, scrawling words onto my own page.

LINK

Send children off to write, reminding them of their options and alerting them to the short texts on their tables in case they want to continue to read and write off from literature.

After two or three minutes during which the only sound was the scratch of pens, I spoke. "Writers, today you'll have forty-five minutes to write. Use those minutes to do some important work. Remember that if you feel stuck for ideas or inspiration, reading a piece of literature can help to spur you on. I've put some particularly powerful excerpts in folders at your tables if you want them.

Then I added, "Right now, will you do some rereading and decide what work you'll do today? Fill in your self-assignment box, and when you know the work you'll do today, you can go off and get started."

When I finish reading, I purposefully do not look up and scan the room, as if giving children the eagle eye. There is something powerful about simply writing in front of others, losing oneself in the page. I know I need to model absolute absorption.

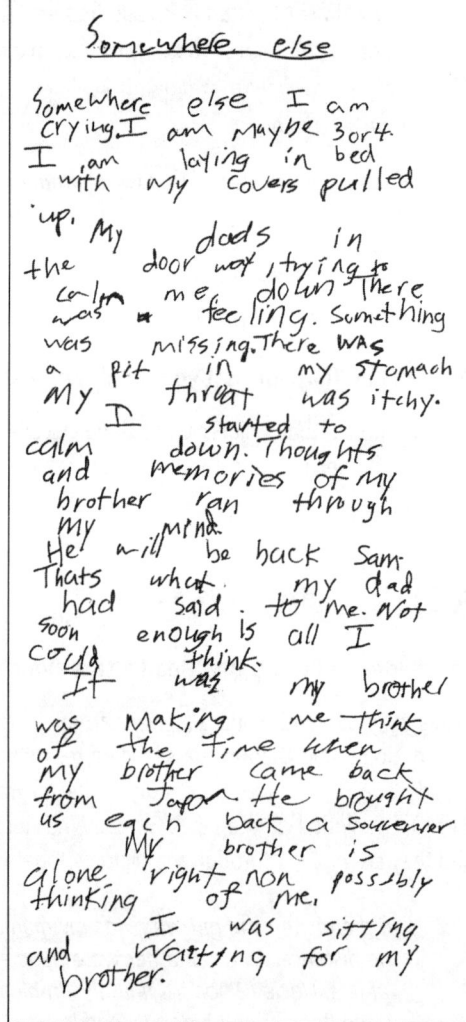

FIG. 4–1 Adam's entry, written during the minilesson after hearing the excerpt read aloud

CONFERRING AND SMALL-GROUP WORK

Writing Guided by Literature

TODAY, MANY OF YOUR CHILDREN WILL CHOOSE TO WRITE OFF FROM LITERATURE, and really, there are a variety of ways this could go. Your first and foremost goal is to get children writing with power and volume and there are a few tricks you might teach them to do this more effectively. The first strategy is something we refer to at The Reading and Writing Project as *echo writing*. In this instance, you teach children to write in a voice that echoes that of an author they admire. They might write to emulate the rhythm of a small patch of writing, the structure of a piece, or even the structure of actual sentences. You might also teach children to literally 'steal' a

---

MID-WORKSHOP TEACHING **Combining and Layering Strategies**

"Writers, can I stop you? I want to celebrate how so many of you have found yourselves in those texts you are reading. When Ali reread 'Eleven,' about a girl who is embarrassed and struggles to deal with this, Ali saw more about herself. She realized that she struggles inside to tell her father (who as we all know has been sick and absorbed by being sick) that she wants him to come back to being a father who cares again about her spelling tests and her soccer goals.

When Max read 'Eleven,' he found something else in it! He found not only a girl who turns eleven and at the same time is also ten, nine, eight, seven, six, five, four, three, two, and one, but Max also found himself—a boy who is moving on to middle school and is still holding tight to a childhood tree fort. We all use mentor texts in different ways to discover things about ourselves.

When writers are inspired to write in the wake of a text, this inspiration usually happens in one of three different ways. First," and I held up one finger to signal the beginning of a list, "they are inspired by the actual topic that the writer writes about. So, for instance, after reading 'Eleven,' I might be reminded of a mean teacher or an experience with a piece of clothing. Second," and I held up a second finger, "they are inspired by the themes or issues the writer puts forth. So, after reading 'Eleven,' I might remember a time when I felt voiceless, or bullied, or like a child smaller than myself." I paused and put up a third finger. "The last way writers are often inspired is by a word, a phrase, or an image that the author uses. 'Not mine. Not mine' might conjure memories. The image of the onion, or of the Russian dolls, one nested inside the next, might inspire me to write. So, today, as you write, remember that there are multiple ways you might be inspired by another author's writing."

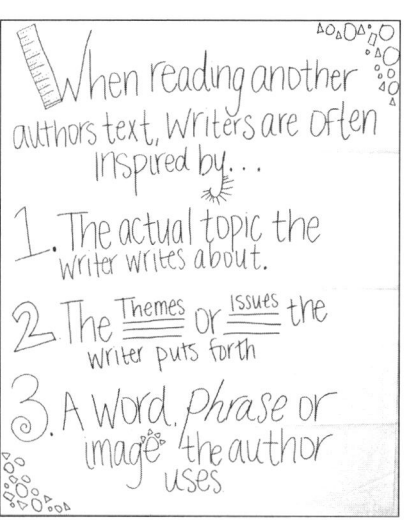

FIG. 4–2

phrase from an author, letting that word or phrase inspire their own thoughts about their lives.

Adam, for example, decided to "write off from" Ralph Fletcher's "Last Kiss." In this memoir, Ralph contrasts his mother and his father—their goodnight kisses and their roles in his life—and ends by saying, "If nothing else, my childhood had symmetry." After reading this, Adam wrote an entry. Later, when I pulled close to see what Adam had been working on, I saw that the entry contained three different attempts to write off from Fletcher's text using his phrase, 'if nothing else' to spur his own thinking about his relationship with his brother. (see Figure 4–3). He explained to me that he read the text, then wrote off from it. Then he reread the text, and again wrote off from it, and the same for the third time.

You may wonder about the fact that Adam borrows phrases from "Last Kiss" and "Eleven," using another author's words to get his ideas going. I noticed this, of course, but kept in mind that Adam is not writing for publication here. He's writing in the privacy of his writer's notebook, fully intending that his purpose is to generate seed ideas. By leaning on other authors Adam is giving himself a scaffold that is allowing him to write much more powerfully than he's ever written, and as long as this dependency is temporary, I'm all for it.

Last, but not least, you might consider harkening back to the work of the personal narrative unit, reminding children that often when a writer writes in the wake of a text, the text reminds the writer of a topic, theme, or issue, giving the writer some content. So, for instance, "Last Kiss" might lead me to memories of times spent with my mom and dad.

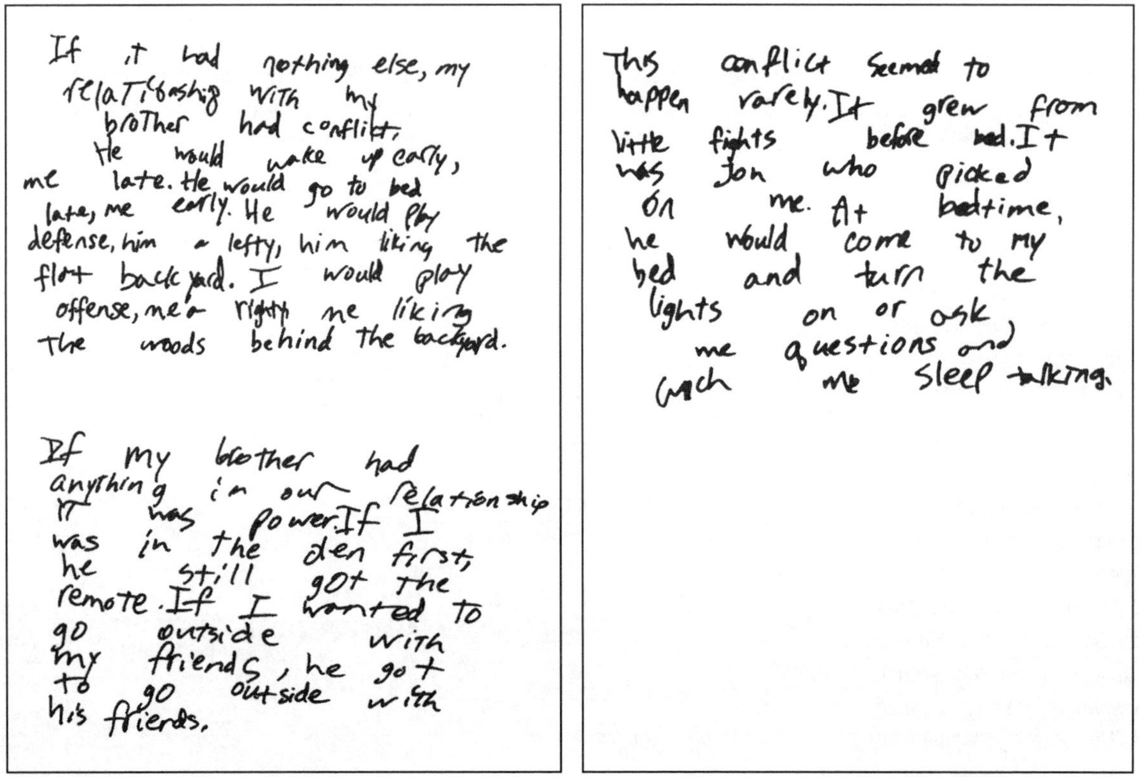

1. If it had nothing else, my relationship with my brother had conflict. He would wake up early, me late. He would go to bed late, me early. He would play defense, him a lefty, him liking the flat backyard; I would play offense, me a righty, me liking the woods behind the backyard.

2. If my brother had anything in our relationship, it was power. If I was in the den first, he still got the remote. If I wanted to go outside with my friends, he got to go outside with his friends.

3. This conflict seemed to happen rarely. It grew from little fights before bed. It was Jon who picked on me. At bedtime, he would come to my bed and turn the lights on or ask me questions and watch me sleep, talking.

FIG 4–3 Adam's entry, inspired by Ralph Fletcher

SHARE

Writing in the Wake of Classmates' Work

Tell children that *all* literature can be evocative, especially that written by friends and peers.

"Today, most of you spent some time writing off of published authors like Sandra Cisneros and Ralph Fletcher. What I want you to know, though, is that we needn't always look beyond this classroom for writing inspiration. What I mean by this is that each one of you can be the kind of writer who inspires other writers."

① 9/04

What Construction workers and handymans and gardners/don't have a single clue about is this: When you build a clubhouse or a swingset in some kid's backyard, or when you plant a big, branch filled, perfect-for-climbing Magnolia tree in some kids front yard, they are gonna love it. And what makes those guys sooo ignorant is you can't bust it down! Even if that kid does not live there anymore!
  I think about how much I miss them. Well, my tree is still there even if I'm not. And hey! I have something a construction worker or any of those guys can't bust down

② Something you can't tear up in photos. Something you can't stain with grape juice and never wear again.
I've got MEMORIES!!
  You can't take away my memories Not in a million years. And when I am old and gray and can't remember my first name, I will still have these memories.
  Wanna know why? Because it is sort of like when you are blind. You can hear and feel better then you could when you could see.
  Since I don't have my clubhouse or my tree, I

③ Can't make new memories with them. And they aren't there to see, hear, feel etc., but they are still there in my heart and soul, and MEMORIES!

FIG. 4–4 Max writes to explore a topic he feels strongly about—his old tree fort—from a variety of perspectives.

SESSION 4: READING LITERATURE TO INSPIRE WRITING

Explain that children will have the opportunity to hear a classmate's writing, and to "write off" from that.

"In just a moment, I will divide you into four groups. You'll go to four corners of the room, where you'll have the opportunity to hear a classmate's writing and write off from it. You might find inspiration in the themes or issues they write about, you might be inspired by a line or two of that writing, or you may be inspired in other ways that you don't quite understand. The only important thing is that you let that student's writing inspire you to write another entry, and that you write it as well as you can."

I divided the children into four groups and sent each one of them to a corner of the room, where a pre-chosen author would read his or her piece aloud before giving the other students a few moments to write in the wake of the reading.

SESSION 4 HOMEWORK

COLLECTING MEMORIES

The writer Katherine Bomer (2005) has said this: "Memories come to people most often while they are doing something else; washing the dishes, driving to work, listening to music, walking the dog. Memory comes in split-second images, it hides in the cracks of daily activity, and to capture it, sometimes we have to sneak up behind, pretend we are doing something else, like scrubbing the bathtub, and memories will come" (*Writing a Life*, 90).

Tonight, and throughout your writerly lives, be aware of the memories that come to you while you are busy doing something else. Record those memories as entries in your notebook, saving them for when you choose a seed idea and begin drafting your memoir.

Session 5

Choosing a Seed Idea

CHANCES ARE GOOD that your writers know enough of the rhythms of writing that they will have been weighing options for the idea that will grow into their memoir before today.

Early in the year, we taught students that writers of personal narratives look for focused, true stories as ideas to grow into pieces. Sometimes, however, a writer may begin with a compelling metaphor, a longing to accomplish a particular purpose, an assigned topic, an excerpt that we want to extend, or with a still amorphous (but very much alive) theme or topic or idea. We need to let our children know that writers do lots of different things, as called for by the demands of the task. In this session, then, you will teach students that writers take first steps with their writing in different ways. The differences reflect different writing tasks, and they also reflect differences in personal style.

Then, too, today you will show children that although writers do make some choices quickly, narrowing in on whatever it is we will write, it doesn't often happen that a writer will, out of nowhere, choose an idea in a single moment of inspiration.

Although writers may start with any one of many "precious particles," as author Malcolm Cowley refers to potential seed ideas, the writer does need at some point to at least try to take a leap of faith, declaring some fragment to be precious, and making the decision to develop this bit.

In this session, you will help writers choose and develop, rechoose and redevelop their themes or ideas. You will help children postpone closure, letting their emerging sense of direction and their image of what it is they will write grow. Earlier in the year, children had fewer strategies for planning a piece of writing and less knowledge of what does and does not pay off when writing. By now, however, you will want children to draw on all they know to rehearse for their writing—because revising as you begin your writing is vastly more efficient than revising as you end it!

IN THIS SESSION, you'll remind students of ways they've chosen seed ideas—or the material that will become seed ideas—during previous cycles through the writing process. You'll help students draw on and improvise off from these strategies to devise a process that works for them.

GETTING READY

✔ An adult to interview (or the transcript of an interview) about how he or she selects a seed idea (see Teaching and Active Engagement)

✔ A list of strategies for selecting a seed idea created from the above interview (see Teaching and Active Engagement)

✔ "Strategies for Writing with Depth" chart (see Conferring)

✔ "Ways to Push Our Thinking" chart (from *Literary Essays: Writing About Reading* unit in Grade 4) (see Share)

COMMON CORE STATE STANDARDS: W.5.1, W.5.3, W.5.5, W.5.7, RL.5.2, SL.5.1, SL.5.3, L.5.1, L.5.2, L.5.3

MINILESSON

Choosing a Seed Idea

CONNECTION

Celebrate the fact that your children already anticipate that they'll shift from collecting entries to selecting a seed idea.

"Writers, I bet I don't even need to tell most of you that the time has come for you to shift from collecting entries to selecting your seed idea—the idea or theme you will help develop into a memoir. Can you give me a thumbs up if you *already knew* that it'd be time, soon, to look back and ask, 'So what am I going to choose?'"

The children all indicated that yes, indeed, they had already anticipated this shift. "What you are showing me is so important. You are making me think that, next year, when you go to work on a story or a poem or an article for the newspaper, you'll know, without me being there, that after collecting some ideas for writing, you need to look back and think, 'Out of all the possibilities, what stands out for me?' You might not realize it, but this is a *huge* lesson, one you need to remember for the rest of your life. Writing will always be more powerful if you take some time to generate a few different possibilities, to mull over them, and to select one choice among many.

"Earlier this year, in our narrative writing unit, you learned that narrative writers often start by selecting one focused moment as the idea to grow into a story. In our informational writing unit, you learned to start by writing about large topics, like Westward Expansion. Only later did you narrow your focus to a subtopic such as the Pony Express."

❖ **Name your teaching point.**

"Today, I want to teach you that the process of developing a full-blown piece of writing has many more layers and can go many more ways than you might have expected. Writers may start with a metaphor, a collection of related stories, or even just a tiny mention of a thought. It can help to study how other authors go about this work before planning for your own process.

◆ COACHING

When your students already know something, it's great to acknowledge this, allowing you to recap what they know and highlight what's new.

You will see that I take the opportunity, again and again, to remind children that they now have a repertoire of strategies for proceeding through the writing process and do not need to rely on my help every step of the way. More importantly, I hope to crystallize in children's minds that this repertoire is transferable—applicable to narrative writing, expository writing, and all kinds of writing.

TEACHING

Briefly describe some ways writers might go about the process of narrowing in on a focused idea or theme.

"As you've been gathering materials for a memoir, you've shifted between collecting, sorting, choosing—and writers do this all the time. Narrowing in on the materials that will become a draft actually happens over a long period of time, as you collect, and as you reread, thinking, 'What do I really want to say?' To understand this process, it can help to study how other writers do it."

Tell students that some will zoom in on one idea or theme today. Others will establish a general direction and develop a focus more gradually.

"You already know that your goal in this unit of study will be to make something—a true story, an essay, an article—that conveys an important message about the whole of your life. You will be writing a memoir. Like so many memoirists, you will spend time choosing (or creating) the form, the structure that will best carry your message. As you think about your structure, you also need to think about your message and your content. In the end, the message and the form go together.

"Some of you will be able to reread your writing today and find your focus. Others of you will establish a direction and begin collecting material, but you may still be unclear what shape your memoir might take or what the primary material will be. But you need to make some choices and to commit at least to a direction."

Interview an adult who will demonstrate strategies that writers use to generate and select between possible directions for an upcoming writing project. From this interview, select and highlight certain strategies that writers can use often.

"So how do writers select their ideas? What I'm going to do right now is to ask Ali to interview me. Will you join her as researchers, keeping track of the strategies I use to decide on the idea I think I'll develop in my memoir? You might want to use your notebook to take a few notes as you listen."

Ali began, "Tell us about how you choose your idea."

I said, "I started by reading the entries I had collected."

Ali gestured for me to continue, so I did. "A bunch of them were sort of related to the way I wanted to fit in when I was a kid, so I asked, 'Do any of my other entries (under the surface) connect to the idea about fitting in?' As a reader, I realized that I had a lot of entries that connected to this issue. Also, I'd listed small moment ideas earlier that fit with the issue."

It is important to teach in various ways. Sometimes you demonstrate by writing publicly; sometimes you share an example that you or an author or a child has written. Sometimes, too, children role-play or reenact in front of the class. And today, Ali and I have decided to model this process jointly. As I play the role of the writer, Ali will interview me about my process, while children join in learning what I have done. You'll want to develop a way to make this same process work in your classroom. Even if you don't have another adult in the room, you might consider putting a transcript of our work on chart paper or the overhead, telling children that you interviewed a friend and thought it might be helpful to research her process. Then again, you might consider bringing a colleague into the lesson with you and doing your own inquiry into his or her process. Another option, of course, is to call upon a child from your class. You'll need to identify a child who has already narrowed his or her idea and help prepare that child to speak about the choices he or she made.

The Struggle to Fit In

- The time Eliza made fun of my dress and said it was antique-looking
- The time I made fun of Elena to impress the other girls in my class
- The time my entire class took a field trip to my house to see my pet monkey, which I had pretended to have, but didn't

Ali then said, "So you reread your entries, saw that a lot were about your struggle as a kid to fit in. Then what?" I continued on. "I also wrote some entries showing my ideas about this. This is a tiny bit of one of them." I read aloud a small bit of writing to the class.

> When I was a kid, I knew I didn't fit in the peer groups, and that haunted me. The funny thing about this is that really, I don't exactly fit in now either, but I don't see it as a goal to do so. I'm not sure when this changed for me.

As students continue to listen, ask them to think about what the writer has done that they might also do.

Then Ali said, "So after you wrote an entry, thinking about your other entries and the issue you were uncovering, what did you do?" Before I answered, Ali said to the class, "Listen to Lucy processing and thinking. What has she done that you could also do? Be sure to jot notes or keep a mental list so you can share what you notice."

I continued. "I knew that fitting in was one possible issue I could write about, but I wanted to go back and mine my notebook some more—to see if there were other issues or themes that have been important in my life. I found a bunch of stories and seed ideas that had to do with my dad, and I realized that my relationship with my dad is an important part of my life, too. I put yellow Post-its on entries about fitting in, and green ones on entries about my relationship with my father. Some of my entries about my dad were also about fitting in, so I put two Post-its on those! After I finished, I thought about which category of entries felt most powerful, and I chose fitting in. Now I have been reading all the entries that relate to my fitting in, and I am getting myself ready to write. I have been thinking about what to say that is deep and true and surprising to me."

ACTIVE ENGAGEMENT

Ask partners to tell each other what they observed the writer doing to select her seed idea.

Ali said to the class, "Talk to your partner. What did you see Lucy doing?" As children talked, Ali jotted what she heard, then called them back together. "What I heard you saying is that there's work that a writer can do to find—and grow—important ideas in one's notebook." Ali pointed to the list she had just created in front of the class.

Although fitting in was a big concern in my life when I was ten, it doesn't preoccupy me anymore, but I decided to focus on this as a topic that resonates for children. I want my writing to help students find the courage to write about some of the struggles in their lives.

Finding and Growing Ideas

- Reread entries and mark the parts that light sparks or stand out.
- Reread marked entries, looking for connections and patterns between them.
- Grow ideas by writing to explore patterns and ideas.
- Don't stop with the first theme you find. Look for other issues or themes that underlie several entries.
- Choose one theme or issue and reread the entries related to it.
- Plan an entry that combines thoughts and stories related to this theme/issue.

LINK

Encourage students to draw on the various strategies they have learned to select a seed idea. Highlight that what works for one child, or one piece of writing, may not work for another. Celebrate independence.

"These are all things that writers do. Above all, writers figure out what works for a particular writing project. They find entries that hold powerful ideas, and imagine the piece of writing it might become."

"Writers, what works for one writer—or for one piece of writing—may not work for another. Right now, plan. What will you try first? Next? Use our chart to help you, but don't be afraid to try something else if you have a different idea. I can't wait to see what you come up with!"

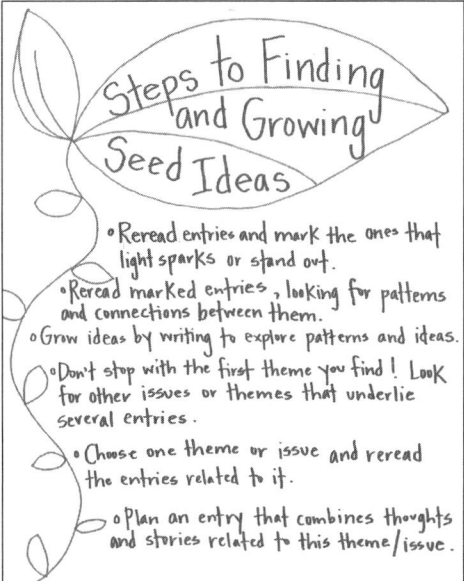

FIG. 5–1

CONFERRING AND SMALL-GROUP WORK

Finding Potent Topics

ONE OF THE REASONS YOU HAVEN'T ASKED CHILDREN to finalize their choices of seed ideas is by postponing this just a bit, you've had time to confer with more children, checking to be sure they've settled on an idea that will yield for them. These conferences are challenging because, of course, you can't listen to a synopsis of a writer's content and be in any position to judge whether that content will yield enough insight and detail to yield powerful writing. Instead, you need to read the child's entries, observe the interaction between writer and topic, and think, "Does this topic/seed idea seem to bring out the best in this writer?"

We have talked about the importance of fostering a safe and supportive writing community, and emphasized that this kind of community is a prerequisite for the kind of risk-taking and honesty that writing requires. But you'll find that some students still choose seed ideas that are, above all, easy or safe. When I conferred with Jill, for example, she told me that she was having no trouble determining her seed idea. "I'm going to write about my mom because I really, really, love her," she said. Her choice surprised me because Jill had collected a few entries about issues that she'd said haunted her. Then, too, as a writer, I know that sometimes it is hard to write about happy, happy times without sounding Hallmark-card clichéd. A writer (I can't recall who) once said, "I don't write about my marriage because I have a happy one," and there is wisdom in this. When I looked at Jill's entry about her seed idea (see Figure 5–2), my uneasiness grew.

Reading her entry, it seemed to me that although Jill might be very committed to a rhapsody about her mother, I suspected that if Jill—who is, after all, a budding adolescent—reached toward honest, deep writing, her writing work would require her to take on a less one-dimensional, all-is-bliss stance on her mother. So I asked Jill if she had any more entries that she'd written about her mom. She showed me an entry describing pumpkin picking together (see Figure 5–3). It was a love-fest; every other line of Jill's entry restated Jill's appreciation for her mother.

MID-WORKSHOP TEACHING   **Reflecting on Seed Ideas**

Share an observation with students about the work they've been doing. Share a strategy to make the work stronger.

"Writers, I want to talk to you about a concern I have. Some of you are filling your notebooks, but losing sight of the fact that you are on a journey to develop deeper, stronger ideas. Step back and take a more reflective stance. Dig a little deeper to uncover what's most important about your ideas." I revealed the following chart:

> Strategies for Writing with Depth
>
> - Try to understand what is so important about your topic. Ask:
>   - What are the reasons I keep writing about this topic?
>   - I've written what's obvious about this; what else can I write?
>   - What do I want to show about myself? What does this say about me?

"I've charted a few questions you can ask yourself when you are working to uncover more about a topic. Try a few today if you are looking to write more about your potential seed."

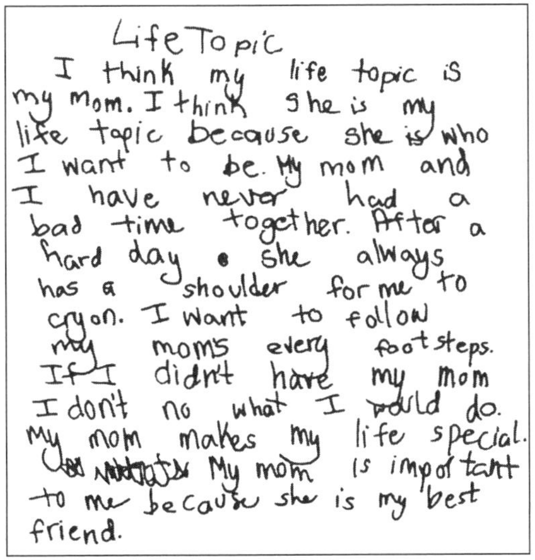

Life Topic

I think my life topic is my mom. I think she is my life topic because she is who I want to be. My mom and I have never had a bad time together. After a hard day • she always has a shoulder for me to cry on. I want to follow my moms every footsteps. If I didn't have my mom I don't no what I would do. My mom makes my life special. My mom is important to me because she is my best friend.

FIG. 5–2 Jill's early 'safe' entry about her mom

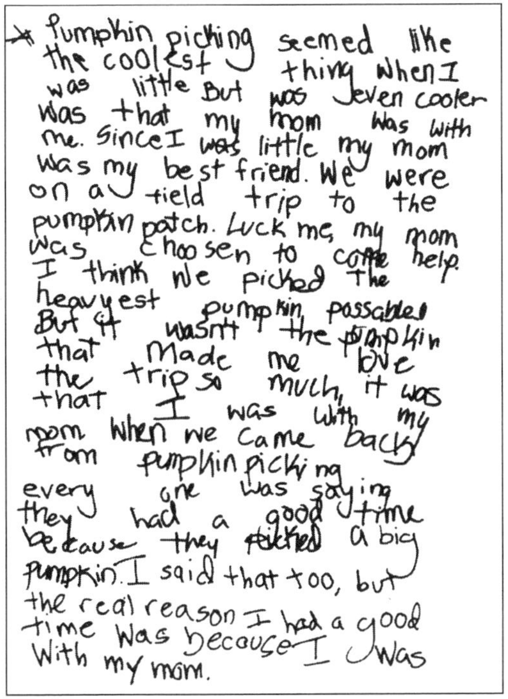

* Pumpkin picking seemed like the coolest thing when I was little But was even cooler was that my mom was with me. Since I was little my mom was my best friend. We were on a field trip to the pumpkin patch. Luck me, my mom was chosen to come help. I think we picked the heaviest pumpkin possable But it wasn't the pumpkin that Made me love the trip so much, it was that I was with my mom When we came back from pumpkin picking every one was saying they had a good time because they picked a big pumpkin. I said that too, but the real reason I had a good time was becouse I was with my mom.

FIG. 5–3 Jill's entry about pumpkin picking with her mom. Once again, she is staying with safer topics.

Jill also told me she'd begun writing an entry about shopping with her mother, because that was an activity they loved to do together.

Continuing my research, I asked, "Jill, remember how earlier I suggested that writers ask deep, probing questions as a way to dive deep into their writing? I'm wondering, have you asked that sort of question about your relationship with your mom?" Jill indicated that no, she'd just gathered more examples of loving-her-mom moments. Because I think it helps children to understand the source of our questions, I tried to explain. "The reason I'm asking this, Jill, is this: you know how the books we read usually have a poignant mix of intense feelings? Characters want things and struggle. The way you are writing about you and your mom makes me think you could turn these entries into a letter to her, into a valentine or a Mother's Day card.

"My suggestion to you as a writer is to ask those questions that can help you dig deeper: Where's the mystery in this topic about loving your mom? If you think of this as a story, Jill, are there any struggles in this story?" I added, "You might also consider whether there are other topics that are important ones for you—topics that contain a mix of feelings or contain some hard parts."

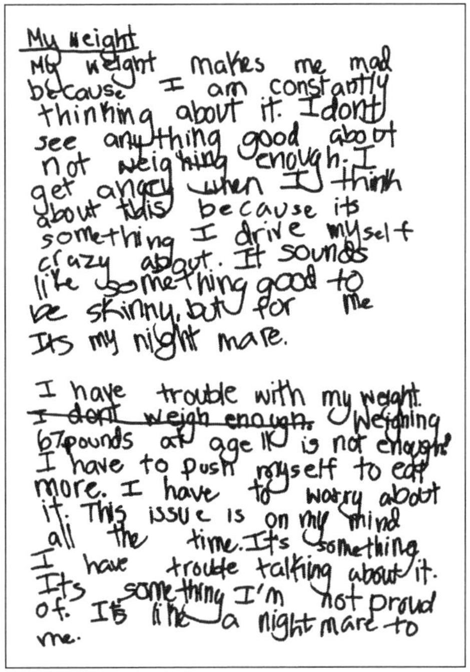

My Weight

My weight makes me mad because I am constantly thinking about it. I dont see anything good about not weighing enough. I get angry when I think about this because its something I drive myself crazy about. It sounds like something good to be skinny, but for me Its my night mare.

I have trouble with my weight. ~~I dont weigh enough.~~ Weighing 67 pounds at age 10 is not enough! I have to push myself to eat more. I have to worry about it. This issue is on my mind all the time. It's something I have troube talking about it. Its something I'm not proud of. Its like a night mare to me.

FIG. 5–4 Jill decided to tackle an issue with which she struggles.

Jill set to work immediately. By the end of that day's workshop, she'd written this entry (see Figure 5–4).

By the time I had circled back to Jill for a follow-up conference, she'd written a storm of intense entries about her struggle over feeling too thin. But then she had put those aside and returned to the story of pumpkin picking with her mom. "I thought about all the choices, and I think that pumpkin picking day was really important to me because I really remember it and it could make a great story," Jill said.

As you can imagine, I was not sure how to respond. We tell

children they are in charge of their writing and that the choice of topics is their own. Jill had made a choice.

I felt as if I was ready to take a parachute jump from a plane. I took a big breath, and went for it. I don't recall what I said exactly, but it went something like this. "Jill, I want you to know right from the start that the decision about your topic will be (and has to be) yours. But let me tell you what I'm thinking. It is safe for you to write about how you love your mom, and about how, one day when you were three or four years old, you and she went pumpkin picking. And I know you could get a good piece out of that because you write well enough that you could write a good piece about anything. But I think you can ask more from this writing project. I think this memoir unit can show you that writing can be a way for you to work out your issues and fears and concerns and struggles—because, Jill, every one of us has hard stuff that we deal with in our lives. And at least for now, you are writing and living inside an incredible community. If there is ever going to be a time and a place for you to write about your issues, your struggles, the real times of your life, it will be right now in this classroom in the company of friends."

I pressed on. "Next year, you will be in middle school, and you and your friends won't gather on the carpet and have community circle and people may not talk as carefully with each other. So I want to suggest that right now, this is a time and a place in your life for you to write about the most important stuff in your life—stuff that isn't perfect, stuff that's on your mind."

"But I know, Jill, that you need to be the one to make the decision. You may decide to stick one toe into a few issues and test the waters. I am going to leave the decision up to you because, after all, you need and deserve the chance to work on something that feels right to you."

End of sermon.

Jill decided to write about her weight. And, in the end, she was very glad to have made that choice. Phew. Sometimes we, as teachers, take risks. They don't always turn out as happily as this one did, but we have to take risks anyhow.

SHARE

Elaborating on Your Seed Ideas

Explain that charts created in the literary essay unit to help develop ideas for essays can be just as helpful when developing memoir ideas.

Speaking to the students at their seats, I began, "Writers, many of you have settled on a choice of theme and are in the process of exploring what, exactly, you want to say. This is a bit like the process you went through last year in the literary essay unit, when you developed a thesis.

"The most important thing you can do now is to write long, getting down all your thoughts and ideas before deciding on a final idea. I've hung up the chart you used last year to push your thinking further," I said, gesturing toward the chart. "In a moment, you and your partner are going to practice using this chart to explore your ideas verbally. So, for instance, I might begin 'I am writing about fitting in. That is . . . I'm writing about how sometimes it was hard for me to fit in when I was a kid.'" I glanced at the chart, in search of another prompt. "But as I'm saying this, I'm realizing that feeling like an outsider at school pushed me to band together with my eight brothers and sisters, turning us into a tighter clan." I stopped, turning my attention back to the children.

"Do you see what I did there? I took my issue—fitting in—and used the prompts from our essay unit to begin to develop my thinking.

Channel writers to work with partners, exploring their ideas, using thought prompts.

"In just a moment, I am going to ask you and your partner to try this work yourselves. You can decide who will go first, Partner A or Partner B. When you're talking, be sure to say as much as you can about your topic, using these prompts to keep you going. If your role is to be the listener, you might help the writer by calling out some prompts to keep her going. Okay, get started." I gave each partnership a copy of the prompts, then moved about, coaching as they rehearsed and developed their seed ideas.

Ways to Push Our Thinking

In other words . . .

That is . . .

The important thing about this is . . .

As I say this, I'm realizing . . .

This is giving me the idea that . . .

An example of this is . . .

This shows . . .

Another example of this is . . .

This connects to . . .

I see . . .

The thought I have about this is . . .

To add on . . .

The reason for this is . . . Another reason is . . .

This is important because . . .

On the other hand . . .

This is similar to . . . This is different from . . .

This makes me think . . .

This proves . . .

SESSION 5: CHOOSING A SEED IDEA

SESSION 5 HOMEWORK

GO OFF THE BEATEN PATH

When you go on a trip, you want to see as much as possible. You want to discover new things. If you stayed close to home and walked around the block, over and over again, that wouldn't be much of a trip. Writing is a bit like traveling. To see new things, it helps to break out from your usual pathway. One way writers do this is by approaching their topic from a new pathway, to look at their topic from a new perspective.

Tonight, take the topic you've decided to write about and try to appreciate it from a different path, to see it from a different perspective. This might mean asking questions of your writing, and I'm sending home the questions we discussed today. But you could also try a new form for your entry. Try writing about your issue using 'pros and cons', or "compare and contrast', or 'then and now'. Go off the beaten path.

> Strategies for Writing with Depth
> - Try to understand what is so important about your topic. Ask:
>   - What are the reasons I keep writing about this topic?
>   - I've written what's obvious about this; what else can I write?
>   - What do I want to show about myself? What does this say about me?

Session 6

Expecting Depth from Your Writing

WHEN I STUDIED MATH, I found that my math midterms weren't difficult because the courses were cumulative. Each new unit built on the material I learned in earlier units, thus keeping that earlier learning alive. My hunch is that all good education is cumulative—that in a well-taught history course, as students study the Great Depression they learn about ways that financial and social disaster compares and contrasts with the depression of 1832.

A yearlong curriculum to support children's growth as writers should also be cumulative. Writers should constantly revisit skills and strategies they learned earlier in the year, using these in the service of more complex, multifaceted operations. This session aims to revisit the earlier sessions in ways that help students write thoughtfully.

Of course, there's no easy sequence of steps that you can lay out for young writers. Compliance will never produce depth of thought! For this reason, you summon children to join you in an investigation. "Which strategies lead to deeper, more insightful writing?" you ask. Writers will profit from approaching writing with an intention to go deep. Your hope is that this session (and this unit) will help them approach a page, wanting not just to fill the page but also to discover new insights, to surprise themselves by saying something they never knew they knew.

I remember working with one first-grade child years ago, who decided that Angela Johnson had taught her, above all, that on every page of her writing, she needed to do something beautiful. This intention, alone, changed everything about that child's writing. In this session, your hope is that students come away resolving that in every entry they will write something that is deep and true and important. You hope, too, that children will approach their writing with a spirit not of compliance but of adventure, willing to climb every mountain until they find their dream.

IN THIS SESSION, you'll teach students that writers of memoir dive deep into their topics by studying how other authors write with depth.

GETTING READY

- ✔ Example of writing that contains several small moments (see Teaching)
- ✔ Example of writing that asks and explores important questions about a Life Topic (see Active Engagement)
- ✔ List of strategies or qualities that pertain to "writing-to-learn" (see Conferring and Small-Group Work)
- ✔ Example of writing that explores a topic using quotes, a memory, a poem, or statistics (see Share)
- ✔ "Strategies for Writing with Depth" chart (see Share)

COMMON CORE STATE STANDARDS: W.5.3, W.5.5, W.5.10, RL.5.2, RL.5.10, SL.5.1, L.5.1, L.5.2, L.5.3

MINILESSON

Expecting Depth from Your Writing

CONNECTION

Point out to students that they have graduated from focusing on strategies for generating writing to focusing on strategies for writing with depth.

"Now that you have narrowed your focus and chosen your seed ideas, the time has come for you to think.

"Have you ever watched a duck swimming across the surface of a lake? It swims along very peacefully for a while, and then suddenly the duck tips its head down and dives deep underwater. Writers are like ducks, in a way. Writers often swim along the surface of a subject for a while, and then all of a sudden, they make a deep dive. I'm hoping you've begun to figure out a bunch of strategies that you can use to help you take deep dives as writers, and that you'll continue inventing and using those strategies throughout this unit and for the rest of your lives."

❖ **Name the teaching point.**

"Today, I want to teach you one way that memoirists learn to write with depth. They study the work of other authors who have used writing to discover deep insights—classmates, published authors, any writer—and they try to name the ways that writer developed deep insights.

TEACHING

Remind students that to learn about the characteristics of any kind of writing, it is important to study an example and ask, "What has the author done here that I can do as well?"

"When you want to learn to write an essay, you read essays. When you want to learn to write information books, you read information books. I'm telling you this because when you want to learn to write with depth, to dive deep, you can study the work of an author who has done just that. As you study that author's writing, you ask, 'What has the author done here?' Then you try it yourself." (See the following list.)

◆ COACHING

I am deliberately beginning this minilesson by requesting children's help in an inquiry that will thread through much of this unit. The query I pose here is, "What strategies can writers use to write with depth?" For now, I will share a few tentative answers, but I also want to set the stage for kids to be collaborators in this inquiry.

Demonstrate how you study a mentor text, modeling a replicable process for children.

"Let's study an entry in which Max uses writing to think interpretively about his own entries. You'll see that Max first reread his own entry. Then he wrote this entry in which he has second thoughts about that entry."

I read the first portion of an enlarged copy of Max's entry (see Figure 6–1) emphasizing some of his sentence starters with an underline.

> *Whenever I used to read the entry I wrote about getting injured on the board-walk, I thought it was about safety. Now I realize it's also about pressure.*

"I'm noticing that Max is focusing in on one entry, one moment, and returning to uncover new themes and insights. But he doesn't settle on the first thought that pops into his mind. He pushes himself to have more than one idea about his life story." I returned to Max's entry.

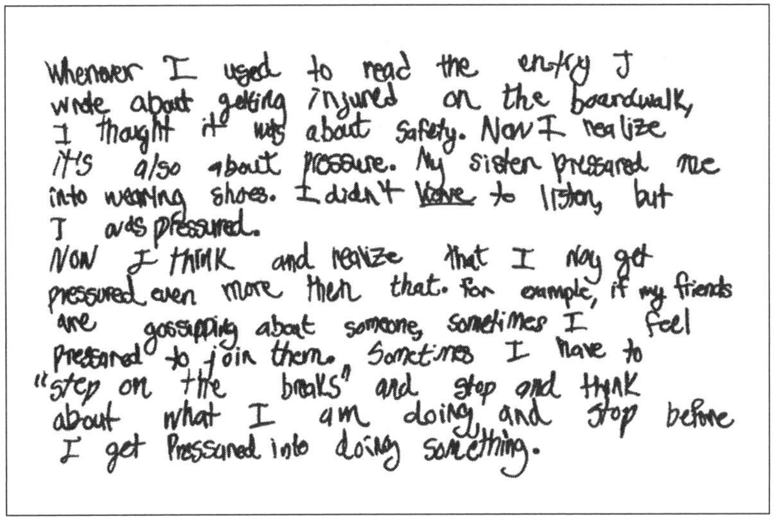
Whenever I used to read the entry I wrote about getting injured on the boardwalk, I thought it was about safety. Now I realize it's also about pressure. My sister pressured me into wearing shoes. I didn't have to listen, but I was pressured.
Now I think and realize that I may get pressured even more then that. For example, if my friends are gossipping about someone, sometimes I feel presured to join them. Sometimes I have to "step on the breaks" and stop and think about what I am doing, and stop before I get pressured into doing something.

FIG. 6–1 Max's entry, in which an idea dawns on him as he writes

> *My sister pressured me into wearing shoes. I didn't have to listen, but I was pressured.*

As I continued reading, my intonation suggested that Max was once again rethinking his original entry.

> *Now I think and realize that I may get pressured even more than that. For example, if my friends are gossiping about someone, sometimes I feel pressured to join them.*

Then I said, "Listen up, because after thinking the original entry is about one issue—safety—then another—pressure from his sister—and then yet another—pressure from his friends, Max now starts thinking about that issue, that theme."

> *Sometimes I have to step on the brakes and stop and think about what I am doing and stop before I get pressured into doing something.*

"To think about how pressure makes him do things, Max talks about stepping on the brakes. He's comparing stopping pressure to stepping on the brakes."

I revealed a list on which I'd recorded the ways Max used writing to think deeply and interpretively about his entry—and his experience.

Revisit Entries, Looking for Themes and Issues

- Look back over other entries and ask, "Are there other examples of this theme/issue in my life?" Search for patterns.
- Push yourself to think otherwise, to interpret the entry differently.
- Think and write about the issue/theme. What ideas do you have? What is this similar to? Different from?

ACTIVE ENGAGEMENT

Ask children to try some strategies in their own pieces, coaching them through Max's moves step-by-step.

"Now that you've studied Max's work, why don't you try some of these same strategies in your own writing? Right now, will you take out your notebooks and open to a clean page?" I waited. "Start with Max's first move. Look over your most recent entry or two and ask, 'What is the issue that's hiding here? What's this really about?' You might borrow Max's phrase to help you get started: 'When I used to read this entry, I thought it was about . . . Now I realize it's also about . . .'"

I gave the students a few minutes to write before interrupting to channel them yet again. "Now push yourself to see that same entry from another perspective. You might try, 'This moment is about . . . But it is also about . . .'"

Again, after a minute or two, I interjected. "Try another move that Max made. What are other moments that connect to this issue? For instance, Max was not just pressured by his sister but also by friends."

I called out another tip. "Max was able to help us understand the difficulty of resisting pressure by comparing it to putting on the brakes. Similarly, Sandra Cisneros described growing older as being like an onion, with each layer (or year) growing and concealing the one beneath it. Is there a comparison you can make to help illustrate something significant about your life?"

"Finally, take the key word or phrase—the big idea or issue that you are exploring. Write about this." Again I gave the students a moment to write. "What can you compare this to?" The room was filled with the scratching of pens.

LINK

Remind writers that their goal is to generate *thoughtful, interpretive* writing. Encourage them to draw from their full repertoire of strategies for doing this.

"Writers, I can teach you strategies for generating narrative or essay writing, but our goal is not just to generate writing. It is to generate thoughtful writing. Our goal is to write like ducks, who may swim along the surface of a subject for a time but who then dive deep. Part of what this means is that you need to approach the page hoping for and reaching

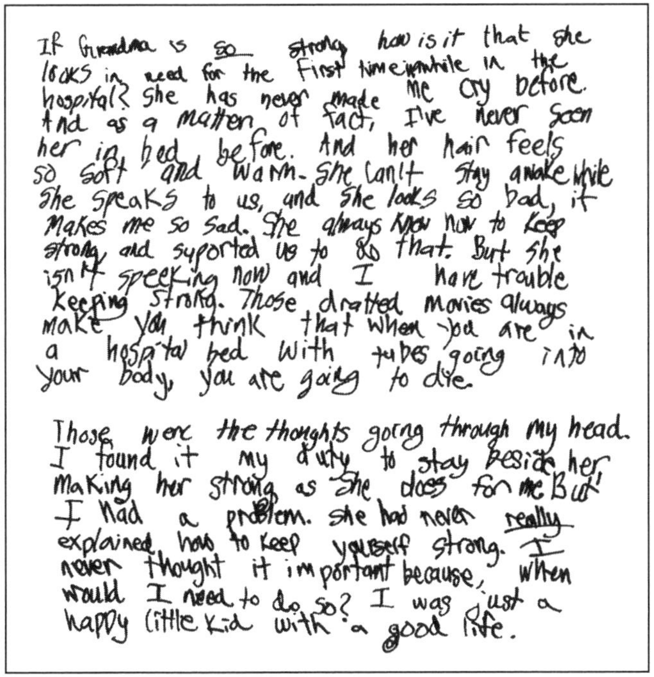

If Grandma is so strong, how is it that she looks in need for the first time in a while in the hospital? She has never made me cry before. And as a matter of fact, I've never seen her in bed before. And her hair feels so soft and warm. She can't stay awake while she speaks with us, and she looks so bad, it makes me so sad. She always knew how to keep strong, and supported us to do that. But she isn't speaking now and I have trouble keeping strong. Those drafted movies always make you think that when you are in a hospital bed with tubes going into your body, you are going to die.

Those were the thoughts going through my head. I found it my duty to stay beside her, making her strong, as she does for me. But I had a problem. She had never really explained how to keep yourself strong. I never thought it was important because when would I need to do so? I was just a happy little kid with a good life.

FIG. 6–2 Max's entry about his grandma

for depth. My hunch is that you need to write with a spirit of adventure and to be willing to risk going off the beaten path. But when this feels hard, and it will feel hard sometimes, one thing to do is to unearth the strategies that other writers have found successful, and try them.

"Today and always, take charge of your writing. Do whatever you need to do so that your writing leads you to surprise, to discovery, to significance. I'll hang our chart on the easel so you can you use it as you write. Off you go."

CONFERRING AND SMALL-GROUP WORK

Naming Specific Goals and Then Tracking Student Progress Toward Them

YOUR STUDENTS WILL BE WRITING A SMALL COLLECTION OF ENTRIES about their seed ideas. Some will be stories such as those they collected earlier this year during the narrative unit—only now, the stories will cluster around an issue or theme that has emerged. Other entries will be reflective, and you may find it helpful to think of these as the material that can be developed, in time, into miniature essays.

You may want to focus your conferring today on the reflective writing. To do this, spend a bit of time before class looking at your students' work and jotting notes about the qualities of good writing you see—and wish you'd see.

You may want to make yourself a little chart, with student's names along the top and a list of qualities down the left-hand margin. Then when you confer with children, the list you've generated can remind you of things to compliment and things to teach. The list of qualities you are conferring towards could be drawn from the fifth-grade Opinion Writing Checklist, or you could make a checklist specifically for this unit.

If I were to make such a list, I'd probably decide to start by focusing on qualities of thoughtful, deep writing. I would start with *honesty*, and this would be one important thing to watch for, to compliment, and to teach toward. I think it is all too easy to write with clichés. When I hold myself accountable for writing the exact truth, my writing is much more apt to take me to surprising places. Specifically, I'd look for evidence that a writer understands that the process of writing involves a writer working toward the goal of putting the truth into words. I'd celebrate any evidence I saw that a writer tried one way to say something, felt dissatisfied, and then tried another way to say that message.

I'd look for *length*, too. As Peter Elbow, the great writing researcher, once said, "Writing is like water. You need to let it flow for a while before it runs clear." There are lots of ways for writers to write longer.

One is to be sure that ideas are elaborated upon. Prompts from the essay unit such as 'The important thing about this is . . .' might help.

MID-WORKSHOP TEACHING   Finding the Mystery in a Topic

"Writers, can I have your attention for a moment? Eudora Welty, a famous memoirist, once taught me a strategy that she uses to write with depth. She gave me this advice (actually, she wrote it in a book, but when I read the book it was as if she was speaking directly to me). She said, 'Write what you *don't know* about what you *know*.'

"She is suggesting that we take a topic we know well and ask, 'What *don't* I know about what I know?' Ask, 'Where's the mystery in this topic?' For example, I could take the topic of fitting in, and I could ask, 'Where is the mystery for me in this topic?' Maybe I'd end up writing about the transition I made when I was going between wanting to fit in and wanting to be out-of-the-box. One thing that is mysterious to me is this: 'Why do I write so often about fitting in when it doesn't matter to me much?'

"You may want to borrow Eudora Welty's strategy. Ask yourself (as I asked myself), 'What don't I know about what I know?' Ask, 'Where's the mystery here?' And then write to discover. I'll add this strategy to our chart." I added the following bullet to our list of strategies for writing with depth.

- Take topics and territories you know well and ask, "Where's the mystery here?"

When helping students write about abstract ideas, I'd want to channel them to sort and categorize. They might benefit from thinking about the parts, the reasons, the kinds. They will certainly benefit from thinking of similarities and differences.

But, most importantly I would want to encourage children to be writers with *purpose*, writing toward the goal of learning more and understanding more. "Remember," I might say, "you are in charge of your own writing process. You need to think about how you can gather entries that will help you to write about the issues and themes of your life. What will you do next? Don't wait for me to tell you what to do, because you are the author of your writing life."

SHARE

Building Bridges from One Idea to Another

Offer one student's writing up for study. Ask children to find, with a partner, something in the writing they could all try to do as well.

"I've made copies of an entry that one of your classmates has written (see Figure 6–3). I thought that we'd try to look together at this entry, asking, 'What exactly has this writer done that the rest of us could do as well?' Read over your copy of Emily's entry, and then make marginal notes showing your observations."

I am still a child and still have childhood memories but when is it over? Maybe it's never over, it is just you believe it's over. On Adam's poetry notebook it says you don't stop playing because you are old–you are old because you stop playing. So maybe if we always believe in this, no one is old. Just because the world says, "You are 90 and that's old" doesn't mean it is true. So like Naomi Shihab Nye says, "Reinvent things." 90 year old people may not be old anymore. I have a picture of an old man in a diaper. Just because your 90, don't mean you can have fun anymore. You will always have a piece of childness in you. And if everyone has memories.

When I was seven, my mom called me a little cub. Because I was a baby. When I was a baby I would lie on my mom's stomach and listen to the beat of her heart and fall asleep. And even now I do the same and I say, "little cub." She says when I'm a hundred I will still be her little cub. Even now I am scared of thunder, scared of monsters in my closet. It feels like I am little always. My sister is the "big sister" so I always feel small. But even my sister is a little baby. There are times in my life where I feel stuck small. But there are many times when I feel big and want to stay a kid forever.

FIG. 6–3 Emily's entry

SESSION 6: EXPECTING DEPTH FROM YOUR WRITING

Collect observations from the class and add some to the class chart.

Children talked with their partners about their observations, and then I asked a few children to say aloud what they'd noticed.

Jonah pointed out that in Emily's entry, as in the entry that Max wrote that the class studied earlier, Emily thinks about a topic in one way, then in another way, then in yet another way. José said that he starts with his idea, and then goes from that idea to one example, one thought, one quote, and another. "You can all do this same sort of work," I said to the class and added several strategies for writing with depth to the chart.

> ### Strategies for Writing with Depth
>
> - Try to understand what is so important about your topic. Ask:
>   - What are the reasons I keep writing about this topic?
>   - I've written what's obvious about this; what else can I write?
>   - What do I want to show about myself? What does this say about me?
> - Return to the topics, ideas, and themes you write about again and again, mining them for new insights, stories, and ideas.
> - With seemingly unconnected pieces of writing, ask, "How DO these connect?" to uncover underlying issues or truths.
> - Write with both Big insights and Small details.
> - Write about the same idea or topic repeatedly, from different perspectives.
> - Imagine how the idea or topic applies to multiple situations in your life.
> - Ask tough questions and try to answer them.
> - Don't worry about finding "perfect" thoughts. Let your pencil fly! Write freely and you will find your way into new, deeper ideas.
> - Take topics and territories you know well and ask, "Where's the mystery here?"
> - Link your topic or idea to one thing, then another, then another (to a quote, a statistic, a memory, a classmate's idea).

SESSION 6 HOMEWORK

CONTINUING TO THINK ABOUT TOPICS FROM DIFFERENT PERSPECTIVES

Writers, when you were younger and less experienced as writers, you probably thought that the content of writing depended upon the subject. But you're older and more sophisticated as writers now, and so you've probably come to realize that as a writer, you can take a topic and then choose the way you write about that topic. We've talked a lot about the fact that a writer needs to decide whether the story about a ride on the Ferris wheel is a story about a child overcoming a fear of heights or a story about a child not wanting to outgrow childish pleasures, for example. As a writer, you need to decide what it is you want to show in a story and then highlight that meaning.

In memoir, the understanding that a story can be told in different ways to highlight different meanings is very important. You can take an incident, for example, and write what you used to think it was about. Then you could write about how something happened to change the way you understood things—perhaps time passed, or perhaps you came to a new realization, or perhaps someone made a passing comment that changed your thoughts—but one way or another, you can write that you came to a new understanding of the situation.

There are other ways to write from different perspectives. For example, maybe you and your friend had an argument, and at the time, you felt angry. You could re-create the argument from that perspective. Then later, looking back, you can recall the entire sequence of events, and from your more distant perspective, you can understand your friend, sympathize with that person, and regret your own role. You could write the story of the argument twice, each time from a different perspective.

To do this sort of work, you will probably want to start by rereading your notebook, looking for an entry that pertains to the territory you've selected. The entry will probably capture one way of thinking about an event or a topic. You may need to recall a time when your perspective on that topic or that incident changed so that you can write from another perspective. You might start your first entry by saying, "At the time, I was mad . . . ," and then write another entry by saying, "But now, looking back, I realize . . ."

Structuring, Drafting, and Revising a Memoir BEND II

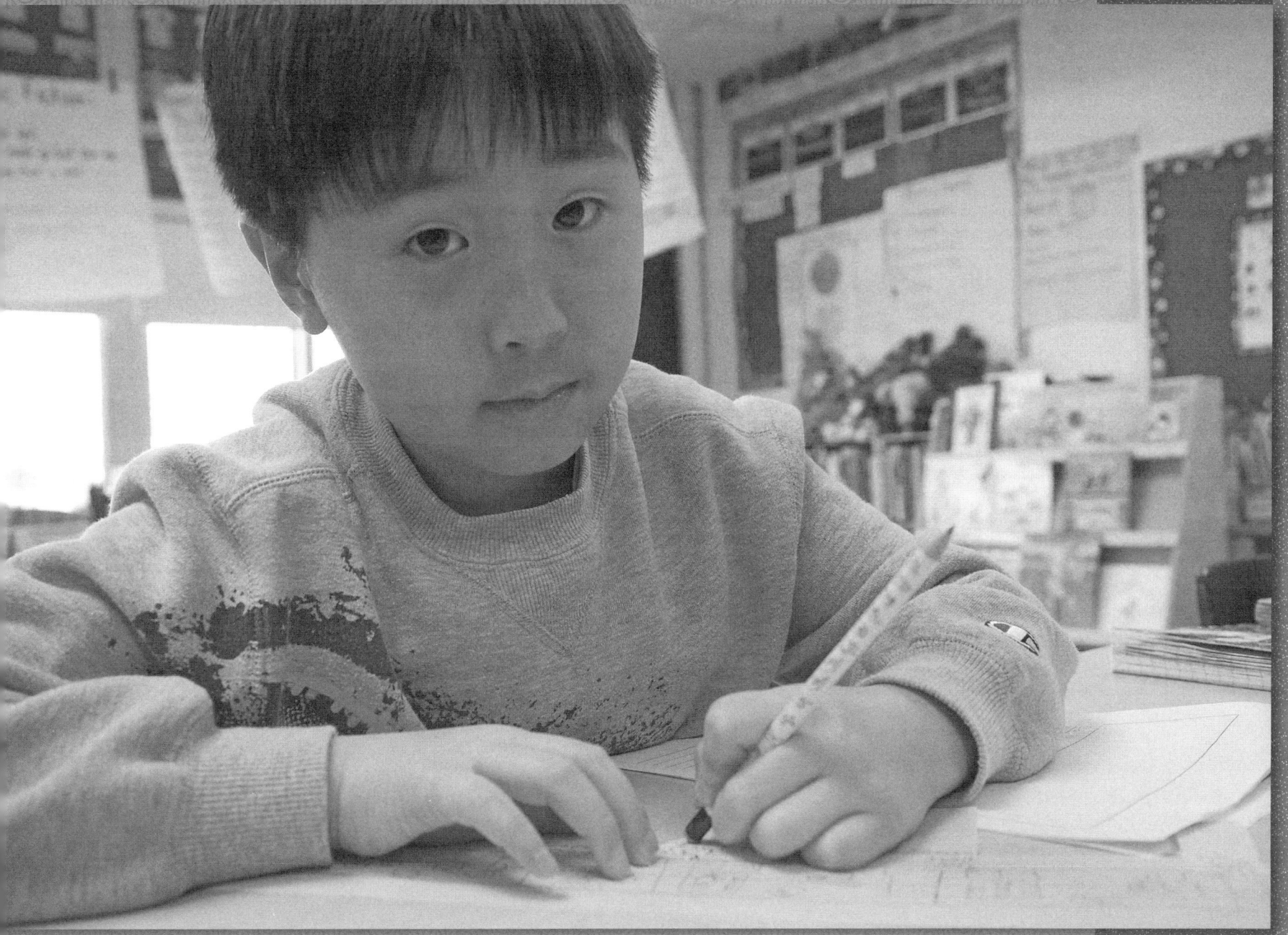

Session 7

Studying and Planning Structures

IN THIS SESSION, you'll teach students that writers study published texts to get ideas for ways to structure their own texts. You'll demonstrate how to study the structure of a text in order to help students learn how to do this.

GETTING READY

- ✓ Excerpt from a memoir organized like a list, such as *Invention of Solitude* by Paul Auster, or another memoir that shows a describable structure (see Teaching)
- ✓ Excerpt from a memoir that uses exposition and narrative writing, such as a story from *The House on Mango Street* by Sandra Cisneros (see Active Engagement)
- ✓ "Ways to Structure a Memoir" chart (see Active Engagement and Mid-Workshop Teaching)
- ✓ Example of a memoir that is structured as an essay such as "Quietly Struggling" (see Mid-Workshop Teaching)
- ✓ Copies of Memoir Writing Checklist (see Share)

BY NOW, YOUR CHILDREN HAVE CHOSEN and developed a seed idea for their first memoir. Before this week is over, they'll have planned, drafted, revised, and edited a memoir, and they'll be ready to start writing a second memoir. Today's session, then, sets the stage for drafting. Your children know that texts can be structured as narratives, as information texts, or as essays. They know the gist of how each type of writing tends to go.

Before they fly the coop at the end of the year, you will want to let them in on the fact that, actually, writers organize their texts in lots of different ways. They may write a traditionally structured narrative or a traditional thesis-driven essay, but they may also structure their text according to a vast range of different templates. Just as painters paint with a palette of colors and can choose the color that allows them to convey their meaning, so, too, writers write with a palette of optional structures and can choose or construct the structure that allow them to best convey their meaning.

In today's session, you will invite children to read texts with an eye for the ways the writers have structured those texts. This sort of analytic reading is valued in the Common Core State Standards, which call for readers to be able to notice how portions of a text relate to each other and to the whole. Students are expected to consider how the structural choices are related to the author's intended meaning, to the central ideas. In this session, you will also introduce children to several potential structures for the texts they will soon write. Don't expect them to immediately grasp and begin flawlessly using the sophisticated memoir structures you'll be discussing. Of course, this work will be a challenge for fifth graders! But remember that you are not only introducing them to ideas and structures that they can practice with now, making the best use of their current abilities and sensibilities; you are also paving the way for future learning and future writing.

COMMON CORE STATE STANDARDS: W.5.2, W.5.3, W.6.1.d, RL.5.1, RL.5.2, RL.5.3, RL.5.5, SL.5.1, SL.5.2, L.5.1, L.5.2, L.5.3

MINILESSON

Studying and Planning Structures

CONNECTION

Celebrate that children have been composing writerly lives.

"There is a saying, 'Today is the first day of the rest of your life.' In many ways, today *is* a turning point in your writing lives. Today you will begin thinking about how the structural choices an author makes can highlight the author's meaning.

"You have learned that writers sometimes structure their texts as narratives, and you know how narratives tend to go. You have learned that writers sometimes structure their texts as research reports and articles, and you have learned ways that these informational texts tend to go. You have also learned that writers can structure their texts as essays, and you know the way that this kind of writing tends to go."

❧ **Name your teaching point.**

"Today, I want to let you in on a secret. Writers structure their texts in lots of different ways. And one way you learn to structure your texts is by reading texts other authors have written and by studying the structures they have used."

TEACHING

Tell children that finding patterns in writing is much like looking out from an airplane, seeing patterns in the land below. To discern patterns, writers need to take in more than what's right in front of them.

"Have any of you ever looked out the window of a plane to see that the world below looks like patchwork? It's funny because when you fly far above the world, you'd think that would mean that you see less, but the truth is that when I've looked at the world from the window of an airplane, even though I see less detail, I also see more. I see patterns. I see component sections. I see the way different component sections fit together. I may see that a city or a swatch of farmland is organized into a grid. I may see that the plots of land are smaller alongside the river; that as distance increases from the river, the plots of land are larger."

◆ COACHING

Your connection and teaching point need not be fancy or elaborate. By now, kids know that if they listen, they'll be rewarded by learning something that helps them with their writing. We hope that often, that knowledge will be hook enough!

You will want to choose mentor texts carefully for this lesson. If you hope to push children toward writing memoirs that are structured like essays, study an example like that. It is important to give children choices in this unit, but you can make deliberate, purposeful choices about what you expose them to!

You'll notice that this has a distinctly different feel than the way you taught children to study texts for craft. At other points in our units, we teach children to pull close and examine the intricacies of what an author has done. Here, to grasp the text as a whole, we teach them to instead pull back.

SESSION 7: STUDYING AND PLANNING STRUCTURES

Demonstrate this with an excerpt from a memoir that has been organized like a list.

"I'm telling you this because when a writer wants to study the ways other authors structure their texts, they read those texts as if they are flying above them, looking down at them. Let me show you what I mean. Let's listen to an excerpt from Paul Auster's memoir, *Invention of Solitude* (1982). Remember, when I reread this bit of memoir, I'm going to look at it as if I'm flying above it. This time I won't be reading to pay attention to the specific details Auster uses or his word choice. Instead, I'll look at large chunks of the text, to see how he has organized his memoir and how the chunks in his text fit together into a larger structure. Okay, let me look at this," I said and began to shift between scanning and quietly rereading the text.

> *He remembers that he gave himself a new name, John, because all cowboys were named John, and that each time his mother addressed him by his real name he would refuse to answer her. He remembers running out of the house and lying in the middle of the road with his eyes shut, waiting for a car to run him over. He remembers that his Grandfather gave him a large photograph of Gabby Hayes and that it sat in a place of honor on the top of his bureau. He remembers thinking the world was flat. He remembers learning how to tie his shoes. He remembers that his father's clothes were kept in the closet in his room and that it was the noise of the hangers clicking together in the morning that would wake him up.*

Point out the structure of the text. In this case, the memoir excerpt is a list, with each part linked to it by a repeated line.

"I am noticing that this part of the memoir is organized sort of like a list. Every two or three lines, Auster shifts to another memory, and the sequence of these memories seems to be random. But Auster links the different memories together with the repeating refrain of 'He remembers . . .'" Then I said, "I wonder if all the phrases describing memories are the same length, and if each phrase about a memory has a similar structure. Let me look back and read on and see. Take a look with me." I spent a moment drawing my finger beneath the lines of each memory, visibly taking note of each one's length.

"I bet many of you are noticing, as I am, that some of the memories have been elaborated upon more than others. Some are given two sentences, some just one.

Debrief.

"Do you notice the way I went back to the text again and again? I didn't say, 'It's a list,' and then move on. Instead, I tried to discover as much as I could about the way Auster makes his lists. In the end, I was able to notice quite a bit about what he does and doesn't do."

I made a point of reading this text to them before today so it would be a familiar text rather than a brand-new one. It's best not to say, "Listen to this new text and as you listen, pay attention to the structure of the text." It is easier to first hear a text and, only afterward, analyze it's structure.

Given that students are trying to see the structure in these texts, it's helpful if you can display an enlarged copy.

When I read a text, looking at its structure, I look for component parts. Is the text composed of a list of items? Does the text contain one small story after another? Is it a single extended narrative? Is it shaped like an essay, with a claim followed by one reason after another? Paragraphs can help me do this. Some kinds of words also signal the microstructures in a text. Some signal words suggest the text is organized chronologically (the word next*) and some suggest the text is organized to highlight contrasting information (words like* yet*). Still other signal words suggest the text reveals a cause-and-effect relationship (*therefore*).*

ACTIVE ENGAGEMENT

Set children up to read a text and notice its structure, jotting observations as they do.

"Let's try reading texts that other authors have written as if we're in an airplane, looking down at the lay of the land— at the map of their structure, okay? I've copied a memoir you know onto chart paper. Please read it quickly, in almost a skimming like way. You'll probably want to look for two or three major chunks in the text. Then look at each of the chunks and ask, 'What kind of text is this section?' Jot your observations about the text's structure in your notebooks," I said, and turned the page of the chart tablet to reveal this excerpt from *The House on Mango Street*.

This text contains both exposition and narrative writing in it. I want to show a possibility that is distinct from Auster's.

> Laughter
>
> Nenny and I don't look like sisters . . . not right away. Not the way you can tell with Rachel and Lucy who have the same fat Popsicle lips like everyone else in their family. But me and Nenny, we are more alike than you would know. Our laughter, for example. Not the shy ice cream bells' giggle of Rachel and Lucy's family, but all of a sudden and surprised like a pile of dishes breaking. And other things I can't explain.
>
> One day we were passing a house that looked, in my mind, like the houses I had seen in Mexico. I don't know why. There was nothing about the house that looked exactly like the houses I remembered. I'm not even sure why I thought it, but it seemed to feel right.
>
> Look at that house, I said. It looks like Mexico.
>
> Rachel and Lucy look at me like I'm crazy, but before they can let out a laugh, Nenny says: Yes, that's Mexico all right. That's what I was thinking exactly.

Notice that here, the text becomes a narrative. It is structured very similarly to "Eleven." This is parallel to the part where Mrs. Price emerges from the coat room, red sweater in hand, to ask, 'Whose is this?' If I worried that children would have difficulty with this, I would have boxed the text into chunks and simply asked students to reflect on the kind of text within each chunk.

Gather students' reactions, and then explain how the text is a combination of an essay and a narrative. Chart some ways to structure a memoir.

I gave children a chance to turn and talk and then called them back to share their observations. Tyler said, "It's kind of like 'Eleven'." I gestured for him to continue. "It has a story," he said tentatively, "but it also has this other part in the beginning that is kind of like the author talking to you. She's telling us her idea."

"Ah!" I said, boxing off the reflective part of Cisneros' writing from the small moment. "So she's doing two different kinds of writing here." After a bit we came to the conclusion that this text begins as an essay and ends as a narrative. "It's a combo," one child said. I began a chart.

Ways to Structure a Memoir...

- Write in a list-like structure, like beads on a string. The beads can be Small Moment stories that are linked (example: times when a writer was shy, or scenes from my childhood alongside the creek). Each memory can be as short as a sentence or two or as long as a page or two.

- A hybrid text that is a mixture of idea-based writing and a story or vignette.

- An essay in which the writer makes a claim and supports it with reasons.

FIG. 7–1 Ways to structure a memoir based on discussion about Cisnero's work

LINK

Remind children that they are the authors of their writing lives, that they have options in the work they do today.

"Today, writers, you need to remember that each one of you is the author of your writing life. You'll need to have written your memoir, revised it, and edited it by the end of this week. For today, plan the work you need to be doing. Some of you may want to spend some time reading and rereading memoir so as to consider alternate ways to structure the draft you'll start today or tomorrow. You'll see that I have left a folder of short memoir on each of your tables, in case studying mentors will help. You can tape a memoir into your notebook and write right onto it—boxing out the component sections, labeling what you think the author is doing.

"Some of you probably feel that now that you know the theme you'll advance in your memoir, you need to gather a bit more material before you can draft.

"Either way, all of you will spend some time thinking about how you will structure your memoir. What might work best for your idea. Some of you will write essays, with a claim, a thesis, and then with parts of the essay showing reasons or examples. Some of you may decide to collect tiny scenes like Cynthia Rylant does in *When I Was Young in the Mountains*. If so, start collecting. It is possible you'll write one story as Cisneros did in 'Eleven' and then write a little essay about it, too. Once you have decided what your work will be today, you can head off to write."

CONFERRING AND SMALL-GROUP WORK

Coaching Writers to Plan

AS YOU CONFER WITH CHILDREN TODAY, you'll be listening to the writer's tentative ideas about the content and the structure of the intended memoir. For example, when I pulled alongside Ali, she explained that her seed idea was still a 'blob' idea, as she called it. She'd decided to write about her direction and plans as a writer (see Figures 7–2 and 7–3).

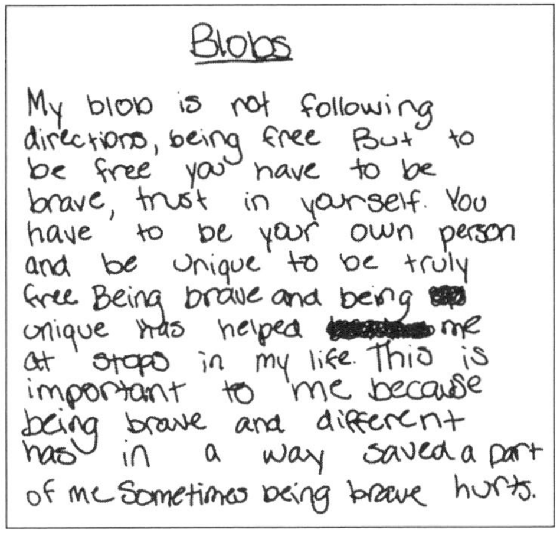

FIG. 7–2 In her entry, Ali tries to name what exactly she is thinking.

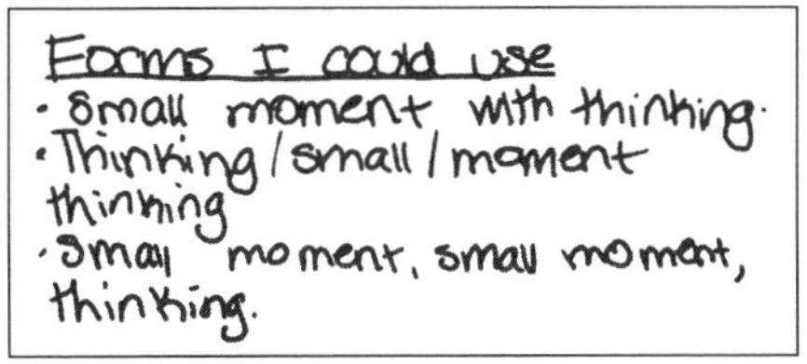

FIG. 7–3 Ali lists structure options.

The process of making the list seemed to have helped Ali. Without any input from me, she'd realized that her final memoir would probably contain a narrative or two. She also realized that, therefore, she needed to collect another memory or two pertaining to her topic. She'd made herself a to-do list (see Figure 7–4) and started to work on the first item.

Ali told me that her plan was to continue collecting more Small Moment narratives, each capturing a time when she had been brave.

By this point in the conference, it was very easy for me to know what I could compliment and how I could teach Ali. I first gushed over the deliberate, planned progression of work that Ali had accomplished. She pointed out that in fact she had already checked off item one on her to-do list. I saw that yes, she'd cranked out a short narrative.

"Ali," I said. "I love that you are so efficient and on task, but very often our strengths are our weaknesses. And although I am pleased you are being the job captain who gives yourself a job to do and I am pleased you are checking off items on the to-do list, I want to caution you to be sure your day doesn't become consumed with little activities and job assignments." Ali nodded. "Yeah," she said. "It is like I spent ten minutes on a quick story so I could do the next step."

(continues)

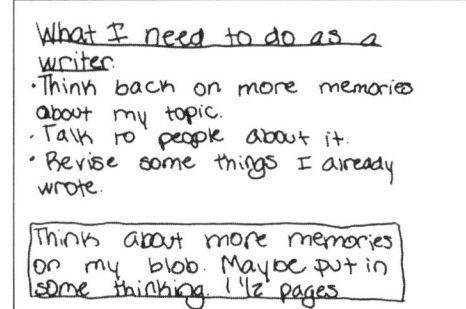

FIG. 7–4 Ali's to-do list

SESSION 7: STUDYING AND PLANNING STRUCTURES

MID-WORKSHOP TEACHING
Memoirs Can Be Structured Like an Essay

"Writers, can I stop you? Earlier today we looked at two texts from an aerial view, noticing how they were structured, and we began a chart of possible ways to structure memoir. I've put a copy of a memoir we looked at earlier in the unit, 'Quietly Struggling' on each table. Will you and your table mates decide its structure and annotate it? Mark up its parts." A few minutes later, I asked children to share their observations. They noted that the memoir had a thesis, topic sentence, conclusion, and so forth. A third way to structure memoir was added to the chart (Figure 7–5).

Ways to Structure a Memoir...

- Write in a list-like structure, like beads on a string. The beads can be Small Moment stories that are linked (example: times when a writer was shy, or scenes from my childhood alongside the creek). Each memory can be as short as a sentence or two or as long as a page or two.

- A hybrid text that is a mixture of idea-based writing and a story or vignette.

- An essay in which the writer makes a claim and supports it with reasons.

FIG. 7–5

I agreed. "And then you spent three minutes writing analytically about it and then five minutes on the next item." I went on to tell Ali that a writer once said, "It is spring in my book. I look up and am surprised to see it is snowing." That author was talking about the feeling he gets as a reader when he is utterly lost in a text, but I think that good writers, like good readers, get totally lost in a text. We dream the dream of a story, and it is as if we are reliving that story. And, for a very long time, we don't hear anything that is going on around us; we are totally absorbed in reliving a moment and capturing it on the page."

In conclusion, I told Ali that she had done a great job taking charge of her own writing life, but I suggested that she assign herself bigger blocks of time, expecting that much of the time she'd get utterly lost in whatever she was doing.

SHARE

Assessing Yourself against a Checklist

Explain to students that they will develop their own hybrid Memoir Checklists, drawing on both the Narrative and Opinion Checklists.

"By now, you are old pros at using checklists to self-assess your writing and set goals. You learned to use the Narrative Writing Checklist to assess your personal narrative writing, you used the Informational Writing Checklist to evaluate and set goals for your pieces on Westward Expansion.

"If this unit were like any other, I'd hand you a checklist and say, 'Here. This is what teachers the world-over agree fifth graders should be doing.' But as we've come to realize, memoir is a complicated genre. In some ways it is a narrative unit: you write stories about your life and dig to uncover why those moments are important. In other ways, it is like an essay unit: you develop *ideas* and *theories* about your life and then write to explore and defend those ideas. We've come to find that memoir is a hybrid, or mixed unit.

"So today, rather than uncovering a premade checklist, you'll use the information in the Narrative Writing Checklist and the Opinion Writing Checklist to make your own Memoir Writing Checklist."

Send children off to work in groups, creating shared versions of a Memoir Checklist.

"In just a moment I am going to send you off to work in your table groups to create a checklist for memoir. You'll see the details for both narrative and opinion in the first two columns, and I think you'll find that you need to draw on both. Let's try one category together before we go off

I have provided you with a pre-made checklist.  *You may choose to simply hand children a copy, though I found the inquiry-based nature of this share to be particularly helpful for students.*

Memoir Writing Checklist

Level 5	Narrative		Opinion/Argument		Memoir	
Structure						
Overall	I wrote a story of an important moment. It reads like a story, even though it might be a true account.	☐	I made a claim/thesis on a topic or text, supported it with reasons, and gave evidence for those reasons.	☐	I wrote an idea about my life and wrote the story of one or more times to show how that idea is true.	☐
Lead	The beginning not only shows what is happening and where, but it also introduces the problem.	☐	My text has an introduction that leads to a claim/thesis. In my introduction, I might give a big picture, tell some background, or find a different way to get my reader interested. I also state a claim and let the reader know the reasons that I'll be developing later.	☐	My text has a beginning that introduces an idea about my life. The beginning might foreshadow what the memoir will be about, or may state my idea clearly.	☐
Transitions	I used transitional phrases to show the passage of time in complicated ways. I might show things happening at the same time (*meanwhile, at the same time*) or flash back and flash-forward (*early that morning* or *three hours later*).	☐	I used transitional phrases such as *for instance, one reason, but the most important reason, an example, consequently,* or *specifically* to help my readers stay with my line of thinking.	☐	I used transitional phrases in two ways: 1. To connect examples and life stories to the idea I have about my life (*for instance, one reason, but the most important reason, an example, consequently, specifically*). 2. To show the passage of time *within* the small moments I tell. I might show things happening at the same time (*meanwhile, at the same time*) or flashback and flash-forward (*early that morning* or *three hours later*)	☐

SESSION 7: STUDYING AND PLANNING STRUCTURES

65

to work in groups." I revealed the 'Overall' category for Level 5, asking children to talk together about what would constitute the Overall standards for Memoir.

I listened in as children read, then discussed the checklist, before calling them back together to share.

Henry began. "I think it's really both, like you said. Our memoirs have stories and they have ideas."

Justin added onto what Henry said. "In memoir we write about an important moment and we write a story. The story is kind of like the evidence to show our idea."

After the children had grappled with this a bit, we decided on the following:

> I wrote an idea about my life and wrote the story of one or more times to show how that idea is true.

Send children off to work independently.

I sent the children off to work in their table groups. With the narrative and opinion right there, they had soon created their own versions of a Memoir Checklist. At the end of the session, we came together as a class to share out our ideas, and co-created the following checklist.

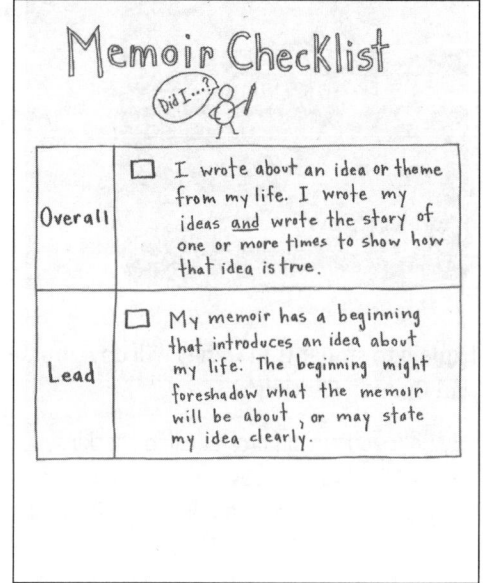

FIG. 7–6   A snippet of the checklist we made as a class.

SESSION 7 HOMEWORK

RESEARCHING FOR MEMOIR

I know that you realize that the people who write articles in *US News & World Report*, *TIME*, *People*, and *Sports Illustrated* all spend time researching those articles before they write them. And when you write reports for social studies, you spend time researching those reports so that you have lots of specific information to weave into your writing. But I am not sure that you realize that almost all writers of almost every genre regard research as an important part of writing. Research is not just something you do for a report on penicillin or Switzerland. Writers research even when they are writing about topics they know well. They research because they know that whatever they write, their writing will be stronger if it is filled with specific, factual details.

So tonight, think of your writer's notebook as a reporter's notepad or a researcher's data collection. Live attentively, trying to collect precise information related to your idea. Collect quotes, details, even articles related to your topic. If you are writing about your teenage sister, try to capture that expression she makes all the time. Go into her closet and count how many pairs of shoes she owns. Record the way she answers the phone. If you are writing about your early days as a reader, go back and reread the books from long ago. Interview your mother to learn her memories of your early forays into reading. You'll probably collect lots—heaps, really—of data.

Session 8

The Inspiration to Draft

I HAVE DEVOTED MY ENTIRE ADULT LIFE to making writing easier for children, helping them realize they have something to say, and finding the words with which to say it. Every word of every book in this series has been written in the hope that somehow we can help children feel ready and able to put themselves on the line.

Yet writing a first draft is one of the hardest things I do. I am still terrified of the blank page. I never fail to feel inadequate to the challenge. Will I—can I—deliver? I hold the pen over the page, poised, and feel as if I'm preparing to parachute from a plane, to dive from a high diving board. My heart is in my throat.

Sometimes the truth is complicated. Sometimes we human beings pursue conflicting goals. This is one of those times. I do want students to write with ease and confidence. But I also want them to be overwhelmed by the awesome challenge of the blank page, to pick up their pens and feel, for a moment, as if they were on the verge of a high dive.

When students are accustomed to writing a lot, as they will be in your classroom, then there is a place for increasing the drumroll leading up to a first draft. And that is the goal of this session. It is crucially important for your students to be both confident and comfortable as writers, *and* also awed and slightly daunted by the magnitude of what it means to confront a blank page.

Then, too, there are important lessons to teach at this critical moment. You will want to remind students that their writing will be stronger and more vivid if they not only write about a subject that they care very much about but if they fill themselves with those feelings of care before they approach the page. Perhaps you'll tell them that many writers find it helps to read beautiful writing just before they write, hoping some of that good stuff rubs off. You will want to remind children that even if they are writing a text that has lots of different components, they can't write all those components at once. They need to decide what subject and kind of writing comes first, and then they need to conjure up what they know about that kind of writing so they can write that one component to the best of their ability. Then, onward. Today, after some more time planning, your students will draft.

IN THIS SESSION, you'll teach students some ways that writers inspire themselves to write better than ever as a way to support drafting.

GETTING READY

- Memoir Writing Checklist from Session 7 (see Link)
- A draft from a student who chose to write about a struggle in his or her life (see Mid-Workshop Teaching)
- A draft from a student who asked, "What do I really want to say?" and narrowed his or her writing accordingly (see Share)

COMMON CORE STATE STANDARDS: W.5.3.d, W.5.5, RL.5.1, RL.5.2, SL.5.1, SL.5.2, L.5.1, L.5.2, L.5.3, L.5.6

MINILESSON

The Inspiration to Draft

CONNECTION

Remind students of the approaching deadline, nudging them to draft if they haven't done so yet.

"Writers, I want to remind you that your memoir needs to be drafted, revised, and edited by three days from now. Some writers call deadlines "lifelines" because the presence of a due date makes them spring to life. Today, you'll need to do that."

✤ **Name your teaching point.**

"Before you begin your first draft, the one written on lined paper outside your notebook, be sure you think hard about how you can inspire yourself to do your best work. Writing well requires talent and knowledge and skill, yes, but also inspiration."

TEACHING

Tell a story about ways to lift the level of first-draft writing. Specifically, teach children that the writer needs to feel an emotion toward a subject in order to make readers feel it, too.

"I want to tell you about a great writer and writing teacher, Bill Zinsser. Zinsser, who has written lots of books on writing well ends his most recent book, *Writing about Your Life: A Journey into the Past* (2005), with a chapter on playing the piano. In this chapter, a musician named Mitchell gives Bill this advice: 'If you feel a certain emotion while you're playing the piano, your listeners will feel it too.' Mitchell elaborated by telling about a time when he was expected to provide the music for a wedding and was given a piano that played like a factory reject. 'I learned it does no good to complain. You think, 'This darn piano,' and you get mad at it and when you get angry you play angry, and you can't project who you really are because you have been transformed into an angry person.' About this, Zinsser said, 'Much of what Dwight Mitchell taught me about playing the piano has nothing to do with music. It has to do with conduct and character.' The lesson, of course, relates also to writing."

◆ COACHING

Milton Meltzer, the great nonfiction writer, said, "In the writer who cares, there is a pressure of feelings which emerges in the rhythm of the sentences, in the choice of details, in the color of the language." I believe that all of this is present also in the voice of the teacher who cares. We can imbue our teaching with the urgency that comes from caring enormously about our message, and in doing so, demonstrate for kids the importance of commitment.

It shouldn't surprise you that when I want to give advice to students, I follow Zinsser's model and convey not only the advice but also the context, the story. I know that the advice will be more memorable if it is wrapped in a story.

"When the day comes for you to write your first draft, you will want to find a place inside yourself from which you can write better than you ever thought you could write. And to do this, it helps for you to think, 'How can I inspire myself to do my best work?'"

Set children up to use the boxes-and-bullet format to take notes as you give a little talk about strategies writers can use to raise the level of first-draft writing.

"Let me share with you some of the ways I try to raise the level of my writing so that my first drafts feel like they are dramatically better than my everyday entries. As I do this, will you take notes? Would one of you be willing to take notes up here on chart paper? And the rest of you, take notes in your writer's notebooks. Your notes will probably need to be shaped in boxes and bullets."

Backing up to reiterate my topic (and signaling to children that this will become their box), I said, "There are many things I do to raise the level of my writing so that my first drafts are more special than my everyday writing." I looked at the charts and notes that were emerging under children's hands to be sure that note-takers had recognized that this was probably an overarching main idea and recorded it as such. "First of all, before I write, I reread wonderful writing. I often reread writing that resembles the sort of text I want to write. In this unit, perhaps I'd read 'Alone' or 'Eleven' or 'Quietly Struggling.' I don't necessarily read the whole text. I am not reading for any one particular purpose. I just want that feeling of awe, grandeur, and intensity to well up inside of me."

I paused dramatically, signaling that another bullet should begin. 'What do I do next? I know! I also reread bits that I have written that I love. Often these are passages I've written that pertain to my seed idea, but sometimes I read one of my earlier publications. Whatever I choose to read, I read that text as if every word is sheer gold. I don't read in a cranky mood, looking for errors. Instead, I pretend the text is magical, and I read it to convince myself that I can write really gorgeous stuff."

"Then, just before I start, I map out a plan. After I sketch a plan, I usually say to myself, 'I'm going to write just the first component, the first bit, of this draft.' I try to think, 'So what *kind of writing* will I be doing? Will this be a narrative?' If so, I recall what I know about writing effective narratives. 'Or will this first section be an essay? If so, will I start with a claim? Will I support it with reasons?'"

"I do all that preparation for writing briefly, devoting perhaps ten minutes to it. And then, finally, I pick up my pen and write a lead. If I like it, I keep going. If I'm not sure that I like it, I pause and try again, hoping to get a solid foundation, a good start, for the upcoming draft. But soon I am writing, writing, writing, fast and furious, until I get to the end of one component, one section, then I pause, then I make plans for the upcoming section."

Notice that several times throughout this minilesson, I coach children to take notes on the minilesson. When children are less mature and fluent as writers, I am not convinced they can listen and jot at the same time. But somewhere toward the end of elementary school, this changes.

The work children did in essay and information writing units, thinking about main idea and supporting information, provides them with skills they can draw upon when taking notes.

You'll notice that as I talk in the upcoming section, I deliberately structure my words so that children will have an easier time capturing my message in boxes and bullets. Notice that to support children's note-taking, my little speech has an especially clean structure.

Notice that once a draft is begun, it's written quickly, all in one sitting.

ACTIVE ENGAGEMENT

Set students up to use their notes as a prop to help them recall and re-create your little lecture. Then ask them to talk with a partner about your talk, adding their ideas to yours.

"In a minute, I will ask you to share your notes with each other. Before you do this, will you and your partner meet, and will you merge the notes that the two of you wrote about my first tip—and as you do this, work together to reconstruct that part of my message? Then read the next bit of your notes—yours and your partner's—and again talk in such a way that you re-create what I said, remembering more than either one of you recorded. Continue in that way to use your notes as a scaffold, a prop, to help you remind yourself of what I said." I gave writers a couple of minutes to teach each other, remembering what I'd said and filling in bullets they may have missed.

Calling them back together, I began, "Now, would you and your partner go back and look over your notes about what I said, asking 'What does she do to prepare for writing a first draft that I may also want to do?' You might also think of strategies I didn't list that you'd like to suggest."

LINK

Encourage writers to set their own goals, using their checklists as guides.

"As you recall, you have a deadline just around the bend. The one thing I want to remind you to do is to scan over your Memoir Writing Checklist. Remind yourself of the qualities of good memoir writing. You might keep this next to you as you write, using it like a little checklist as you compose your writing. Go ahead and set your self-assignments for today, and then get started!"

CONFERRING AND SMALL-GROUP WORK

Choosing the Right Story and Blending External and Internal Storylines

BY THE TIME I REACHED TYLER, he had already rewritten his entry about his grandmother so that it was now a first draft. His entry had begun: One time I was going to my grandmother's house and I was so excited. I got there with my brother and we were wondering what we could do. So we took our jackets off and started talking to Grandmother. In his draft, Tyler tried to write about his special relationship with his grandmother and to zoom in on one fun time they'd had together. It was immediately clear to me that he had made an effort to write his draft as a compelling story, one imbued with feeling. (See Figure 8–1.) His draft continued:

> In New York City there is always something you could do. So we decided to go to the lunch place. When it was time for lunch we went to Dr. Jekyl and Mr. Hyde. This restaurant was scary and that is why I liked it. It was funny/scary and had good food.

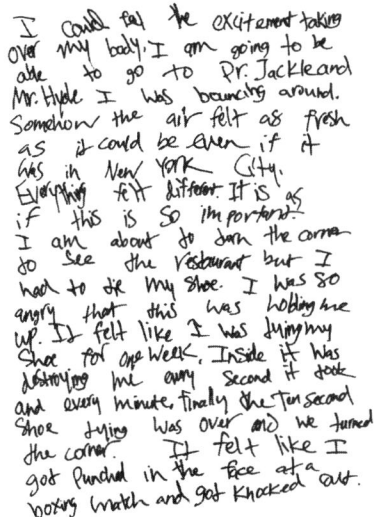

FIG. 8–1 Tyler writes his first draft, working hard to make it a compelling story.

SESSION 8: THE INSPIRATION TO DRAFT

> I could feel the excitement taking over my body. I am going to be able to go to Dr. Jekyll and Mr. Hyde. I was bouncing around. Somehow the air felt as fresh as it could be even if it is in New York City. Everything felt different. It is as if this is so important. I am about to turn the corner to see the restaurant but I had to tie my shoe. I was so angry that this was holding me up.

Although Tyler's draft was significantly better than his entry, the draft still didn't seem to be a memoir. I worried that Tyler's efforts to "write a good story" had lured him away from writing in a way that conveyed some big ideas about his life. His exaggerations also made me not trust his text. This wasn't the first time that I'd seen a child make an effort to tell an event with excitement and end up distorting the truth of it. Looking up from reading what Tyler showed me, I asked Tyler what he felt about his draft. "So what are you thinking?" I asked.

"I think the draft is better because I was filled with feelings—I was hungry when I wrote it!—and I *showed* my excitement to get to the restaurant. I didn't *say*, like, 'I was excited to go out to lunch'; instead, I *showed* it by the part about tying my shoe and 'Arrrrrg! I want to stop doing this and get to the restaurant!'"

"Did that shoe-tying bit really happen?" I asked.

"Well," Tyler said. "It is one of those true but not true parts. I don't really know if it *did* happen or not, because it was a year ago, but I *was* happy to be going out for lunch 'cause it is a cool place."

Tyler's responses were helping me construct a sense of him as a writer. In conferences, I make a point of pursuing multiple lines of inquiry. So I asked, "What are you thinking you should do next?" I added. "Is this going to be part of a larger memoir? Are you thinking of stretching this out, or of laying other events alongside it, or embedding this story within a larger idea or theme, or what?"

"I gotta put some other things with me and my grandma because this isn't really that much about us; it is mostly about the lunch place," Tyler answered.

(continues)

MID-WORKSHOP TEACHING POINT   Truth-Telling

"Writers, can we gather for a moment in the meeting area? I know that is unusual, but what I have to say is so important that I need all of you to pull close," I waited until everyone had taken a seat on the carpet. The room bristled with some tension. The children clearly wondered what was powerful enough to alter the normal routine.

Jill sat beside me at the front of the meeting area. "Writers, I need to talk to you about Jill," I said. "Last week, when I conferred with Jill, she was thinking about writing about her relationship with her mother, telling specifically about pumpkin picking with her mother. Jill had some good writing on that topic, and it is something she feels strongly about.

"But in her notebook, Jill also had some entries about a problem that haunts her like a nightmare, a problem that is so difficult that she doesn't like to talk much about it. Jill and I got to talking, and I suggested that this year, you guys are such a close community, that maybe Jill could take the gigantic leap of faith and write about the problem that haunts her." Then I said, "Can you talk to the kids about this, Jill?"

As Jill started to talk, children shifted in their seats and one or two whispered to each other. Sitting beside her, I signaled for her to wait. "Wait 'til their eyes are on you, 'til you have their full attention." After the room grew quiet, Jill began to talk. "I realized that pumpkin picking with my Mom wasn't really on my mind or anything, so I'm writing about my weight." And she talked about it.

I added, "Class, earlier we talked about bravery and how there are lots of kinds of bravery. Ali, you are writing your essay on that, aren't you? I think that Jill has just shown us one kind of bravery, don't you? Jill has a draft and is willing to share it with us. So let's listen. As you listen, will you jot down things that you notice Jill doing in her writing that make her draft a powerful one?"

Jill glanced up just once and then began to read (see Figure 8–2).

Throughout the class, hands shot up. Jack spoke first. "I think you are brave to write about that because it is so personal. And I don't think you should worry about being thin because your age is a time for changes and it will probably change, because I grew like, four inches in a year!" he said.

Max added, "When you wrote that you hide under your blanket like when you were five, it sounded like Sandra Cisneros in 'Eleven' talking about all her different ages." Others followed.

After a few minutes I brought the class back to the central point. "Let's take Jill as a mentor. All of us have the courage to tackle the real topics that are on our minds. The truth is, we will end up writing in powerful ways when we select a subject that has some angst, some struggle involved in it. So if any of you are writing all-is-perfect entries, you may want to think, 'Where's the struggle in this subject?' and 'Is this the truth of what has been on my mind lately?' Tackle the hard stuff, and your writing often becomes more powerful."

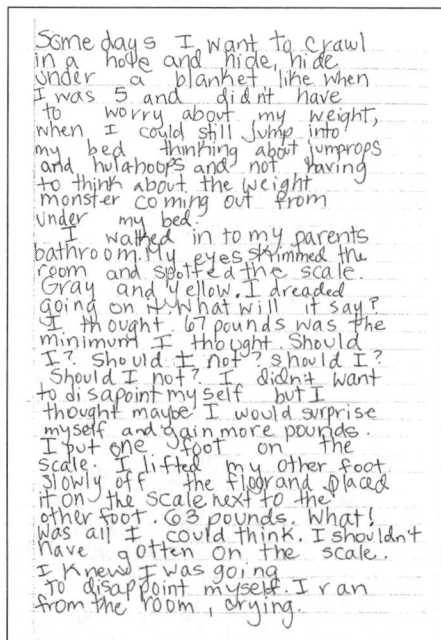

FIG. 8–2   Jill wrote powerfully about a personal topic.

This comment made me think Tyler felt that his relationship with his grandma was really the theme. I decided I now had enough background to be helpful. "I love that you didn't just copy your entry and call it a draft, but instead you deliberately worked to draw on all that you know about writing effective stories. I can see that you wrote the draft with a problem and a solution and you angled it to convey a feeling," I said. "But, Tyler, what I love best is that even after all that good work, you have the courage to look back on what you have done and to say, 'I'm not sure this really shows what I want to show, which is my relationship with my grandmother.' That is incredibly thoughtful, and I definitely agree that although this is a well-written story that shows how hungry you were, the details about how hungry you were probably won't be the heart of a memoir about you and your grandmother."

Then, in an effort to be sure Tyler didn't veer off course again, I said, "Can I help you get started on writing about a moment that shows what you want to show about your relationship with your grandmother?"

I asked Tyler if he had an idea for another event—one that might show the relationship even more. He said he was thinking about writing how his grandmother went on a roller coaster ride with him. Recalling the harrowing trip I'd once had on a roller coaster and wanting to rally Tyler's energy for the idea he'd proposed, I said, "Oh my gosh, Tyler. Your grandmother went on one of those rides?" Then I added, "I went on a roller coaster a few years ago and it was brutal. My head was practically jerked off my neck. I nearly lost it! I can't imagine your grandmother on that ride!"

"She didn't want to. She yelled her head off," Tyler agreed. Then he confided, "I think she did it just for me."

"No wonder you want to tell this story! It is so revealing of your grandmother, isn't it!" Shifting, I said, "Can you tell me how the whole thing happened? What happened first?"

"We were standing in line, watching the ride, and the people were screaming. Then we got on."

"Tyler," I said. "Tell it in smaller steps. And, Tyler, you want to tell what you saw and did—the external story—*and* what you felt and thought, too—the internal story." To get him started, I said, "So stand up and show me exactly what you were doing as you stood in line, watching the people."

Tyler acted to show that his eyes followed the roller coaster as it traveled along the rails. Prompting him, I provided words for his actions. "I stood in line . . . " Then I said, "That's the external action; what were you thinking, feeling?"

"I was amazed at the roller coaster," he said. When I prompted him to shift and tell what he did or saw next (returning to the external story line), he said, "My eyes were following the roller coaster like, like, it was the strongest magnet in the world!"

"That's beautiful," I assured Tyler. "Write it!" and I dictated the words he'd said while he recorded them. Soon Tyler had written this (see Figure 8–3).

"Tyler," I said. "Do you see how, at the start of this, you shift between the external story line, telling what you did or saw, and then the internal story line, telling what that made you feel or think?" I reread the draft, underlining the external and letting the internal stand.

> <u>I stood in line to get on the roller coaster</u> next to my grandmother amazed at the roller coaster. <u>My eyes follow it as if it was the strongest magnet in the world, and every second it got closer, closer, closer.</u> And nothing can stop me from getting on it. And before I know it, <u>the roller coaster zoomed right next to me as it almost knocks me off my feet.</u> I am so excited <u>I jump up and down like a kangaroo.</u>

"The draft has a pattern that really works," I said, as if this had been his invention. "It goes like this: (1) I do or see something, something happens in the external world. Then (2) I respond by thinking or feeling. Then (3) I do or see something, something happens in the external world, and it continues.

"This is going to be a drop-dead amazing piece, I can just tell. It is amazing how a little story about you and your grandmother riding the roller coaster can become a window into your relationship, which, you're discovering, is really the theme of your memoir. Would you work on this now and maybe at lunchtime—because you are onto some important work—and bring it to me soon so that I can use it in a minilesson to teach all the other kids?"

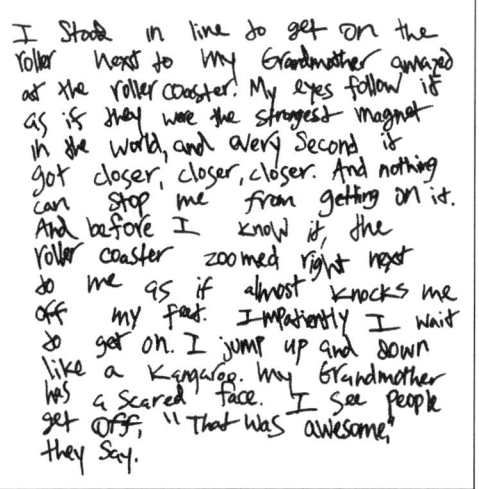

FIG. 8–3 Tyler explores internal vs. external story.

SHARE

The Courage to Redraft

Tell the story of one writer who collected an excess of entries and drafts and then paused to ask, "What do I really want to say?" and used that question to lead him to start an entirely new draft.

"Writers, I want to talk with you again about courage. That seems to be the subject of the day! I want to tell you about another writer who showed great courage today, and that is Adam.

"Adam, as you know, has been writing about his relationship with his brother. Before I conferred with him today, he'd collected about ten long entries about moments he has spent with his brother. For example, he had written an entry which began like this."

> My brother and I go to restaurants. We always play a game named napkin. Whoever sits down first says, "Napkin." If you are the first one to say this you get one point.

Adam had also written an entry about Jon teaching him to be a goalie and about Jon writing to him when he was at camp and on and on the list goes. When I asked Adam his plans, he said he thought he'd recopy the entries and find a refrain that could hook them together. Instead of saying 'Alone is . . . ,' he'd say something like, 'My brother is . . .'

"But as we talked, Adam said something really important. He said, 'I don't know if these *really* show what I feel.' I asked him to say more, and he talked about how he's feeling like his childhood with Jon will soon be over. Then Adam did something really brave. He put all those entries aside and pulled out a clean sheet of paper. 'I'm going to try writing just one really long story about the day when he leaves,' Adam said. 'I'll pretend it already did happen, and stretch it out and put all my feelings in.' Then he added, 'If it doesn't work, I will go back to my other entries.'"

"How many of the rest of you have put aside your initial entries and had the courage today to write a whole new draft—not just a copy and correction of your prior work?" Half the class signaled that they'd written some new work. "Those writers had a lot of courage. Let's listen to their new work, okay?" I organized the class so one or two children would listen to each child who had written a whole new draft.

This quote by Don Murray hangs alongside my desk as a personal reminder: "Emptiness is the starting point of writing and I have to remind myself of that. After all, I don't want to write what I have written before, and write it in the same way. I have to remember that in despair, in terror, in hopelessness, I have come to the beginning of my writing. Now I can find a new country to explore."

One of the readers was Adam. He read a piece to two listeners that began like this (see Figure 8-4):

I intervened. "Even though you haven't heard the end of the draft, give each other feedback."

For the next few minutes, children talked to each other. Two of them told Adam about the emotional power in this piece, and about the power of his stretched-out moment.

Coach students to share further thoughtful suggestions about the draft presented.

"Writers," I said. "It will be important that people help you feel like you have made a good decision; you guys have just done that. Thank you. But it is also important that people give your writing the respectful attention it deserves, and this means helping you to make it even better. These are *first drafts*. And they deserve smart, honest responses. So give each other the honor of your thoughtful suggestions." They did.

FIG. 8–4 Adam's initial draft about his brother

FIG. 8–5 Jude redrafts his memoir to include a repeating refrain patterned after Paul Auster's refrain.

SESSION 8: THE INSPIRATION TO DRAFT

SESSION 8 HOMEWORK

CONFERRING WITH YOURSELF TO MAKE A WRITING PLAN

Writers, tonight I'm going to ask you to confer with yourself, just like I confer with you and then to continue drafting. I've jotted some of the questions I often ask, that you might ask yourself:

Questions to Ask in a Writing Conference
- What was the last thing you decided to do, to work toward? How did it turn out?
- Why, exactly, did you do this? What else could you have done to reach the same goal?
- What else, other than that work, have you been doing, and how has that worked out?
- Do you have specific plans for what you might do next?

Tonight, as you have a conference with yourself, will you ask yourself also, "Am I being a brave writer? Did I risk writing a whole new draft, instead of just copying and connecting entries? If not, will I take the risk now?" Ask also, "Am I writing the truth?" There are lots of ways to be brave and lots of ways to answer these questions.

Create a plan for your work. Write a planning box that reflects your decisions and plans. And then begin the work that you lay out for yourself.

Session 9

Becoming Your Own Teacher

Dear Teachers,

Take stock of your class and decide what you need to teach today. We've written some ideas for one way today might go, but be sure to consider other options. If nothing emerges that seems more essential, you might encourage children to step up to the role of being their own teachers. You will name for children what it is that you do when you confer with them and remind them that each writer needs to confer with himself or herself. Tucked into such a session, you could remind your students to draw on all that they already know—to review options, and to make plans.

MINILESSON

You might begin this session by explaining that, as much as you try, it is hard to provide all the conferring time they need. "Writers, I wanted to share with you a problem that I have been having and ask for your help," you might begin. "I'm finding that in this unit of study, it is hard to keep my conferences short and efficient. You've written a whole lot of entries, all of which pertain to this writing project, so even just reading what you've written takes time. And you've put so much thought into your plans, that it also takes a lot of time to hear and understand your agenda. I love conferring with you, but I am not getting to as many of you as I'd like."

Then, solicit children's help. "Here is my request: would it be okay if I taught you a bit more about how to confer with yourself? I'll still confer as much as I can, but if you can each confer with yourself, then you won't be waiting for me. This would not only help with my problem; it would also mean that whenever you write, for the rest of your lives—when you are at home or at camp or in middle school or at your grandparents' house and you decide to tackle a writing project—you'll know how to not only be the writer, but also to be the writing teacher."

For your teaching point you might say something like, "Specifically, what I want to teach you is this: when a writer can't go to a writing teacher, the writer needs to become

COMMON CORE STATE STANDARDS: W.5.3, W.5.5, W.5.10, RL.5.1, RFS.5.4, SL.5.1, SL.5.4, L.5.1, L.5.2, L.5.3

his own writing teacher. Before you can be your own writing teacher, suggesting next steps for yourselves, you need to pay attention to what you have already done. A good writing teacher looks backward in order to look forward."

Set up a mini-inquiry. Ask children to study you as you confer with one child in front of the class. You might say, "Writers, how about if I confer with Justin right up here, in front of you, and meanwhile, you and your partner keep shared notes on what you see me doing? After I confer with Justin, I'll ask you to look back on what I did in this conference and think, 'Is this something I could do for myself?'"

As you confer, be sure to highlight whatever you hope your students will notice. You might begin with something like "So, Justin, how's your writing going? I haven't talked to you since we had that conference about you needing to not only write big, but also to write small about your ideas." If you think your students need help extracting the replicable moves you are making, you might shift out of the role of teacher so as to comment, "Did you guys notice how I started with a big question about how writing is going for Justin? Make sure you get that down. Some of you also noticed that I'm checking in on the goals Justin set for himself last time." Then turn back to the student and continue on with the conference.

As the student explains what he or she is working on, you'll want to model looking closely at the relevant section of his or her text, studying it with the student. "Justin," you might say, "you said that you are working on supporting your claim with a variety of evidence. Can you show me some of that evidence?"

After you model exploring several lines of inquiry, you might turn to the children again and say, "So now my research is done. Watch what I do next." Then, shift from researching the writer to giving a compliment and teaching. You'll decide whether you need to stop sporadically to point out significant teaching moves, or whether you can expect students to extract these.

Once you have completed the conference, consider asking students to debrief with their partners, naming what they saw you do that they could also do in a conference with themselves. Listen in on what they say, and use it to compile a list of questions writing teachers ask.

You might say, "Talk also about whether you can imagine conferring in similar ways *with yourself*." Then, after they talk and you compile a few notes, you could intervene. "Let's chart questions you saw me asking that you could ask as well." The chart might look something like this.

Questions Writing Teachers Ask

- What was the last thing you decided to do, to work toward? How did it turn out?
- Can we look at places where you did that work?
- What else have you been doing, and how has that worked out? Can we look at places where you did that?
- What are your specific plans for what you might do next?

You might end this lesson by giving children time to confer with themselves, resulting in each student developing a self-assignment. "Writers," you can begin, "many of you have been taking about thirty seconds at the start of each writing workshop to decide on the work you are going to do each day and to write your self-assignments. But I hope that today has helped you to realize that it is important for you to take a little bit more time to function as a writing teacher for yourself, making sure that you are on the best possible course. Try asking yourself some of the questions that I ask in conferences: 'What was the last thing you did and how did it turn out? What else have you been doing, and how has that worked out?'" Point to the chart as you repeat these questions to remind them that the chart is a resource for them. "As you ask these questions, remember that you need to notice what you have done well. Sometimes you'll stumble almost accidentally onto doing some really good work, and if you don't stop and notice what you've done and dedicate yourself to doing more of that, then it becomes just a one-time lucky accident, instead of a new discovery that happens again and again.

CONFERRING AND SMALL-GROUP WORK

As you move around the room, you may discover students who seem to be going along just fine, making plans for themselves and writing up a storm, but when you pull up alongside them, you notice that the drafts they are making are not as thoughtful as you would hope. Some writers, for example, have written a *lot*, often using a lot of details, but they don't seem to select details that create an effect or make a point. If you come across a group of children like this, you might pull them together into a small group.

You might begin by saying, "Writers, I've noticed a lot of you have added in tons of details to your memoirs. You can congratulate yourself on writing with specifics, as this shows that you have the muscles you need to write really well. But effective writing can't just be a storm of detail, hurling toward the reader. The details need to be chosen and controlled to create an effect."

Continuing, you could say, "A detail can be true and yet not advance the idea you want to get across. I had a student last year who wanted to convey his worry over his mother's illness. He told about visiting her in the hospital. He had to wait for visiting hours. But he added in details about the exciting video game he played while waiting—and only later realized that distracted from his message. Look over your writing for details that are true, but that don't help you create the effect you want." Children worked on that for a while.

MID-WORKSHOP TEACHING

You might use today's mid-workshop teaching point to shine the spotlight on a few students who are working with particular independence. You might spot students using the charts in the room to remind them of strategies or help them out of a rut. You might feature a student who uses his checklist to guide his work, checking each item off as he accomplishes it. By showcasing independence, you create a classroom full of resourceful writers.

SHARE

You might consider wrapping up today's session with a nod toward transference. Gather students around the class charts you've developed thus far in the unit, as well as those from other applicable units, especially essay and narrative. You can ask children to bring their Narrative Writing Checklists with them to the meeting area, as well. Then, remind students that yesterday's learning is today's best practice!

"Learning," you might say, "is similar to the way Sandra Cisneros describes growing up. She writes that when you are 11, you are also 10 and 9 and 8. In the same way, when you learn a new writing strategy on Friday, you should also be using what you learned on Thursday and Wednesday and Tuesday and Monday." You might tell children that their learning is a bit like an onion, or the rings in a tree, and that it pays off to stop once in a while and ask, "Am I doing everything I know how to do? Am I using all the strategies I know for powerful writing?" Chances are they aren't, and you'll encourage them to make action plans for how they'll transfer all they know to their current piece of writing.

HOMEWORK

For homework, you'll definitely want children to complete their first draft of their memoir so that they'll be able to devote at least some time to revision.

Best Wishes,

Lucy and Ali

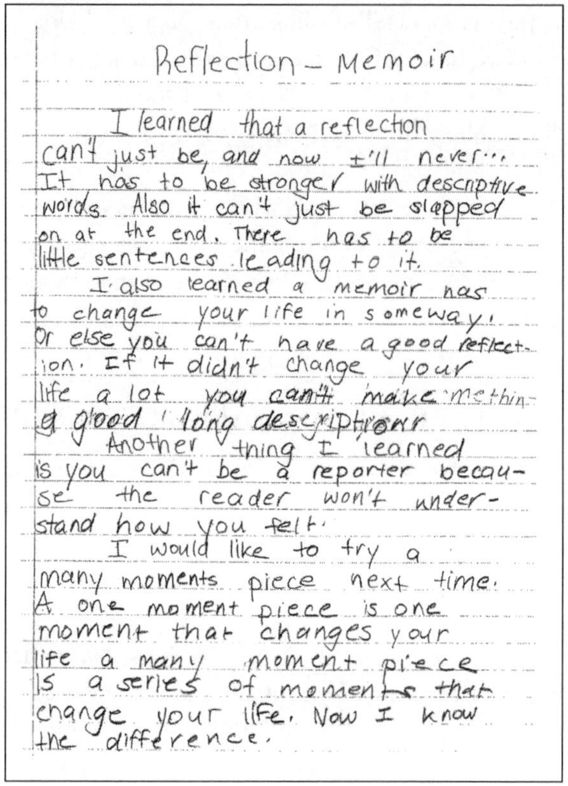

Reflection – Memoir

I learned that a reflection can't just be, and now I'll never... It has to be stronger with descriptive words. Also it can't just be slapped on at the end. There has to be little sentences leading to it.

I also learned a memoir has to change your life in someway. Or else you can't have a good reflection. If it didn't change your life a lot you can't make something good long description.

Another thing I learned is you can't be a reporter because the reader won't understand how you felt.

I would like to try a many moments piece next time. A one moment piece is one moment that changes your life a many moment piece is a series of moments that change your life. Now I know the difference.

FIG. 9–1 Emily reflects on the lessons she has learned in this first round of memoir.

Session 10

Revising the Narrative Portion of a Memoir

THE MOST IMPORTANT LESSONS that you will teach your students are not ones that are simply taught, then checked off from your list—"Done!" Instead, the most important lessons are the ones that your students revisit over and over, in a cycle of continuous study, with your teaching and your students' understandings becoming more complex and sophisticated over time.

It should not surprise you, then, that this session revisits lessons you have taught often. From the start of the year, you have emphasized that writers need to ask, "What is my text really about?" The central claim in an essay frames the entire text. In stories, however, the meaning should be no less omnipresent. It is particularly essential that the stories embedded into memoir carry longer meanings. In this session, you will remind students that based on the writer's answer to the question, "What is my writing really about?" the writer will tell the story differently. You have already taught them that if the writer is writing about riding a Ferris wheel and the point is that the writer still cherishes childhood pleasures, then she may describe how she stood in the ticket line, surrounded by a sea of little children, none higher than her waist, and realized that old as she is (ten!), she still appreciates childhood pleasures. On the other hand, if the Ferris wheel story is about the writer appreciating the chance to look out over the entire fairgrounds, the writer will probably bring out the internal thinking that occurs when the Ferris wheel approaches the top of its spin.

Today you take these lessons another step and suggest that writers revise their stories so that the main character (who in this instance is the author) goes through an internal journey of feelings that parallels (and is in response to) the story's external journey of actions. This means that if the writer wants her memoir to convey that she still appreciates childhood pleasures, she can do better than putting that one unchanging feeling throughout the anecdote—at the beginning, middle, and end. Instead, she might revise her draft to reveal an internal journey that shows a conflict and a resolution.

IN THIS SESSION, you'll teach students to remember that if their memoir contains narratives, those stories need to carry meaning.

GETTING READY

✓ A published text that shows internal and external story lines, such as "Mama Sewing," from *Childtimes* by Eloise Greenfield (see Teaching)

✓ Chart of internal and external timelines for text above (see Teaching)

✓ Copies of a student's writing containing internal and external story lines for each student (see Active Engagement)

✓ Example of writing that shows specific action (see Mid-Workshop Teaching)

✓ Excerpts of writing that show how skilled writers capture feelings (see Share)

COMMON CORE STATE STANDARDS: W.5.3.b,d; W.5.4, W.5.5, RL.5.1, RL.5.2, RL.5.5, SL.5.1, L.5.1, L.5.2, L.5.3

MINILESSON

Revising the Narrative Portion of a Memoir

CONNECTION

Reiterate all the options your children have as memoirists, and then tell them they have no option when writing a memoir but to reveal themselves through it.

"Writers, you have lots of choices as a writer of memoir. Your memoir can shine a spotlight on your relationship with your father, on the tree fort in your backyard, on your childhood struggles to learn to read. You can structure your memoir as one story, a necklace of related mini-stories, an essay, or even a collection of poems. You have lots and lots of choices as a writer of memoir.

"But as a memoir writer, you have no choice but to reveal yourself. The point of writing a memoir is to make a statement about yourself—about the kind of person you are. So yes, Max can write about the tree fort that used to be in his backyard, but *really*, his memoir needs to be about a boy who is nostalgic for that tree house. And Adam can write about his brother Jon leaving for college, but *really*, the memoir needs to be about Adam, the younger brother, who is left behind. And Ali can write about her father's bravery as he lies in bed, recovering from an awful injury, but really, Ali is writing about the girl who stands beside her father's bed. And Tyler can write about a grandmother who is so loving that she rides a scary roller coaster with her grandson, but really, this needs to also be a memoir about what that grandmother's generosity means to that grandson.

"Sometimes, after a day or two of drafting, you find that you have been focusing so hard on getting down the external story, the story of *an event*, that you've forgotten this needs to be the story of *you as a person*. You need to write not only the external story of what happened to you, but also the *internal* story of what you thought and wondered and remembered and worried."

❖ **Name your teaching point.**

"Today I want to teach you that even within a memoir, both the external events *and* the internal feelings will usually evolve across a timeline, a story mountain. When you write a story, you know there will be a sequence of actions—that one thing will happen, then another thing, and another. But you may not always be aware that there needs to be a parallel sequence of *reactions*, of feelings and thoughts, dreams and fears. Writers often have to redraft their memoir so that each point on the external timeline affects the central character on the inside, creating a parallel internal timeline."

◆ COACHING

You should be able to feel the drumroll in your language. "You have choices about one thing, you have choices about another thing, but you have no choice but to . . . "

Draw on precise examples from students in your class.

Whenever you can name what your students are doing in ways that are beautiful, you'll lift the level of their work and their self-concepts. It is important to do this. Notice that when I want to speak beautifully, I use techniques that we teach children—in this instance, parallelism. My list is parallel and detailed.

Some people think it is important to simplify the teaching point by consolidating it into a single sentence. I advocate for clarity over brevity.

TEACHING

Reiterate the teaching point in different words, emphasizing that writers approach the narrative section of a memoir thinking, "What feeling do I want to show in the beginning? In the middle? The end?"

"I want to remind you that when you plan the sections of your memoir that contain a narrative (depending on the structure you've chosen, the narrative might be your whole memoir or one tiny piece), you need to plan for how you will show the journey of feelings that you experience as you moved through time. You can't just show the external series of events. Instead, you also need to show your reactions to each event as it unfolds. This helps the reader understand how you feel and what this moment reveals about you."

Illustrate your point by reading aloud a short text and showing children the external and internal story lines in it.

"In 'Mama Sewing,' Eloise Greenfield has very clearly organized the *external* story line of her piece. In a similar way, all of you write with very clear external story lines or structures. But what I noticed last night when I was reading 'Mama Sewing,' trying to learn from this mentor text, is that each event in the external story line affects Eloise, and the effects that the events create are a big part of the memoir. More than this, I noticed that the way Eloise is affected—the way she feels as a result of various events—creates the *internal* timeline of this memoir.

"In 'Mama Sewing,' the text is a story that jumps over long spans of time. Eloise Greenfield writes in this way to show that her understanding of her mother has changed over time. Listen as I read 'Mama Sewing.' Let's think, 'What is the first external event?' 'What is the internal response to that external event?' Then think, 'What's the next external event, and the next internal response?' " I read this aloud.

> Mama Sewing
>
> *I don't know why Mama ever sewed for me. She sewed for other people, made beautiful dresses and suits and blouses, and got paid for doing it. But I don't know why she ever sewed for me. I was so mean.*
>
> *It was all right in the days when she had to make my dresses a little longer in the front than in the back to make up for the way I stood, with my legs pushed back and my stomach stuck out. I was little then, and I trusted Mama. But when I got older, I worried.*
>
> *Mama would turn the dress on the wrong side and slide it over my head, being careful not to let the pins stick me. She'd kneel on the floor with her pin cushion fitting the dress on me, and I'd look down at the dress, at that lopsided, raw-edged, half-basted, half-pinned thing—and know that it was never going to look like anything. So, I'd pout while Mama frowned and sighed and kept on pinning.*
>
> *Sometimes she would sew all night, and in the morning I'd have a perfectly beautiful dress, just right for the school program or the party. I'd put it on, and I'd be so ashamed of the way I acted. I'd be too ashamed to say I was sorry.*
>
> *But Mama knew.*

Notice that as these units of study unroll, students revisit the same concepts of good writing over and over, each time dealing with them with increasing sophistication. So at first they asked, "Where is the heart of my story?" Next, they learned to ask, "What is my story really about?" and to comb their answer through the whole text. Now you are teaching them that their internal as well as their external story unrolls in a progression. The internal story evolves as much as the external one.

"What do you think?" I asked. "Jot two tiny timelines—the external and the internal one." Students jotted for a second, and then I said, "I agree." Turning the chart paper tablet to reveal the chart I'd made of the external and internal story line in this memoir, I said, "The memoir tells one thing and then the next that happened on the external story line. Each event affects Eloise in some way. The way she is affected—the way she feels as a result of various events—creates the internal timeline."

Timelines in "Mama Sewing"

External Timeline	Internal Timeline
• Mama sewed for me when I was little . . .	• . . . my response was that this made me happy.
• Mama sewed for me when I was older . . .	• . . . my response was that this made me irritable.
• Then Mama made me a beautiful dress for the school dance . . .	• . . . my response was that I was ashamed of my earlier behavior toward her.

Highlight the fact that the external events move the story forward. The character's responses to those events constitute the internal story line, conveying the impact the events have on the person or on the relationships.

"When you lay these timelines side by side, you can see how Eloise has changed her way of understanding her mother as a result of this series of events from her life. At the start of the story, Eloise appreciates her mother's sewing. But as the story line unfolds, Eloise goes through a journey of feeling. When Eloise is a teenager, she has no patience for her mother or for her mother's sewing. Her feelings have evolved. Then, one day, Eloise wakes up and finds a beautiful dress that her mother worked on all night to sew, and she becomes ashamed of the way she has treated her mother.

"In this memoir, and in many memoirs, the internal story is important because this helps us see what the character realizes about herself and about her relationships. Even if your memoir is shaped more like an essay, and storytelling is one small part of it, it is still important to make sure that those small stories reveal something important about your internal self."

Acknowledge the ways different strategies apply to memoir that are structured differently. This strategy will be applied in a more, whole-scale way to memoir that are almost entirely narrative. Those that are predominately exposition will still contain anecdotes and students will want to bring forth the internal "stories" in those micro-stories.

ACTIVE ENGAGEMENT

Tell students about a child who deliberately shifted between the external and the internal story and whose internal story line follows a clear sequence. Ask children to track the journey of feelings on a copy of the child's text.

"I know many of you are already imagining ways you'll rewrite the sections of your memoir that contain a narrative so you bring out the internal journey of your feelings. I'm going to ask Tyler to read aloud the start of his draft about a time when he and his grandmother went on a roller coaster ride. You each have a copy of it. As you listen, notice the way Tyler records the *external* event (sometimes in just half of a sentence) and then his *internal* response to that event. Then he records the next *external* event and his next *internal* response to that event. As you listen, keep in mind the evolving *internal* story line. How does Tyler feel at the beginning? After a bit? Later? Soon you'll have a chance to talk about Tyler's journey of feelings."

Tyler read the beginning of his draft aloud (see Figure 10–1).

> I stand in the line, my eyes drawn to the roller coaster as if it were the strongest magnet in the world. I follow the cart as it swoops and swirls. It jets along the tracks over my head. "I can't wait," I think.
>
> I count how many people are ahead of me in line. Nothing is going to stop me from getting on the ride!
>
> "The Intimidator," my grandmother reads from the sign. I look at her and see that she is clutching her pocketbook in her hands and brushing the dust off her vest. I start to worry.
>
> The roller coaster cranks to a stop near us. And the people get off. As they flood past us, I hear someone say, "That was awesome." And, "Let's do that again." Out of the corner of my eyes I see my grandmother sigh with a scared face. I worry more.
>
> We step into the cart. "Grandma, you don't have to go on. It's a pretty big ride," I say, wanting to get her off the ride. I hear a click click as the handlebar locks against our stomachs. I feel like my grandma is trapped in her worst fear. "This is our last chance. Do you want to get off?"

"Do you see all the places where Tyler has given you a glimpse into his internal feelings? He lets you in on how he reacts to each part of the story. Turn and talk to your partner about the places where Tyler did this. How does it help you learn about him as a person?" I coached in as partners talked, helping them to notice that Tyler's evolution of emotions leads readers to understand how much he cares for his grandmother.

I've deliberately chosen to spotlight Tyler's piece because the external story of a roller coaster ride is so dramatic and action-filled that the internal story might easily have been lost. Yet Tyler has managed to write an equally powerful internal story, and I want the other children to learn from this.

FIG. 10–1 Tyler's draft

LINK

Highlight the importance of redrafting. Remind writers that when they work on the narrative sections of their memoir, they need to plan for a journey of feelings and to remember that the external story line is intertwined with the internal one.

"The Newbery award-winning children's author Jack Gantos once said that for every draft he writes, he *rewrites* it at least fifty times. Fifty is a lot, and I'm afraid we won't have time for anything close to that many drafts, but it *is* important to hold yourself to large-scale redrafting at least a few times. You'll remember from our personal narrative unit that this doesn't mean crossing out a line here and adding in a word there. Instead, it means that you set aside your first draft and write a brand new version. Then you compare drafts and make choices.

"As you work on the drafts of your memoir, many of you will spend some time working to write a story—the story may be a big part of your memoir, or just a small piece. Either way, remember that when you write a story, there is a sequence of events that moves the story forward through time. And with each event, the main character will begin to see and think and feel differently. Each point on the external timeline of a story will affect the character—in this case, you—on the inside and, as a result, the internal story line will be created. You have just today and tomorrow to finish this text, so don't waste an instant!"

CONFERRING AND SMALL-GROUP WORK

Writing about Internal Changes

I PULLED MY CHAIR ALONGSIDE ALI, who was rereading the draft of the narrative section of her memoir (see Figure 10–2). "I tried to divide it into tiny chapters based on my feelings," she said, "but it was mostly one feeling because Dad wasn't able to do anything but lie there."

Ali was writing about the feelings she experienced during her father's long convalescence after major back surgery. She had produced dozens of drafts of both a vignette about how she'd gone into the room where her father lay, wanting desperately to feel that he still cared about the little events of her school life. She'd also written many reflective ruminations, modeled after the initial expository section of "Eleven."

"Can you tell me about the journey of feelings that you are trying to show?" I said, and Ali told me that she hoped her draft first showed hopefulness as she tried to interest her Dad in the details of her life, then showed loneliness and sadness as she responded to his disinterest, then showed that she tried to feel better by leaving to watch TV but found that the sadness lingered.

"So what are you planning to do next?" I asked, and then I learned that Ali had decided that she needed to stretch out each feeling more. For example, she'd written a flap to insert into her final paragraph (see Figure 10–3).

(continues)

FIG. 10–2 Ali's initial draft describes a visit to her father's bedside.

MID-WORKSHOP TEACHING
External Actions Can Be Windows to the Internal Story

"Writers, can I have your eyes and your attention? I've been reading the revisions that you're making to your memoirs, and I can see that your writing is becoming much more powerful as you concentrate on telling your internal stories. Many of you are adding in lots of internal thinking. I want to remind you of something. You can also convey the internal story by using very specific actions that show how you were feeling! The internal story isn't just telling your feelings. You can use actions to convey feelings. For example, Rie is trying to show that she feels embarrassed and out of place in dance class. She shows this to her reader at the very beginning when she walks into the dance studio, pulls out her ballet shoes, and then quickly shoves them back into her bag because she doesn't want anyone else to see them. This tiny action is a window into Rie's feelings. So as you revise, remember, you can convey the internal story with external actions, too."

After some time I got up and left his side. I stood outside the door and looked at him for some time. Waiting. Expecting him to talk to me. Expecting him to push his pain behind him. If I stood there long enough he would get up and run and play ball with me and we wouldn't have to wait. Wait, that was my least favorite word. I went downstairs.

FIG. 10–3 Ali tries to chronicle her reactions to her dad's illness.

Ali had also built up the internal story of what she felt as she stood outside the door of her father's room, waiting, willing him to react to her and to get over his injury. When I arrived, she had been in the midst of writing this insert.

"Ali," I said. "You are doing really important work, aren't you? It gives me goose bumps. And I absolutely love the way you are thinking about the 'chapters of your feelings' and trying to show how your feelings evolved across the sequence of this piece—from hopefulness, to loneliness, to whatever it is you are showing yourself feeling when you stood outside the door after you left (perhaps anger). I also love the way you are planning your work, giving yourself assignments."

Then, shifting, I said, "Can I give you just one tip?" Ali nodded. "You may want to watch the ratio of external actions and internal feelings, because as you stretch out the sections in which you write what you are feeling, you may find yourself writing one sentence of actions—I stood beside my dad's bed—and then a huge paragraph of feelings and thoughts. What you can do to solve this is to invent small actions you could have done at the time. For example, you could say,

> I stood beside Dad's bed. I thought . . . I felt . . . I reached out and touched Dad's hand, running my finger over his bumpy veins. I remembered . . . A breath of wind rippled through the curtains. For a moment I glanced outside. I wondered . . .

I pushed the door open. I didn't go in yet, not yet. I thought of what I was going to say. I knew I was going to say what I had said for the past two weeks: "When will you be better?" I wasn't just putting off what I was going to say. I was preparing myself. I didn't want to run away like my brother.

I walked in about two feet, then I started to turn around. I stopped mid-turn. "No Ali, stay" I said inside my heart. I jumped on to the bed and crawled over to his side. "When will you be better?

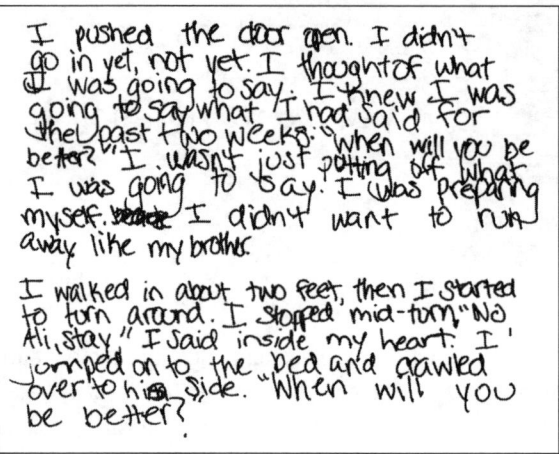

FIG. 10–4 Ali intersperses actions with reactions in this revision.

"Do you see how that version intersperses actions in between the thoughts and feelings?" Then I said, "Let's try it. Start with when you walked into his room. Slow down and tell tiny, tiny actions so you keep up the balance of an action, then a feeling or a thought, then an action. " Then I said, "Start, 'I pushed the door open. I didn't go in, not yet. I thought . . . '"

Ali picked up where I'd left off. Soon she'd gotten a strong start on another draft (see Figure 10–4).

"You got it!" I said. "And after this, remember to, yes, think about the journey of your feelings as you've done here. And also remember to braid your writing so that you weave the external story to the internal story."

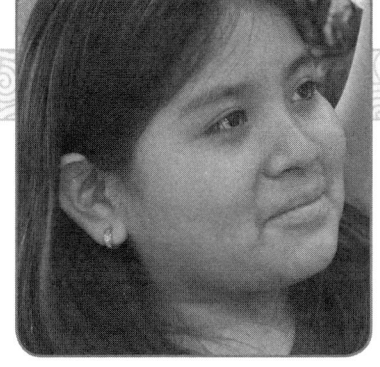

SHARE

Finding the Words to Capture Complexity

Contrast the way novice writers describe feelings—usually summarizing the generic feeling in a single word—with the way that skilled writers capture feelings. Share examples of the latter.

"Writers, in this session we have talked a lot about the importance of writing not only what was happening *to* you, but also, what was happening *in* you. I want to remind you that it is not easy to put feelings onto the page. What novice writers sometimes do is they try to find a single word that will sum up a feeling, and they write, 'I felt sad,' or 'I felt lonely,' or 'I was worried.' But writers like you, who study the qualities of powerful writing, know that usually when you want to convey a feeling, you need to do so by writing sentences or paragraphs that capture the feeling. And you know that a writer takes seriously the challenge of helping people know the specific way the writer experienced that particular feeling.

"Once I worked with a fourth-grader, Gerthruder, who wrote about getting up late in the night and feeling afraid as she made her way down the hall toward the bathroom. Listen to how she captured her particular experience that night of being afraid."

> It was terrifying getting closer to the bathroom and feeling like my heart was running ahead to the light switch.

"And once a boy named Birger wanted to describe what it felt like just after he learned that his cat had been run over by a car. He described himself walking out toward the scene of the accident, and he captured his feeling by writing":

> It was hard, smelling the fresh Spring air, and thinking that a part of me had just died.

Ask children to share with their partner instances in which they captured their feelings in print or to help each other do this if they haven't yet had a chance to do it.

"Right now, would you and your partner look over your drafts and find places where you've tried to put a feeling you had onto the page. See if you found a way to capture the precise, the particular, experience you—and only you—felt. And if you haven't yet done this, help each other. Turn and talk."

FIG. 10–5   An excerpt from Ali's draft

SESSION 10: REVISING THE NARRATIVE PORTION OF A MEMOIR

SESSION 10 HOMEWORK

REVISING TO CONVEY MEANING

Writers, tonight I'm going to ask you to continue the revision work you began today. Revising to bring out what is truly important about a moment or theme is no easy task! Tonight take some time to pick up where you left off. Some of you have written memoirs that are one long story and are working to show how your feelings grow and change across the story. Others of you have a few tiny moments embedded in your memoir. You need to focus on angling those stories in a way that shows what they are really about.

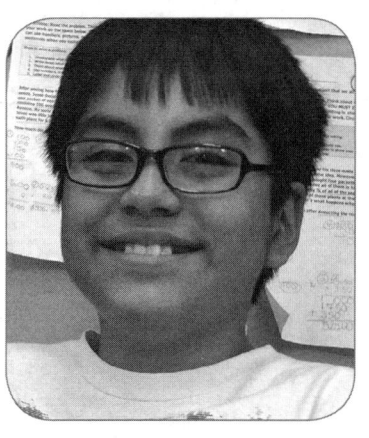

Session 11

Editing for Voice

ear Teachers,

Today marks the end of the second bend in this unit, and so it is important that the work students do today feels not only rigorous but also celebratory. Students review, revise, and edit their drafts for a final time, but they do this work right in the last draft. It would require a lot of time for them to recopy their almost-final draft, and there will be time enough for this at the very end of the unit. For today, there is time for reviewing and fixing up, and time also for celebrating. Students will, however, take stock of the work they've done over the course of this bend, and you may decide to also allot time for reflection on the genre of memoir itself, as we lay out in today's share. Tomorrow, students begin a new piece, and the writing cycle, too, begins anew. Be sure they understand, then, that this is a turning point in the unit.

It will be important to remind your students to use their memoir checklists to make some quick improvements to their writing, and you'll remind them also to use everything they know about writing conventionally to edit.

Encourage them to draw on their editing toolbox. As children use these checklists, hopefully they'll develop goals, and will work in the service of those goals. A child who tends to write with unclear pronoun references might make that his goal; a child who struggles with spelling might aim to spell the class set of high-frequency words correctly and to use the words she knows how to spell with words she doesn't yet know.

MINILESSON

You might begin by reminding students of some of the editing tools they already know. Earlier this year, students wrote personal narratives and worked with an editing checklist to check their own writing. You may bring out that checklist again to remind them of the work they did in the narrative and informational writing units. "Remember way back in the beginning of the year when you worked with a checklist to remind yourself of how to

COMMON CORE STATE STANDARDS: W.5.1, W.5.3, W.5.5, L.5.1, L.5.2, L.5.3

make your personal narratives longer? Last month, you kept up similar editing work in your informational writing. Let's take a look at that checklist again and see if you remembered to do all these things in your memoir." You can have students quickly look over their writing as you read off the items, putting up a thumb for each item they have done. The Editing Checklist is available on the CD-ROM.

> Editing Checklist
>
> 1. I have checked that this makes sense and that there are no words or parts missing.
>
> 2. All my sentences are complete, and I have checked for run-ons and fragments.
>
> 3. I have used correct capitalization (for names and the beginning of sentences).
>
> 4. I have used commas and quotation marks for dialogue.
>
> 5. All my verbs and subjects agree, and my verbs are in the right tense (past, present, future).
>
> 6. The words all seem to be spelled right. They look right, and I have checked the ones I was uncertain of.
>
> 7. I have checked for frequently confused words (to, too, two; there, their).
>
> 8. I paragraphed and indented.

You may decide to add to your students' editing toolbox by teaching them to edit not only for correctness but also for voice.

An essential goal is that children feel they are on a shared journey, learning powerful new things during what can feel like a humdrum stage of the writing process. One way to make today's work feel significant is to link it to something that has more pizzazz—something like writing with voice. Many published writers agree that there are few qualities of good writing that matter more than this hard-to-define quality. I write with voice when the imprint of my personality comes through my words. If you, my reader, can sit where you are—perhaps you are at your desk in your classroom on the fourth floor of a school in the heart of Los Angeles, or perhaps you are in the middle seat of a plane flying from Miami to Puerto Rico—and if you can pick up this page, read the little black letters that march across it, and feel as if I'm there with you, telling you something that matters to me, then I have written with voice.

For your teaching point, you might say, "Today I'm going to teach you one more thing writers do when they edit. You can listen for voice by reading your writing and pausing to ask yourself, 'Does this part sound like me? Is this written in a way that only I could say it?' Then once you've noticed places where your voice is strong, think about ways to make other parts of your writing just as strong."

If this is what you decide to teach, you will want to model how writers reread their writing, listening for places that are particularly powerful, places that sound like them. You can use your own text to demonstrate.

As you reread your piece in front of the class, you might stop and think aloud, "There I am. This part sounds real!" Name what you have done. "This sounds like me because I used parentheses to make an aside comment. I do that when I'm talking!"

You may also want to show students how to take a part that sounds wooden and rewrite it.

During the active engagement, instruct students to reread their writer's notebooks, looking not only for places where they've written about important topics, but looking also for places where their writing feels alive. Tell them about the powerful quality of voice, and ask them to look for places where they think that they, as human beings, can be heard behind—or through—their words, and encourage them to find ways to do this in other places in their writing.

You may wonder how voice relates to mechanics. The one seems almost spiritual, the other, mundane and workaday. But remember how magic happens. The wizard doesn't make his magic potion by adding a handful of pearls into the finest apricot wine. He mixes the most basic, earthly ingredients—three hairs from a rabbit's ear, the top of one yellow acorn, goat's milk. In writing, too, powerful effects come not from fancy phrases but from mixing the most basic ingredients—words and commas, white spaces and parentheses. Writers know this and so we take time, fooling around with our print.

In order to help your children approach editing and revision work, not just today, but always, caring about how their words sound, encourage them to reread their drafts, looking for places where their writing feels alive. Tell them about the magical quality of voice, and ask them to look for spots in their writing where they shine through their words, spots where they say, "Ah, yes. This is me." Then they can notice what they've done to create that effect—maybe it's as simple as the presence of a detail—and they can notice places where their writing feels wooden. How can they make those portions of their writing feel more alive?

Your attentiveness and respect for the tools of writing well will make a world of difference. Teach students that powerful effects come not from fancy phrases, but from basic ingredients—words and commas, white spaces and parentheses. Writers take time to tinker around with their word choice to make their writing clear, to make it true.

CONFERRING AND SMALL-GROUP WORK

You will probably have several goals for conferring today. One goal might be for each child to have a personal agenda, a set of goals related to conventions and mechanics and voice. One child should know that he tends to write with unclear pronoun references and needs to keep that in mind; another should aim to spell the class set of high-frequency words correctly and to use the words she knows to help with words she does not know how to spell. Yet another might aim to be more personal in his writing, using punctuation and word choice to make that happen.

SHARE

You'll want to find a way to celebrate during today's share. Ask children to reflect on what they have learned in this bend, naming the specific lessons they will carry into Bend III. What have they learned about the genre of memoir? How have they become stronger as writers? You might consider giving children an opportunity to share their first drafts with their peers. Perhaps partners could share. Alternatively, you might do what we call a "museum walk"—spreading the pieces of writing across the room and allowing children to wander from desk to desk, reading each other's writing.

    Best wishes,
    Lucy and Ali

SESSION 11 HOMEWORK

READING OUR WORK ALOUD

Many published writers agree that there are few qualities of good writing that matter more than voice. I write with voice when my personality comes through in my words. If you, my reader, can sit wherever you are (perhaps you are at your desk in your classroom on the fourth floor of a gigantic school in the heart of Los Angeles, or perhaps you are in the middle seat of a plane flying from Miami to Puerto Rico) and if you can pick up this page, read the little black letters that march across it, and feel as if I'm there with you, telling you something that matters to me, then I write with voice.

Tonight, take some more time to think about voice. Read an entry or two to yourself, a family member, or a friend. Does the writing sound like you? Can you read it strong and powerfully? If not, consider doing a bit more editing to bring out your voice!

A Second Memoir BEND III

Session 12

Seeing Again, with New Lenses
Interpreting Your Own Story

IN THIS SESSION, you'll teach students to study themselves as they would characters in a book, uncovering ideas and theories that can lead to new memoir ideas.

GETTING READY

- ✓ "Thought Prompts to Help Us Better Understand Ourselves" chart and "Thought-Prompts to Help Us Better Understand Character" chart (see Teaching)
- ✓ Excerpt of your own writing that the students are familiar with (see Teaching)
- ✓ Examples of published writing that contain inspiring images or symbols (see Mid-Workshop Teaching)
- ✓ "Ways to Structure a Memoir" chart from Session 9 (see Share)

TODAY MARKS THE START OF BEND III. You won't be surprised that your goal in this session is both to rally youngsters for a return engagement with memoir, and to up the ante. So often in schools today, students and teachers, too, have just one opportunity a year to delve into the challenging projects. Students write one historical fiction story, do one research project on ocean life, write one memoir. The problem is that when the work is complicated and demanding, significant amounts of scaffolding are needed in the first engagement with a challenging project. That work is important, but it is also important for learners to work with more independence and more fluidity.

During this third bend in the unit, students will cycle through all parts of the writing process again—they'll generate entries again, plan again, draft again, revise again. Of course, it will be important to encourage them to draw on all they already know how to do as they proceed through this process.

Today students will return to a very brief bout of generating entries. They undoubtedly have many untapped possibilities in the early sections of their notebooks, and one option is for them to mine those early entries. This session channels students to use prompts that may lead them to structure this next memoir as an interpretive essay. Specifically, you teach them that the prompts they've become accustomed to using when they write essays about characters in novels can be transferred to the writing workshop, becoming a source of reflective ideas ("I used to be. . . , but now I am . . ." 'My feelings about . . . are complicated. On the one hand, I'm . . ."). Such prompts will encourage students to grow theories about themselves and about the people in their lives that are not unlike the theories they've grown about characters in books.

COMMON CORE STATE STANDARDS: W.5.3, W.5.4, W.5.5, RL.5.1, RL.5.2, RL.5.3, RL.5.10, SL.5.1, L.5.1, L.5.2, L.5.3

MINILESSON

Seeing Again, with New Lenses
Interpreting Your Own Story

CONNECTION

Set students up to anticipate the work ahead. Remind them that memoirists write and support theories about themselves like essayists write theories about characters.

"Writers, over the next week or so, you'll have the chance to use all that you learned from the memoir work you've done so far to write a different memoir, in a different structure. So if your first memoir was a narrative, for example, this next one might be an essay.

When you want to grow ideas for a memoir, it helps to reread all the writing you've done earlier. When you go to develop ideas for a memoir, it can help to ask, 'What is my theory about myself?' Just as you can develop theories about characters in books, you can develop theories about yourself."

❖ **Name your teaching point.**

"Today I want to teach you that just as you study characters in the books you read, you can study yourself in the stories you tell. You can look back over your entries to come up with bigger theories about who you are as a person."

TEACHING

Explain to students that the prompts they use to develop ideas about characters in literature can be used to develop ideas about themselves.

"Some of the thought prompts that you use to develop theories about characters in books can also be used to develop theories about yourself as well." I unveiled a chart of prompts for developing theories about characters in books.

Model using the charted prompts to explore theories about yourself and entertain possible ideas for a memoir.

"This chart will look familiar because you used a similar one to study characters in Literary Essay in fourth grade. Right now, I'm going to show you how you can use these same ideas to think about yourself as a character in your memoir."

◆ COACHING

Think about how important it has been for you to teach not just one unit in your writing workshop, but several. With experience, your teaching becomes more deliberate, more nuanced. Your children, too, need opportunities to do something again—hence this invitation to write a second memoir.

Make sure that you are drawing on what kids already know how to do in reading. Your goal is not to teach a million new ways to think about themselves, but instead, you are saying, "You already have ways to think about characters in books. Just bring those ways of thinking into your writing."

Thought Prompts to Help Us Better Understand Characters

- Some people think (this character) is . . . But I think . . .
- Early on, (the character has this problem). Later, (the character changes).
- My ideas about this character are complicated. On the one hand, I think . . . On the other hand, I think . . .
- This character's experiences/relationships/struggles can teach us . . .
- At first I thought . . . But now I realize . . .

Thought Prompts to Help Us Better Understand Ourselves

- Some people think I'm . . . But really I'm . . .
- Early on, (I had this problem). Later, (I changed).
- My ideas about myself are complicated. One the one hand, I think . . . On the other hand, I think . . .
- Experiences/relationships/struggles can teach us . . .
- When _____ first happened to me, I thought it was about . . . But now I realize it was really about . . .

"Help me try this using my own notebook entries. I'm going to see myself as a character in a story—my story. Using this chart, what can I uncover about myself that might later lead to a strong memoir?"

I began flipping through my notebook and settled on my entry about getting the lead in the Civil War play, an entry the children know well. "You all know the entry, which later became a personal narrative, about the time I got a lead role in the Civil War play, right? I'm going to go back to this story again, but this time I am going to grow theories about myself using some of the prompts.

"Let me think." I looked at the chart, reading the first prompt from it. I tried a few alternatives, "Some people think I've always been confident, but really I was insecure as a kid." "Some people think getting a part in the play is all about achievement, but really it's all about socializing with a new group of kids.

"Let me try another. My ideas about myself are complicated. On the one hand, I'm a person who has no problem performing to a big audience, but on the other hand, I worry about the judgment of my peers.

Debrief in ways that highlight the replicable work you've done.

"Do you see how I did that? I went back to an entry I'd read often. This time I borrowed a lens that we've used to think about characters in novels, and that lens helped me develop new theories about myself. Any one of those ideas could become the anchor to an essay-like memoir."

You will probably return to a moment students know well. This is not the time to regale them with new, fancy stories from your life. Instead, it is a time to show them the effect of bringing a new lens to bear.

ACTIVE ENGAGEMENT

Help students use the prompts to develop ideas, insights, and theories about their own lives.

"Writers, take a moment and try using the same strategies to grow theories about yourself. You can start with an entry as I did, or you can just use a prompt from the chart to get you thinking. Either way, scrawl some ideas, some theories about yourelf right now."

I gave the children a few minutes to try this and then asked them to share their ideas with a partner. I listened in, taking note of strong examples to share with the class. I called them back. "It is amazing how much you can discover when you really study yourself, isn't it? Emily was realizing that her ideas about herself are complicated. On the one hand, she wants to be mature and grown up. On the other hand, she wants to stay little forever. Ben jotted that though most people think he is tough, he actually gets nervous sometimes. I bet you are all imagining how these theories might become part of a second memoir."

As children work, you might coach in by voicing over a few prompts. "'When _____ first happened to me, I thought it was about . . . But now I realize it was really about . . .' Go ahead, try that one." You'll likely choose a comment or two to share with the whole class, and others you'll simply whisper quietly to a few students who seem stuck.

LINK

Send children off to explore new thinking.

"By the end of today, you need to select an idea for your second memoir. So let's not waste a minute of today's workshop. You have armloads of strategies for finding issues and themes and for collecting materials—stories, observations, details, examples—that can go in a memoir. And now you know that you can bring prompts you've used to think about characters from the reading workshop into your writing, to study yourself as a character. The theories you develop about yourself will probably be the backbone of your memoirs. Remember that this memoir needs to be structured differently than your first memoir."

CONFERRING AND SMALL-GROUP WORK

Coaching Writers to Grow Theories about Themselves

YOU MAY FIND THAT SOME OF YOUR STUDENTS seem to be skimming across the pages of their notebooks instead of rereading carefully. For these children, you'll want to emphasize the fact that themes and insights are hidden in even the smallest of moments, and for this reason, it is worth slowing down and sifting carefully through their entries. You might show them how you read a page of your notebook, underlining and highlighting parts of an entry as you go. One way to make sure students reread slowly is to put speed bumps in their paths. Simply showing them how you stop at the end of a paragraph or page and say, "I'm not moving on until I dig up an idea or a topic here," will give them the image of how to grow ideas as they read.

You'll find that it helps to teach children to write marginal questions and comments alongside their entries. Diana's entry described how, as a child, she shaved one eyebrow off and then decided it looked awful, so she shaved the other off as well. In her margin, she wrote, "Why do I always do weird things like this? Am I the only one in my family who does this stuff? When my mother was little, did she do weird things like this?" Those questions turned a silly memory into an exploration.

Simply teaching writers to notice repetition across entries, underlining the repeating parts, can be powerful. It's often helpful to nudge children to remember that a memoir asks, "So what?" and "What does that show about me?" Olivia had written an entry about her relationship with her siblings (see Figure 12–1). After reading Olivia's entry, I complimented her on what seemed like an effort to dig deep and then gave her a tip. "Ask, 'What does this show about me?'" I explained. Soon she'd written a new entry (see Figure 12–2).

> I have a deep responsibility for my brother and sister. I have a deep responsibility for them because I love them but I also do it because my parents love them. If my parents ever saw them dead or hurt it would be painful for them and me.

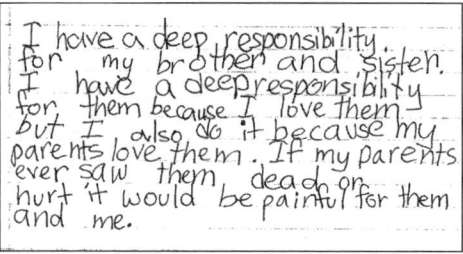

FIG. 12–1 Olivia's entry

MID-WORKSHOP TEACHING **Uncovering Images**

"Today is a day of discovery. Many of you are finding new ideas.

"Another way to develop theories about yourself is to look for *images* that stand for something important to you. The writer named Camus once said, 'A man's work is nothing but this slow trek to rediscover, through the detours of art, those two or three great and simple images in whose presence his heart first opened.' When you reread your notebook, look for images—for pictures, objects, scenes, places—that capture something important. My suggestion is this: don't think too much. Don't try to go through a logical process of weighing one image versus another. Just reread your notebook looking for images that somehow capture your attention.

"Sandra Cisneros found little wooden Russian dolls, one inside another, as one of her images. One of my heart-opening images is the stump that stood alongside the playground at my elementary school. That stump became our chariot, our castle, our underground railroad station. As you read them, look for images that matter. Think of an image that says something about who you are, what your family is like, what you care about—and write about it.

Early on I didn't always like spending time with my brother and sister. It seemed boring. Later I learned that I need them. If they were gone I would be lonely and have nobody to play with, nobody to cheer me up, because they are a part of the key to life for me. We are like a puzzle and if a piece is missing and never found you could never finish it.

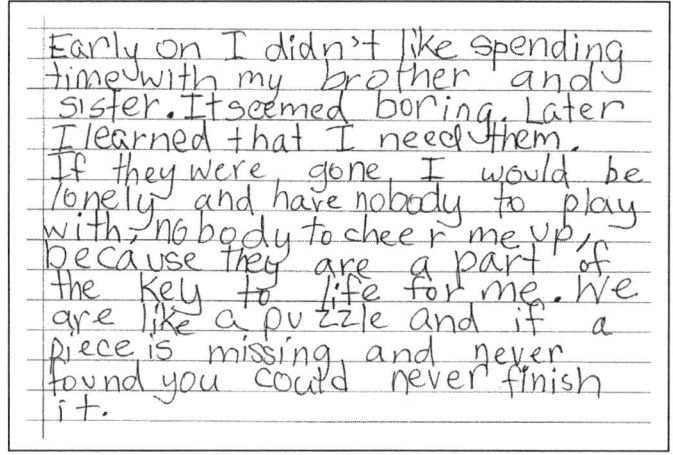

FIG. 12–2 Olivia deepens her entry.

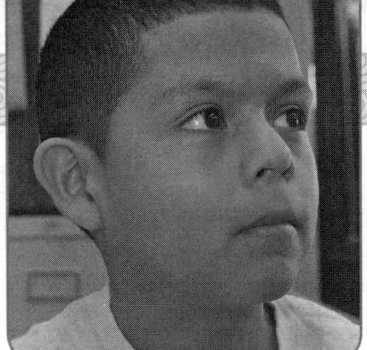

SHARE

Planning Drafts

"WRITERS, I KNOW YOU HAVE LOTS OF IDEAS for the content of this next memoir. You'll also want to think about how this memoir might be organized. I've put our 'Ways to Structure a Memoir' chart up for you to reference. Make a little plan for yourself so you are ready to hit the ground running tomorrow."

As students worked, I coached them along. "For those of you who are writing essays, remember to write a claim—it's hard to be an only child—and then try adding the word 'because' and see if you can generate reasons. If that doesn't fit with what you want to say, consider whether you want to discuss *times* when your claim is true: 'It's hard to be an only child on holidays, in the summer, and most of all when my parents are away on trips.'"

I added, "Some of you will be structuring your memoir like 'Eleven,' with a story section and a discussion section. Others will be writing a memoir that looks more like 'Quietly Struggling.' No matter what structure you choose, make sure you have a text that resembles it nearby." Then I said, "You have five minutes to think about your structure. Go!"

After five minutes, I channeled children to talk and then convened the class. "Chris is writing about the role of baseball in his life. His thesis is, 'My ideas about baseball are complicated. On the one hand, baseball has always made me feel tense. On the other hand, baseball has always made me feel needed.' His first body paragraph will tell how baseball has always made him feel tense. He'll explain his idea to his reader first, and then write a small story to show how his thesis is true."

Ways to Structure a Memoir...

- Write in a list-like structure, like beads on a string. The beads can be Small Moment stories that are linked (example: times when a writer was shy, or scenes from my childhood alongside the creek). Each memory can be as short as a sentence or two or as long as a page or two.

- A hybrid text that is a mixture of idea-based writing and a story or vignette.

- An essay in which the writer makes a claim and supports it with reasons.

FIG. 12–3

SESSION 12 HOMEWORK

GENERATING MATERIAL RELATED TO YOUR SEED IDEA

Writers, Pulitzer Prize-winning writer, Don Murray has advice for writers. He says, "If I am going to make you care about my subject matter, I need to care deeply about it first. I have to find in what I write some echoing cord of my own being: my fears, hopes, language, appetites, and ambitions." Tonight you need to collect more material that you can draw upon tomorrow when you draft another memoir. You'll reread old writing to find some that will be relevant, and you'll write new entries as well, entries that pertain to your seed idea, your thesis, or central idea.

I've seen you flip halfheartedly through your writer's notebook and your drafts. Your whole stance says, "Boring. Boring." as you flip through your pages. I understand that those pages can seem boring. They're old now. But my message to you is this: you can decide to care about your own writing. Tonight, practice deciding that your new memoir topics are unbelievably important. Here are a few processes for revving yourself up so you *do* care about your writing. Try whichever might help you.

- Reread an entry and find the line word or paragraph in it that at least sort of matters to you. Copy that part over and reread it, this time telling yourself that this is really huge, that now that you think about it, this actually does matter. Psych yourself up like an athlete before a big competition. After you have decided that this bit does matter, write off from it. Make it bigger. A great deal of power in writing comes from finding the strong parts of our writing and making those parts bigger.

- When you and I go about doing the details of our lives—say, washing dishes—we always have a choice. We can do that action as if it is monotonous, or we can try to be awake to whatever we are doing. Reread some of the writing that pertains to the theme or issue you'll address and notice when you described yourself doing something, anything, in a half-awake fashion. Tape a new sheet of paper over that part of your draft and plan to reexperience whatever it was you wrote about. Were you shampooing your dog? If so, do that action—not really, but in your mind's eye—but this time, be awake to whatever you are doing. Then, write to capture all the new details you experience.

- Reread writing connected to your theme or issue and find a place where you wrote using the one-size-fits-all words that anyone could have used. Try rewriting that part of your text, this time holding yourself to the goal of being exactly, precisely honest. You will find that you tap into a new source of power when you reach for honesty.

Session 13

Flash-Drafting

Dear Teachers,

Today, students may need to spend a bit of time planning and rehearsing, but you'll also encourage them to get started drafting. Writers always have a choice, when drafting. They can progress slowly and deliberately through the different parts of their draft, or they can write quickly, relying on revision more than planning. In the end, there is probably no one best way to proceed, but because we've seen so many children devote days to cranking out a rather wooden, mechanical draft, we tend to be on the side of flash-drafting instead. Writing an entire draft before each one is fully ready to do so is only a good idea if the writer embraces large scale revision.

In this session, you encourage many of your students to write a flash-draft, starting and finishing the entire draft today, in preparation for major revisions tomorrow. You encourage them to approach their draft with a big picture of their piece.

The wonderful thing about writing a daft from start to finish in a single day is that it is far more disposable. That is, the student is not attached to his writing because he did not labor over it for days. Remind students that if the draft they write today isn't all they hope for, that's okay. They will have time to fix up their drafts another day.

MINILESSON

Students have already gone through the writing process once in this unit—and many times throughout their writing lives—so you can expect that they have the process in their bones. Remind them of this. Tell them they already know a ton about writing memoir that will help them as they draft today. You might say something like, "Have you ever seen the show *Iron Chef*? On this show, chefs have to cook three superb dishes within a certain amount of time. They choose a dish they have cooked many times before, so they don't need to look back at a recipe after each step. You can see the chefs thinking over what they need to do, what they already know about the recipe, and then they get cooking right

COMMON CORE STATE STANDARDS: W.5.3, W.5.4, W.5.5, W.5.10, RFS.5.4, SL.5.1, L.5.1, L.5.2, L.5.3

away. They don't waste time worrying about each little thing. They keep the bigger picture of the dishes in mind and can cook fast and furiously. Just like those chefs have recipes in their bones, you have the writing process in yours."

For your teaching point, you might say something like "Today I want to teach you that sometimes writers decide to get their writing down quickly—not because they're in a contest, but because flash-drafting can help writers get the whole of a piece down right away which sets them up to know how to revise."

In the teaching component of your minilesson, you might translate the larger lesson to an agenda for today. "Some of you will decide to flash-draft a new memoir today. Others may wait and do this tomorrow. When you flash-draft, you keep a big picture of your piece in mind and write furiously to get your entire memoir down on paper."

You might quickly demonstrate how you look over your plans, thinking aloud about your memoir as a whole. "I decided to structure my memoir as an essay built around a couple of Small Moment stories that fit with my main point. I have a few stories in mind." You'll want to summarize the specifics of your idea briefly and then begin drafting-in-the-air, saying a bit of your piece aloud to give students a sense of how their drafting work will go today. You can then pause and remind students. "See how I looked my plan over quickly, thought about how my memoir would go, then started drafting?"

For the active engagement and link, you can get students drafting in the meeting area. "You can all do this work right here and now. Look over your plans, think about the big picture of how you want your memoirs to go, and then, when you're ready, start flash-drafting."

CONFERRING AND SMALL-GROUP WORK

As students flash-draft, they will need, above all, the time to write. A few will linger in the planning stage a bit longer, and you'll want to help move them along. Research what these writers are doing. Are they simply being meticulous about planning each and every part of their memoir (in which case a quick "don't be afraid to give it a go and flash-draft" admonition might help)? Alternately, do they seem to be struggling with memoir structure itself (in which case you'll want to pull out the sample memoirs you showcased in an earlier session and reteach a bit)? You may decide to pause at each table for a moment, notice what the writers are doing, and give non-verbal cues; a thumbs up or a nod to acknowledge hard work or a shrug of your shoulders to prompt a student who has stopped writing. You might also decide to voice over tips that you hope will help sustain your students' writing. Above all, use this time to assess. Consider circling the room, Memoir Checklist in hand, noting what children are doing well and what they will need support with. Now is a perfect opportunity to plan ahead for the whole class, small group, and individual teaching you'll do in the days ahead.

MID-WORKSHOP TEACHING

Your mid-workshop teaching may be delivered through voice overs alone. Prompt them to write quickly, focusing on volume. You might notice some students not getting a lot of writing accomplished, perhaps because they are worrying about writing texts that are weighty enough, and are therefore stopping to check each sentence. You might even find students who feel so pressured to write in a profound way that they are frozen. Discourage them from fretting over the small things and channel them to get a complete draft done today. To provide the students with some momentum, you might use the following (or similar) prompts.

"Remember, keep your big picture in mind and write, write, write!"

"Your pencils should be flying across the page!"

"Productivity matters. Writing a lot matters. Just keep writing and you might surprise yourself with what you uncover."

"Don't worry about perfection. That comes later. Right now, just get the broad strokes, the big parts of your draft down."

SHARE

During the share today, you will want to celebrate your writers' hard work. You might say something like "That was amazing. I didn't see any of you walking around or even looking around. Every writer was hard at work. Your pens didn't stop moving down the page!" Then, encourage students to take a step back from their drafts and do a bit of self-reflecting. You might ask them to hold their flash-draft up against the Memoir Checklist they created the other day, asking, "In what ways does my writing measure up?" and then, "What should my next steps be?" Encourage students to rely on their partners to listen for the elements on the checklist as the writers read their pieces. Ask students to set goals for their writing for the days ahead.

Best Wishes,
Lucy and Ali

SESSION 13 HOMEWORK

REREADING THROUGH THE LENS OF MEANING

Tonight, will each of you take your writing home and reread it? Before you read it, ask yourself, "What is it I most want to show in this memoir? What am I trying to get across to my reader?" Then, read through the lens of meaning. Read each part, asking, "Does this part help to show what I'm really trying to say? What about this next part?"

The work you wrote today is a draft—plan on rewriting it from top to bottom, and begin to make plans for the next draft. Then get started doing some large-scale revision. Will you redo the first body paragraph? Will you rewrite the first half of your draft? Today is not the day for revisions that are wedged into a draft with carets and Post-its. Today is the day for big, large-scale revisions.

Session 14

Revising the Expository Portions of a Memoir

IN THIS SESSION, you'll teach students that when writers write about ideas, just as when they write about events, it is important to find or create a structure that allows them to say what they want to say.

GETTING READY

✓ Example of writing that contains both exposition and narration (see Teaching)

✓ Example of writing that shows multiple writing strategies (see Active Engagement)

✓ Drafts of the same memoir written two different ways (see Share)

COMMON CORE STATE STANDARDS: W.5.1, W.5.3, W.5.5, RL.5.1, RL.5.2, SL.5.1, L.5.1, L.5.2, L.5.3

EDUCATION IS A CYCLICAL PROCESS. Children learn to do something in a concrete, rudimentary fashion, and then they cycle back and relearn that strategy, this time discovering more sophisticated ways of working. When your students were less experienced writers, you tended to teach them a writing form and then they brought their content to that pre-set form. Now that your writers are more sophisticated, you can let them in on the fact that writers often think about what they want to say and only then step back to consider what the main parts are to that message or how those parts fit together. That is, writers usually begin with the content and find the form that matches that content.

Your students have experience thinking about ways to structure their content. During the sequence of units in information writing, they've learned that if, for example, they are writing about a tiger, it is important to sort information so that facts about the tiger's habitat go on one page and facts about the tiger's enemies go on another page. In this session, you will teach children that even when their topic is less concrete, they still need to think about how to organize it. Even when the material for an essay is one long story, and then lots of thoughts about that story, writers profit from looking over those thoughts, asking, "Can these be divided into groups?" Writers ask themselves, "Are some of these thoughts about one thing? Are some about another thing? Do both categories go into the draft, and, if so, in what sequence?"

This session invites children to think about their thinking. It does so by telling a rather long story about one child—Ali—who has been writing the story of visiting her invalid father in bed and feeling a chaos of conflicting feelings. As Ali wrote this memoir, she sorted through her feelings and wrote countless drafts. The thinking and writing work that Ali does will be too complex for some students. You may decide to tell the story of a child's work that seems more within the zone of proximal development for your writers. Keep in mind that it is important for students to have horizons. This session can help you and some of your kids reach toward big dreams for the conceptual work they can do as they draft and revise the expository sections of their memoir.

MINILESSON

Revising the Expository Portions of a Memoir

CONNECTION

"Writers, memoir are made from stories and idea, above all. My hunch is that in a minute you could list four things that make for great stories. You ready? Go! List across your fingers."

The room buzzed. "Writers, you know a lot about stories, and they are part of memoir. But memoir also contain ideas, and I'm not so sure you can list four things that make for great idea writing. Try it. Go!"

After children talked for a minute, I said: "Do you see that it was harder for most of you to name what makes effective idea writing? That's the reason for this lesson."

"I have emphasized all year that writers show, not tell, but of course the truth is that writers show *and* tell."

✤ **Name the teaching point.**

"Today I want to teach you that when writers revise the portions of their memoir that explain their ideas, they think about how those ideas link, one to the next. They want their ideas to be easy to follow."

TEACHING

Use an example of one student's work to show the steps a writer can take to shape expository sections of a text.

"Often during this part of my minilesson, I tell you about a famous writer. Today I want to tell you about a writer who is famous in our community, and that is Ali. I want to tell you about the way Ali worked to make the essay part of her memoir as good as it can be. Will you take notes on what Ali did as a writer that you could do as well and later you can talk about this?

◆ COACHING

I might have used "Eleven" to demonstrate how we carry our earlier selves with us throughout life. When we teach children to write memoir, it is essential that we encourage them to put all of who they are, and all of what they know, into their pieces. Memoir writing is about discovering and revealing something essential about oneself, and this sort of discovery happens not over a few weeks or years, but over a lifetime.

SESSION 14: REVISING THE EXPOSITORY PORTIONS OF A MEMOIR

"As you recall, Ali's work on this memoir began with her writing about the day she walked into the room where her father was lying in his hospital bed. She tried to tell him about her spelling test, only to find him looking blankly back at her. Standing there, at her father's bedside, Ali felt a lot of different feelings as she struggled with the fact that because of his injury, her father wasn't there for her.

"Ali was trying to write not just the story of one time, but to write a piece that conveys who she is as a person. Early on, she tried using the prompt 'And the thought I have about this is . . .' to grow some ideas about this (see Figure 14–1). She inserted thoughts she generated into her story."

1. The most important thing I learned was that silence is very powerful. Because silence can say a lot without saying anything.

2. Feeling a small braveness inside yourself is a very strong feeling. Because it makes you think.

3. Wait. That was my least favorite word. But I couldn't help myself. Hadn't I waited long enough?

"Then, later, when Ali wanted to develop the thinking section of her writing, she took each of these and wrote longer about it."

As you chronicle what one child did to write the expository sections of her essay, pause to debrief, highlighting the points you want children to abstract from this example.

"Ali could show you all of those entries, but there are a dozen efforts to write about the ideas. And the first thing I want you to know is that, in the end, she didn't jam all the ideas she had about various subjects into one paragraph. Instead, she made a choice. She said to herself, 'How could I categorize my thoughts?' and she decided she had two main topics—one about the agony of waiting for her father to get better and the other about bravery. And she decided that one of these ideas was going to be the framing idea for her essay, and the other would be just tucked into her story. She could have chosen either one of these as her framing idea, but she chose bravery. Later, when you read the story of her walking in and standing by her father's bedside, you will see that in three or four places she wrote tiny paragraphs in which she tucks her thought patches about waiting into the midst of her story."

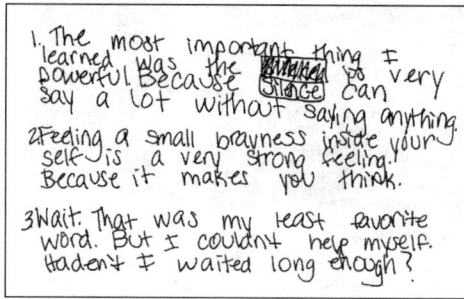

FIG. 14–1 Ali theorizes about one of her narrative entries.

Notice that so far, Ali has used a thought prompt to generate a few ideas. She'll then write longer about each of these.

One of the things that you may notice is that the writing process that students have experienced—gathering entries, selecting a seed idea, developing that seed idea, and so forth—repeats itself as one writes the components of a text. For example, Ali has essentially experienced the entire writing process to write a bit of reflective writing at the start and finish of the memoir.

Show that after the child generated some ideas off of her narrative writing, she took those ideas and expanded on them. Name the strategies the writer used, emphasizing that the writer generated lots of material.

"But let's look at what she did with bravery. She wrote a lot of stuff, writing freely, and much of this writing stood on the shoulders of Jacqueline Woodson's and Sandra Cisneros' writing. You'll hear that Ali borrowed some of the structure of 'Alone' and of 'Eleven' to get herself going, talking about bravery. Listen." (See Figure 14–2.)

> Some days I wake up to bravery like a chicken cawing at the sun, like slurping down fresh squeezed orange juice. Like that.
>
> Brave is how I go to sleep some days, listening to the crickets outside my window, hugging my bear real tight.

"Then there was this version."

> When you're being brave really brave like Superman, you don't always know it. Not right that very second.
>
> Sometimes it takes a few minutes to realize, a few thoughts. A few gazes before you know, "Hey, I was just being really brave by standing up to my fears." It could be that you won't know your braveness until the next time that you are the least bit brave. That is just the way the system of braveness works.

"So when Ali wanted to go from entries to a draft, and to write something about braveness, she needed to decide two main things: what did she want to say, and how would her writing be structured? To make this decision, she did what writers the world over do. She reread, thinking, 'What is the true idea I want to get across?' And Ali came to the realization that 'Standing beside my father's bed, I was brave.'

"Then Ali had almost a conversation with herself. She said, 'Of course, I wasn't brave in a Superman way.' So pretty soon Ali had an even more specific idea she wanted to get across to her readers: 'When my father was an invalid for so long, I acted in brave ways. This wasn't a Superman kind of bravery, and in fact I didn't even realize until recently that I was being brave!'"

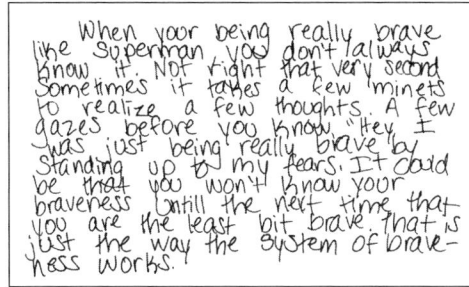

FIG. 14–2 Ali riffs on bravery.

By now, Ali has also echo-written, using lines from published writing to prime her own pump. Then she stopped to ask herself how she wanted her writing to go. To answer, she reread, asking, "What is the main idea I want to get across?"

ACTIVE ENGAGEMENT

Review the steps this student took to structure her writing and timeline her thoughts, steps that you hope other writers might also take.

"Writers, I hope you have learned a lot of things from what Ali did. Let's go back and talk about all you've figured out that she probably did." The children talked, listing what they saw Ali do.

After a few minutes, I intervened. I used my fingers to list off each step in turn. "First, Ali wrote a story. She knew she needed her writing to say something important about herself and her life, so she reread her narrative and used the thought prompt 'This makes me think . . . ' or 'This makes me realize . . . ' to write a few tiny bits of ideas, bits that could be inserted into the draft.

"Then, it seems like Ali made each of these ideas longer. She reread her ideas and realized that they could be sorted into two main topics: waiting and bravery. She decided that her thoughts on one of those topics could get inserted into key spots in her story and that she wanted to have an introductory and a closing bit of writing in which she wrote about her ideas, with the story inserted in the middle.

"Then Ali reread what she'd written about bravery and figured out one claim she wanted to make. When her dad was sick, she acted in brave ways—not a superman sort of bravery, but bravery still.

"Ali thought of what she might say about bravery, thinking what she might say first (which would be something sort of obvious that everyone agreed with) and then what she wanted to say next (which would be building off that idea) and next. Finally she wrote a paragraph in which she said one thing, then the next, then the next! Phew! That's a lot of thinking, isn't it? But this is important work."

A beginning

Some people think being brave is jomping off a cliff, running into a burning building and saving a person, diving in front of a bullet. Well I think being brave is also telling off a bully, not running away from something you're scared of waiting. And at first you may feel like you let someone important in your life down that you weren't as brave as you wanted to be. It could be you don't hardly see your braveness. That is what I think being brave is.

An ending

~~When you're~~ done falling off a cliff, when you're out of surgery to check for infections from when you were shot with a bullet, people clap and cheer for you and on your return home, news camerds are waiting to interveiw you. those people's sign of bravery are on the outside. But when you walk away from a bully that you left behind wide-eyed, or when you stand close to the thing you were once scared of, those peoples' signs of bravery is the feeling of proudness, the feeling of people claping that is on the inside of you. My sign was little sparkles, like a fairy sprkling her golden dust over me.

FIG. 14–3 Ali's beginning and ending

LINK

Set children up to go off and revise using a multitude of strategies.

"Of course, some of you will tuck everything that I taught you today into your tool kit to use later, and for now continue doing other work. You are in charge of your writing, and I know that right now, some of you have other work that demands to be done. That's as it should be. Right now, why don't you set yourselves goals for today?

"If and when you do decide to work on the idea-based part of your memoir, you'd be wise to try using some of Ali's steps to develop and organize your thinking."

CONFERRING AND SMALL-GROUP WORK

Elaborating with Lists

WILLIAM WAS BUSY REVISING as I read the first paragraph of his memoir. He began with exposition, and I could see that he tried to make it organized and concise. His beginning went like this (see Figure 14–4).

"I can see that you tried to make your lead direct and to the point. That's important. Your ideas aren't going to get swamped by too many words."

"Yeah," William said, "I tried to make it short. It was much longer, but it was too confusing. I couldn't even understand what I was saying." We both laughed.

"That's so true, William. Longer writing does not always make better writing. But I sort of wonder if what you've written is too brief. I think that there's a way to say more and still keep your idea focused. When writers say more, they are often able to make their ideas clearer and sometimes even a bit deeper. Are you game for some tips?"

William picked up his pencil, ready to write. "Sure," he said.

"One way that writers say more about their ideas is by listing brief examples."

"Try it," I said and gestured toward the second line of his lead where he'd written that he wants more of his mom's attention.

> Some people think that oldest children don't need attention. But I'm an oldest child, and I miss my mom's attention.

FIG. 14–4 William's beginning

MID-WORKSHOP TEACHING   Studying Mentor Texts

"Writers, can I have your eyes and your attention? If you are writing about your thinking and you feel like your writing is not as strong as you'd like it to be, remember that to lift the level of writing, writers study what other writers have done. They think, 'What do I like that this writer has done?' and 'How could I use a similar technique in my writing?' We have lots of models that you can learn from in this class. You can learn from the lead and ending that Ali wrote, which we studied earlier today. Or you can learn from the opening section of 'Eleven' or 'Quietly Struggling.'

"Remember, one way to study a writer's craft is to reread the text and to simply notice parts that make you go, 'Wow.' So, for example, I could reread the part where Sandra Cisneros says, 'Because the way you grow old is kind of like an onion or like the rings inside a tree trunk or like my little wooden dolls that fit one inside the other, each year inside the next one. That's how being eleven years old is,' and I could say, 'Wow.' And then I could try to name exactly what it is that she did that I could try also. So, for example, I think that Cisneros decided to use images of real-life things that show her big idea. After naming this technique, then I could look at my own writing and I could say, 'So where might I try the technique Cisneros just used? Where could I use an object to show a big idea I want to communicate?' And I could revise with her technique in mind."

(continues)

"Okay," William said. He read the line out loud: "' I'm an oldest child, and I miss my mom's attention.'" He thought for a couple of moments, rereading his idea out loud. Then he said, "Maybe it could go like this."

> I miss the way she used to run the bathtub for me and make sure the water was just right. I miss the way she used to sing to me until I fell asleep each night.

"Wow! Let's see what that sounds like all together." We laid out William's draft and together pieced the work he had just done with his lead.

> Some people think that oldest children don't need attention. They think that being the oldest means that you want to be independent and mature. They think that being the oldest means that you want to shine all your attention on younger kids who might need more guidance. But I'm an oldest child, and I miss my mom's attention. I miss the way she used to run the bathtub for me and make sure the water was just right. I miss the way she used to sing to me until I fell asleep each night.

"That seems to really work, William. You've said more without swamping your idea, and those extra thoughts elaborate on your idea in a way that feels clearer and deeper, don't you think?"

> Some people think that oldest children don't need attention. They think that being, the oldest means that you want to be independent and mature. They think that being the oldest means that you want to shine all your attention on younger kids who might need more guidance. But I'm an oldest child, and I miss my mom's attention. I miss the way she used to run the bathtub for me and make sure the water was just right. I miss the way she used to sing to me until I fell asleep each night.

FIG. 14–5 William's revised beginning

SHARE

Writing Ideas about Your Stories

Share the way one child writes a narrative about her life and then writes reflectively about that narrative. Highlight what the child did that is replicable. In this case, the child wrote first from one perspective, then from another.

"Writers, I want you to listen really carefully to the work Claudia has been doing. Claudia, as you know, has been writing about the day she visited the nurse's office in her school and had to tell the nurse that she doesn't have a dad." Claudia took a seat in a chair at the front of the meeting area and said, "Well, I got my story part written yesterday. This is it." (See Figure 14–6.)

You will notice that often, I either share children's work or I have them share it, but then I extrapolate the points I want to make rather than trying to elicit these from the child. I can imagine that you might want children to assume a teaching role for their classmates more often. Just keep in mind that the point of the share session cannot always, and only, be to make the one child in the spotlight feel proud of herself. Granted, that will happen. But if twenty-eight children have stopped their work to listen, the intervention must be helpful to those kids who are listening.

FIG. 14–6   Claudia's draft

SESSION 14: REVISING THE EXPOSITORY PORTIONS OF A MEMOIR

> I sat in the bean bag chair in the nurse's office feeling all queasy and sick and about to throw up. My head started turning and everything started to blur. The nurse came over and touched my forehead with her hand. She shook her head and took a deep breath. "Is your mom at home?" she asked.
>
> "No she's at work," I said weakly.
>
> "What about your dad?" she asked. I just sat there unable to answer. What about my dad? I closed my eyes and touched my forehead with my own hand. My seashell bracelet scratched my skin and I immediately remembered that day on the beach with my dad when we collected shells in our blue-striped bucket.
>
> "Hey dad, I found one and it's a beauty," I said as I held the shell up for him to see. I ran to him. He kissed my forehead and took my hand.
>
> "I don't have a dad," I said to the nurse. I sunk down lower into the bean bag chair and fought hard to keep from crying.

"Today, Claudia began to work hard on writing her *ideas* about this narrative. Just like explorers explore a new land, writers explore their topics. Watching Claudia work, it reminded me of a person holding a piece of sea glass in her hand, turning it this way and that way. Claudia was sort of holding her memory of that visit to the nurse's office in her hand, thinking about it one way and then another way."

Extrapolate from the one case in point whatever it is you hope your students learn from the example.

"After she wrote, 'The thought I have about this is . . .' and wrote about the entry one way, she purposely tried to think about it in a whole different way. Then afterward, she reread everything she'd written, and now it was almost as if she was fishing for something she felt was really good: a good line, a good idea, a good image. She liked most of this entry but then decided to reread it and look for the best part of it. She decided to look for the surprising part, the part that wouldn't be obvious to most people. So this is what she chose."

> The thought I have about this is . . . there are so many times in my life when I need my dad and he's not there. Like in this story, I needed him because I was sick. I try to remember things about him when I'm feeling bad, but that sometimes just makes me feel worse.
>
> Sometimes people ask me what it's like to live in a new country and what's hardest about living here. They always think that learning a new language or eating different foods is what's hard, but none of that is hard for me. What is hard is that I had to leave my dad and I haven't seen him in three years.

"After she reread this, Claudia said, 'Well, my story shows that I needed my father but he wasn't there. That's kind of obvious. But I don't really say anything about how leaving Poland was hard, because I had to leave my dad, and I haven't seen him in three years.'

"I told Claudia that she is really smart to identify which of her ideas is especially interesting, and I pointed out to her that she could, if she wanted to do so, start right in with her observations about how people think the hard part of moving is learning a new language, and they don't realize that the hardest thing can be that sometimes you need to leave people you love at home. To help Claudia get started I said, 'I could imagine, for example, that you might begin your memoir by saying, "When people hear that I moved from Poland to the United States, they always ask me, 'Was it hard to learn a new language? Was it hard to get used to a different way of eating?' But none of that was hard for me. What was hard for me . . . "' And then you could continue.

"Claudia added onto that oral version of her draft, saying, 'What was hardest for me is that now I don't have my dad when I need him!' Then she said, 'That's it. That's it exactly!'"

Ask all the writers to look at the expository parts of their own writing and to consider if the structure is right for that section of their text.

Then I said, "Writers, can you look at the thinking part of your writing, or at entries when you explore your thoughts on your idea. And can you do as Claudia and Ali have done and think, 'What am I really trying to say?' Ask yourself, 'Is there a way that I can divide my ideas into a couple of categories? Are all of these categories necessary right in this part of the text? Should I be saying one thing? And even if I am saying one thing, what might come first in my writing? Next?'"

When I nudge kids to consider a new way of structuring their writing, I'm hoping they'll see that sometimes a simple shift in angle can bring their writing to life. By suggesting that Claudia begin with the expected reasons a person might struggle when leaving a native country, I'm giving her a way to make her own, personal reason stand out.

SESSION 14 HOMEWORK

REREADING THROUGH THE LENS OF BALANCE

Memoirists know that it is important to consider the balance of thinking and storytelling in their memoir. One way to do this is to read over your memoir with the lens of balance. Your first read through might be to read over your ideas or thinking, and to see if you've included story examples that demonstrate the ideas you write about. Then, you can read your piece a second time. This time, read your stories and ask, "Is it clear what this story is really about?" Have you explained the ideas, lessons, and themes that go with the life story you wrote about?

Depending on the structure of your memoir, you may have mostly story, mostly idea-based writing, or a combination of both. The important thing is that you have a little of both, and that both your ideas and stories go together to help the reader understand what your story is really about.

Session 15

Reconsidering the Finer Points

IN THIS SESSION, you'll teach students that the best details are the truest.

GETTING READY

- Example of writing that could be rewritten to include revealing details (see Teaching)
- Example of writing that includes emblematic details (see Active Engagement)
- Transitional Phrases: Moving from Exposition to Narration (see Share)

IF YOU THINK OF THE PEOPLE YOU LOVE and allow yourself to just sit for a moment, holding the image of those people in your mind, you will probably find yourself savoring particular details. I find myself tenderly taken by my son's teenage spread in our bathroom. His tidy line of cologne, hair spray, zit medicine, and mouthwash says so much to me about the drama of being sixteen years old. When I think of my son, details such as these act like Aladdin's magic lamp; I hold one of these details in my mind, and lo and behold the detail conjures up the person, as real as life. Tiny details make our writing intimate.

Of course, to be truly powerful, the details need to act as Aladdin's lamp not only for the writer, who knows the people, the places, represented in the details. Those details also must have magical conjuring power for readers.

In this session, then, you will help writers realize that details matter. In previous sessions, you emphasized that a memoir always reveals a person, the author, and you helped children think about ways they can develop their internal story line to convey a journey of thought and emotion. In this session, you will remind children that writers bring themselves to the page not only when they write their thoughts and feelings ("I remembered . . ." and "I worried . . ."), but also when they select details that reveal who they are and what the world in which they live is like for them.

You will teach students that writers do not include a detail—say, the color of their kitchen counter—simply because the detail happens to be true. The details in a brief memoir must be those that are emblematic. Writers choose which details to include and which to exclude by thinking, "How does this detail help create a portrait of me and of my life?"

COMMON CORE STATE STANDARDS: W.5.3.b,d, W.5.4, W.5.5, RL.5.1, RL.5.2, SL.5.1, SL.5.4, L.5.1, L.5.2, L.5.3

MINILESSON

Reconsidering the Finer Points

CONNECTION

Celebrate the way children have created a progression of feelings across the narrative sections of their memoir.

"Writers, perhaps the most famous of all memoirs is a book called *Walden* by Henry David Thoreau. In a book on memoir, Zinsser points out, "*Walden* isn't really a book about how Thoreau spent his days at Walden Pond. It's about what went through his head for two years at Walden Pond. In the same ways you've learned to write the internal story of your experiences." (4, 2004)

Today I want to talk to you about the smallest parts of your memoir—the details. If you write these well, they reveal you, your family, your world.

Tell about a writer who included details simply because they were true, explaining that writers learn to choose details with care, selecting ones that are emblematic.

Some of you have heard me talk about a student, Diana, who'd written, 'I walked up to my brown front door, and went in. I left my book-bag by the door and walked through the kitchen.

"I asked her why she decided to say that she walked to her *brown* front door and she looked at me like I was nuts. 'Because it is brown,' she answered, exasperated by my question. I could tell from her voice that she wanted to add, 'Duh.'"

I persisted. "I totally understand, that your front door *is* brown. But I still need to ask, 'Why did you put that in your memoir?'

"I'm telling you this story about Diana because writers don't add details into their drafts simply because they are true. It is no doubt *true* that Diana's door is brown. And that it includes a doorknob. And hinges. And maybe there is a slot for the mail. Maybe there's a plant on the doorstep. Lots of details will be true details, but writers don't include details just because they are true. They include details because they are important to a text. And in a memoir, usually this means the details say something about the kind of person you are, the kind of life you lead."

◆ COACHING

Zinsser begins his book, Writing about Your Life, *by saying that one of his premises is "think small." He adds, "write about small, self-contained incidents that are still vivid in your memory. If you remember them it's because they contain a larger truth that readers will recognize in their lives." (6, 2004)*

This point harkens back to the Narrative unit of study, when I reminded children that the details they include in a narrative must be those that are true to that moment in time, from the narrator's vantage point. A child who runs across a lawn and into the front door of her house is not apt to make a mental note that the front door is brown, unless it had been painted that day. This detail, therefore, is jarring in the mental movie a writer hopes to create for the reader. In this minilesson, I am highlighting a different aspect of this same point.

❖ Name your teaching point.

"Today I want to teach you that writers reveal themselves not only by bringing out their internal thoughts, but also by spotlighting details that reveal whatever it is they want to show.

TEACHING

Point out that the details in televised mysteries always end up being significant to the solution. Similarly, details in a memoir always end up revealing bigger meanings.

"In my family, we watch that television show, *Monk*. At the start of this mystery show, some extraneous detail always happens—a cat runs across the living room, a neighbor brings a cake by—and I have learned (finally) that those details are never included in the story by accident. They always turn out to be part of the solution to the mystery. That's how mysteries go, and, frankly, that's how well-written texts go."

Share ways the writer you described earlier could have rewritten her writing to include revealing details.

"When Diana and I thought some more about the sentence she'd written—'I walked up to my brown front door, and went in the house'—we realized that if she *did* want to write about walking up to her house and going into it, she could have done so in ways that revealed what her family is like, what her life is like. She could have said, 'I walked up to the front door, past the discarded bikes and hula hoops left over from our last day of summer, our last day of play.' Or she could have said, 'I raced off the bus and started to tear across the lawn toward the house. Then I glanced up and saw a figure behind the living room curtain. "Is Dad home?" I thought, moving quickly from the carefully manicured lawn onto the cement path.' That is, she could have chosen details that create a portrait of her family."

ACTIVE ENGAGEMENT

Share an example of a writer who used detail to paint a family or a life. Ask children to point to (and to talk with partners about) places in the text where the author used emblematic details.

"My son Miles once wrote a memoir about visiting his grandparents—my parents—at my childhood home. I've made copies for you (see Figure 15–1). I'm going to read the start of Miles's memoir aloud. Would you follow along, and, as you do, notice and mark places where Miles uses details that reveal something about the sort of person he is and the sort of family he belongs to. Then you'll have a chance to talk with your partner about craft moves that Miles made that you could also make in your own writing." I began to read.

Whenever possible, I show children that elements of writing are all around them—even on television! You may decide to show a bit of a video clip now and again in a minilesson.

Notice that in this teaching component, I am not demonstrating how a writer might go about doing the work. Instead I am simply showing children the difference between problematic and good writing. You may decide your children need you to share specific strategies for accomplishing the goal you detail here. That is, you may decide that you need to demonstrate how Diana (or you, in your own writing) can go about producing the more effective version.

A Family Portrait

As we approached my grandparents' sprawling farmhouse last Christmas, my brother and I went silent. In single file, suitcases in hand, we marched down the ramshackle brick path. The storm door slammed shut as we entered the mud room, then trooped up the short flight of stairs, past the boxes of apples, home-laid eggs, the dog food, and into the kitchen.

Catalogs were strewn across the tables, Christmas cards dangled from the walls. Dogs lay curled under tables and chairs, and cousins of all shapes and sizes–thirty-four in all–perched on every surface. In the corner, Virginia's parrot squawked, "Hello Charlie, Hello Charlie," as he swung chaotically in his cage.

Virginia, the matriarch of the family, furtively scanned the room. In a conspiring tone, she asked, "Did you hear what happened to Bradley?"

We had all heard the news. Nevertheless, the room grew silent.

"He wrote a lousy essay and got waitlisted at Harvard."

We shook our heads in collective pity. No one spoke. It was as if church bells had rung and the clan was grieving. Bradley had blown it.

One of the important things to notice about Miles's description is that even though the paragraph is part of a story, he is still advancing one idea and providing supporting details. I doubt if he thought of that as he wrote it. I suspect, instead, that he made a movie in his mind and replayed that movie, selecting the particularly apt images. Still, every detail Miles selects adds to a single impression of ramshackle chaos!

Pausing at this point, I said, "Would you turn to your partner and point out particular places where Miles used details that revealed something about him or his family?" Children talked in partnerships.

Ask children to imagine that they are writing a narrative about entering their home. Channel them to tell this narrative to each other, weaving in revealing details.

Rather than eliciting from children a list of what they'd noticed, I decided to challenge them to follow Miles' model. "Right now, would you think about your own home, your own entrance way? Remember the first things you see and do when you arrive home. And would Partner 2 turn and tell Partner 1 the story of a time when you arrived home and walked into your place? Use details not because they are true, but because they reveal whatever it is you want to show about yourself, your family, your home."

LINK

Remind writers of the options they have for proceeding. They may need to reflect on what their memoir aims to show. They may decide to rewrite their draft to include more revealing details.

"Writers, can I stop you? Mystery writers include details that will later turn out to help solve the case, and memoirists include details that help to make the text we write into a statement about ourselves.

"You can decide what the implications of this minilesson are for you. Some of you may decide that you need to think a bit more about how your text is a window onto yourself. You may need to pause and think, 'What is it I want to show about myself?' and 'What do I want my reader to know about me and my family?' Others of you may have begun a draft and may decide that before you get any farther, you want to rewrite the start of your text so that you are more careful to choose details that reveal yourselves. Others of you will keep this advice in mind as you write, or when you get ready to rewrite. Before you head off to work, will you talk for a moment with your partner about how you will use the advice from today's minilesson? Then when you feel clear about what you are going to do, you can get yourself started."

CONFERRING AND SMALL-GROUP WORK

Conduct Research to Understand Struggles

AS YOU READ THROUGH YOUR CHILDREN'S WRITING, be aware that your reading will probably be more powerful if you assign yourself a lens through which to look. For example, you may decide to look closely at the work of two writers who seem to you to be struggling with this unit, and also at the work of two writers who seem to you to be soaring in this unit. Your task might be to think about what it is that the more successful writers are doing that could, perhaps, be taught to the two who are struggling (and to others). "What are the really essential differences between those who are soaring and those who are struggling?" you'll ask.

As you read through your children's work, you will want to find places where their writing takes your breath away. Children profit from specific examples, and of course, it is transformational when a teacher says to the class, "I want all of you to study the important work that so-and-so did," and that child is a classmate! It is especially important that you find instances where a struggling writer has done something that you hope everyone will learn from. Look especially hard to find treasures in the pages of your more novice writers.

As I do this work, time after time I find that the novice writers who are struggling (and not all do) are those who spend most of their time writing about generalities. The call to write big important ideas can derail some students from writing detailed, chronological narratives, which was something they could do with success in earlier units. Children who struggle probably also have trouble with the open-ended nature of the unit and are trying so hard to write something big and significant that they write in clichéd generalizations, one after another.

The units on personal narrative writing taught children to write tiny, tiny focused narratives, and this new unit is, after all, asking children to write about themes and issues. One way to do this is by writing tiny focused narratives, shifting sometimes to write also about overarching themes. It should not surprise you if some children have been pulled into writing in generalizations. Revision is a perfect time for them to tighten their narratives!

MID-WORKSHOP TEACHING **Inventing Details**

"Writers, can I stop you? As many of you know, Jack is writing a story about a time in second grade when he froze with fright when he was asked to read aloud in front of the class. He said to me, 'I'm stuck. I want to write with details but I don't have a good memory.' Then he added, 'I can remember how I felt, which is embarrassed, but I can't remember what book I was reading or what Mrs. Buckley said or hardly any details!'

"I wanted to thank Jack for bringing this up, because I am sure it is something many of you are dealing with. What I want to tell you is this, Jack. (The rest of you should listen, too.) What you do is this: you make up the details. The secret is that you invent the details that reveal the truth of your life.

"I'm pretty sure that when Miles went to write about that particular Christmas Eve at his grandparents' house, he did not recall the exact words the parrot squawked. He made them up. Miles supplied the detail that the bird called, "Hello Charlie. Hello Charlie" from all the Christmases he has ever spent with my family.

"So, Jack, you can make yourself stand in front of the classroom to read aloud or you can sit yourself on a rocking chair. You can decide what book—and what page of the book—you will read. The details may not be true with a small *t*, but they will be True with a capital *T*."

(continues)

SESSION 15: RECONSIDERING THE FINER POINTS

You could couch this teaching in a bigger principle. For example, you could teach children that whenever a writer decides to tackle a particular kind of writing, she must pause for a moment, thinking, "What do I already know about how to achieve this challenge?" That is, once a child has taken on a particular writing task, the child needs to take the time to access what she already knows about how to do that task. For example, if the child is writing a focused narrative in her notebook, then she needs to recall what she knows about how to do this well. Having said this, you can then remind children that in this case, it can help to make and revise a timeline or a story mountain, it can help to think about what the story is really about and to start it in a way that links to the real meaning of the story, it can help to start with dialogue or with a small action, and so forth. In this way, you will help children understand that the work they are doing in this unit stands on the shoulders of all the work that has come before. If a child's memoir has a more essay-like structure, you might pull out an old chart about ways to move seamlessly between narrative and exposition, giving one example, then another, then another, all the while reminding students that the same moves they used as essayists can be used as memoir writers.

SHARE

Linking Exposition and Narrative: Transitional Phrases

Remind students to draw on all they know about transitioning between ideas and story.

"I want to remind you that memoirists move from ideas to story and back to ideas in their memoir. Just because you are writing about ideas, just because Ali is writing about bravery, and William, about being an oldest child, this doesn't mean that all your memoir need to be exposition. You can shift into a story if you want. 'Eleven' goes that way."

"If you do shift from idea-writing to story, remember to use a transitional phrase. Here are some transitional phrases." I revealed the following chart (see Figure 15–2). "You've used these kinds of linking words in personal and literary essays. Right now, will you read them over with your partner and then take some time to look back at your memoir? Ask yourself, 'Did I use transitional words and phrases to carefully lead my reader from idea, to story, and back to idea?' If not, you might take some time, right here in the meeting area, to try to add in a few of these phrases."

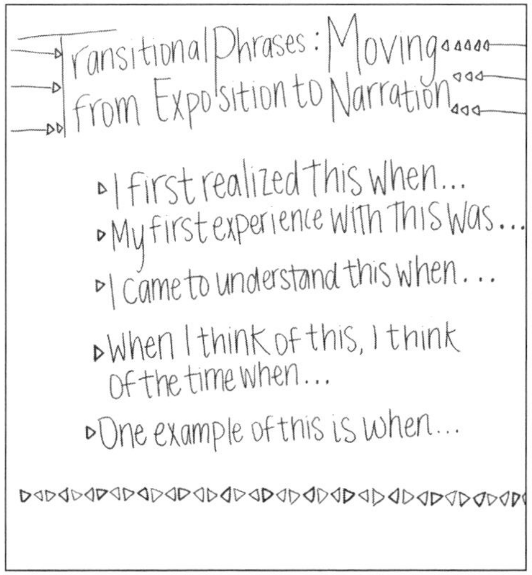

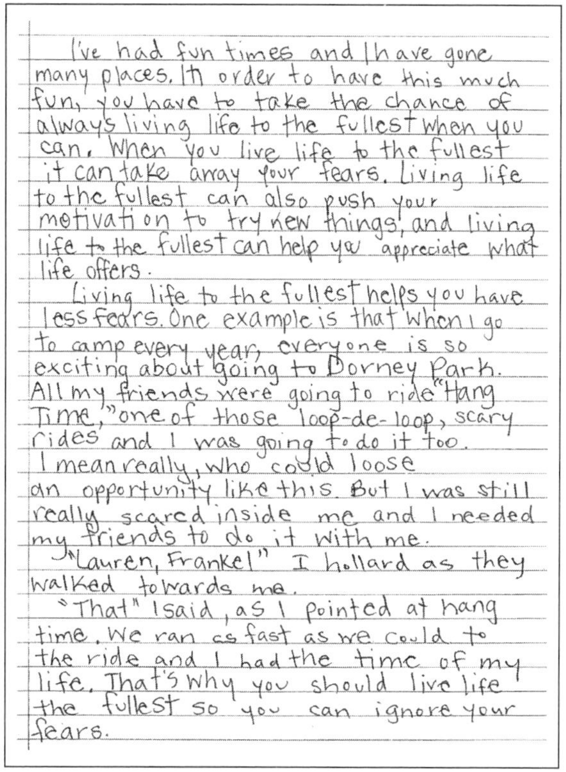

FIG. 15–2

FIG. 15–1 Henry uses transitions to move from ideas to narration in his memoir.

SESSION 15: RECONSIDERING THE FINER POINTS

SESSION 15 HOMEWORK

UNPACKING BIG MEANING FROM TINY EVENTS

Life whizzes along so quickly that each moment often blurs into the next. At the end of the day we might recognize that something big has happened to us and that perhaps we're different in some way, but it's sometimes hard to unearth the particulars inside of each moment. The writer Natalie Goldberg says, "Writers live twice. They go about their lives, as fast as anyone . . . But there's another part of them that they train towards. The part that lives everything a second time." That's what we do as writers. We train ourselves to slow down the crucial moments in our lives. Listen to Gary Soto's beautiful description of his inner journey, bike riding down the street and around the bend. ("The Bike," *A Summer Life,* 1991)

> My first bike got me nowhere, though the shadow I cast as I pedaled raced along my side. The leaves of the bird-filled trees stirred in a warm breeze and scuttled out of the way. . . . Going down the block was one thing, but taking the first curve, out of sight of Mom and the house was another. I was scared of riding on Sarah Street. Mom said hungry dogs lived on that street and red anger lived in their eyes. Their throats were hard with extra bones from biting kids on bikes, she said.
>
> But I took the corner anyway. . . . After a few circle eights I returned to our street. There ain't no dogs, I told myself.

We stand back from an event, remember, and ask ourselves, "How did this moment change me? How am I different because of it?" And then we write, slowing down time and showing how change occurred inside of us in this tiny bit of time. Tonight think about places where you might try something similar to what Gary Soto did—writing the whole timeline of even the smallest of actions, being sure to include both the internal and external story as you do.

Session 16

Rereading Your Draft and Drawing on All You Know to Revise

JUST AS THERE IS A STORY LINE to a narrative, there is also a story line to a unit of study, and specifically, to this unit of study on writing memoir. At this time in the unit, you will want your writers to focus less on the content of their writing and more on the craft. You want them to be less consumed with the question "What shall I tell about myself?" and more consumed with the question "How can I write this so the text works?"

Early in the unit, most of your students relied on narrative structures; now many of them are working more with exposition. Some students are inventing structures to fit their message. The timing for all of this work is right. Your fifth graders are changing, and are ready for more independence. This unit works to give them their independence.

The independent writer needs to read her own writing first as an openhearted, receptive reader, ready to be touched and moved by her own words and to sense the potential they hold. Such a reader notes her own response to the text, asking, "Where does the meaning pop off the page with freshness and energy? Where is the meaning crystal clear and startlingly significant?" Such a reader knows that a great deal of a writer's craft involves finding what works and building upon this.

The writer also needs to read her own words as a stranger might, no longer filling in all that the writer knows but hasn't yet said, and as a busy person might, ready to set the page down if ever the pace sags and the meaning becomes mired. The writer, too, needs to read her own words, ready to pull back in askance and say, "What? This makes no sense." Such a writer cannot give the draft just a cursory glance. Instead, this writer reads each word, each sentence, and asks, "Where is this vague? Where does this say two contradictory things?" This writer-turned-reader needs to read precisely and exactly and with ruthless attentiveness.

IN THIS SESSION, you'll teach students ways that writers reread their writing intently, to learn from it how they need to revise.

GETTING READY

- ✔ Student's writing folders, in the meeting area and containing their drafts from Bend II and Bend III (see Connection)
- ✔ Drafts of one student's writing, one with revision annotations and the other with the revisions (see Teaching and Active Engagement)
- ✔ "Ways to Structure a Memoir" chart (see Share)
- ✔ Copies of memoirs used throughout the unit for students to study (see Share)

COMMON CORE STATE STANDARDS: W.5.3, W.5.5, W.6.1.d, RL.5.1, RL.5.2, RL.5.4, RL.5.5, SL.5.1, SL.5.3, L.5.1, L.5.2, L.5.3

MINILESSON

Rereading Your Draft and Drawing on All You Know to Revise

CONNECTION

Find a way to compliment the students on their involvement in their writing work.

"A friend of mine told me a story the other day. Her daughter, Rachel, is a high school student, taking a class in developmental psychology and working with children. The teacher of this class decided she wanted the high school students to realize that having a child is a big responsibility—something best left to adulthood—so she purchased a baby doll that is programmed to cry, to need to be burped, to fuss, to need constant attention. Last weekend, Rachel's homework assignment was to care for that baby all weekend and to keep a log of her responses. She did it: getting up five times in the night, carrying the baby with her everywhere. But she came out of the weekend saying just the opposite of what the teacher wanted her to say. 'It felt great to have a child!' she said. 'I didn't mind at all giving the baby all that attention. I can hardly wait until I can have my own child!' That wasn't the lesson the high school teacher meant to teach, but it was an important lesson for Rachel nonetheless. She learned that she has a greater capacity to care, to be invested (even in a doll!) than she'd imagined possible.

"I couldn't help but think of all of you as I heard this story, and the time and work you've put into your memoirs. You have been *so* involved, *so* invested, and the evidence of all this is in the folders I asked you to bring to the rug today."

Let children know that today they will pick a draft for final publication.

"Today you have a decision to make. You've taken two memoirs through the drafting and revision process, and this morning you will pick one to bring to publication.

"You might be thinking, 'How can I pick? I like them both!' and I wouldn't blame you. The memoir you don't choose will stay in your folder, and there will be plenty of time in your writing life to bring it to publication. But today I'm asking you to pick the one single memoir you want to put out in the world."

I gave children a few moments to go through their folders and make a decision and then called for their attention again. "Place the memoir you have chosen before you, and let's get started."

◆ COACHING

I know, I know. This is an odd story to tell kids. Call it an attention grabber! Minilessons can get to feel rather similar, one to the next, so sometimes we go a bit "out there" for the sake of being interesting. You'll see that my real goal is to wax sentimentally over the kids' amazing dedication to this work. I find I can't be mushy for long, so I'm using this little tidbit of news as my way in. Watch how I get from this odd (but true) story to my point, and realize you can find ways to tuck almost anything you find interesting into a minilesson!

Here, I reinforce the idea that all writing matters. Even the pieces that don't make it to publication are important, and there are always opportunities in a writer's life to revise, edit, and publish past writing. But today I want children to "go with their gut" and choose one piece. In my experience, children often make wise choices—choosing pieces that represent their stronger writing and that have an important message they want to convey.

❖ **Name your teaching point.**

"The hard work you do as a writer needs to change as you work through the writing process, and this often involves moving from the role of writer to the role of *reader of writing*. Today I want to teach you how to do the special sort of reading writers do when they read their own writing. They do not skim over it as if they've seen the draft a hundred times. Instead, they examine the draft in all its particulars. If you read what your draft actually says (and if you read also for what it *could* say), then your page will teach you how to write."

TEACHING

Tell children that when you near the end of a writing project, you often shift into being a succession of different sorts of readers of your writing.

"I think this quote from Annie Dillard really gets at what I mean. 'Who will teach me to write?' a reader wanted to know. 'The page,' Annie Dillard answered . . . 'The page that you cover so slowly with your crabbed thread of your gut . . . that page will teach you to write'" (*The Writing Life*).

"Once I can see the end of a writing project, I sometimes feel tired and am tempted to call it a day. I have learned, however, that this is a time instead for me to shift from being a *writer* to being a *reader*. I usually take my writing and go sit in a different place. I bring a different color pen with me or a fresh pack of Post-its. (I think I'm trying to dress up, almost, as if I am no longer the writer of this piece.)

"I deliberately decide what sort of reader I'm going to be, and then I read my writing as that reader. Usually, I first read as a bighearted, responsive, involved listener. I expect to be blown away by parts of the writing and to see incredible, amazing meaning in it—sometimes meaning that isn't yet on the page. I usually look up from that first experience of the text and say to myself, 'This particular section is huge and important. You have no choice but to develop it!' Sometimes I just find tiny places in a draft where it is clear there is more, under the surface of the story; more that deserves to be heard and said. So I mark those sections. 'Slow down,' I might jot in the margins, or 'Say more.'"

You will have noticed how often this reading with a deliberately chosen lens enters into our teaching of writing. The ability to do this, of course, is equally essential for readers.

Show your children how a student in the class went about rereading his draft as one kind of reader, then as another kind of reader. Role-play being the child, reading in one way, then thinking aloud and annotating the writing.

"I helped Adam get a head start on this work yesterday, so that today he could show you what he's done as a reader of his writing," I said, putting half a page of his draft on the overhead projector. "He has chosen to publish the first memoir he wrote, about his brother leaving for college. Adam reread this piece of writing, trying to be a really responsive reader, one who feels what the piece gets you to feel. Let's all be Adam," I said and read this aloud.

> "Nooo, please can't I go," I pleaded. My mom just ignored me. I knew she would but I was desperate.
>
> My brother walked outside where my mom and I were standing. Our eyes met. Sadness seemed to flow straight into me just like the sound of Jon's bassoon when he practices. I ran to my brother. He embraced me in his tight hug. I pulled him closer.
>
> It was already happening. My eyes stung.

Then, talking as if I were Adam and still looking at the draft, I jotted, "Those last minutes can be really important and sad." Then I looked at the page and said, "This is a great scene to show. But I should slow it down and show more. I've got to show the packing more. I have to think about what specific things Jon could have packed in that might say something about our relationship. And I should slow down the hug even more, too, and show what I felt at the start of it and in the middle." Then, continuing to role-play Adam, I read on.

> I am in camp, running up a hill. The scene of my brother pulls me forward. The sun is shining but shadows are keeping me cool. As I run my feet push the rocks aside, as I run faster my feet start to slip. When I look up my brother is on the top of the hill. He opens his arms. I am happy and a smile spreads across my face. Tears almost pour out but I control myself.
>
> I tried to blink back tears but they were inevitable. Tears started pouring out over my eyes. I looked up and saw tears in my brother's eyes. I was surprised at this.

Role-playing Adam, I jotted another note in the margins of the draft. "It's great to put what I was remembering into that moment, but I should think about more memories, more times Jon and I had, remember them, and put them in, too."

There will be lots of times when the material you have with you to use in a minilesson is an artifact of another person's writing. In this instance, I have Adam's annotated draft; in another instance, I will have a writer's published text. Either way, I always have the choice of teaching through demonstration or teaching through explaining and showing an example. In this instance, I teach through demonstration, playing the role of writer, reenacting what he did as he progressed through the process.

Show how you can then shift into being another kind of reader, approaching the same draft differently. Again, shift between reading aloud, thinking aloud, and making marginal annotations.

Now shifting out of the role, I leaned toward the children and said, "Then Adam reread, thinking less about that time in his life and more about the words he'd written. This time, he read every sentence and tried to translate that sentence into a mental movie so that he could be sure that the words conveyed exactly what he wanted to show happening.

"Adam did this and realized there were places where his sequence of action wasn't clear. Watch how he did this rereading." And I began slowly reading each bit aloud, registering what it said in my mind, then reading the next bit.

> "Nooo, please can't I go," I pleaded. My mom just ignored me. I knew she would but I was desperate.

"I'm not sure what exactly is happening here. The action isn't clear. It is hard to start the mental movie because what, exactly, is going on?" I read the next sentence or two aloud. "So let me read on, still pretending to be Adam."

> My brother walked outside where my mom and I were standing. Our eyes met.

As Adam I said, "This is clearer, but I didn't say we were packing up the car or any of that. (And then, class, Adam continued rereading his work that way.)"

Tell children that writers also read in different ways, summarizing a few pieces. Then show the child's earlier draft and revised draft, asking the class to talk with partners about the revisions they notice.

"Adam, like most writers, also read the writing in other ways—to make sure it rang true, that it felt absolutely emotionally honest (because sometimes to make a good story we hype something up in a way that is not exactly precisely honest). And he read his draft like he was in an airplane, flying over, looking at the structure and thinking, 'How else could this have gone?'

"Adam left these marks on his first draft and then rewrote it. I'm going to read Adam's next draft of this section (see Figure 16–1), and then would you and your partner talk about what you notice Adam has done differently as a result of his reading?"

> "Nooo, Please can't I go," I pleaded. My mom just ignores me. I knew she would but I was desperate.

> "Nooo! Pleeease can't I go," I pleaded. My mom just ignored me. I knew she would but I was desperate. *[Jon]* My brother walked outside *[with a suitcase to the car]* where my mom and I were standing. *[He turned around.]* Our eyes met. Sadness seemed to flow straight into me just like the sound of Jon's bassoon when he practices. I ran to my brother. He embraced me in his tight hug. I pulled him closer. *[Reword it. TOO FAST.]* It was already happening. My eyes stung. I tried to blink back tears, but they were inevitable. Tears started pouring out over my eyes. *[list]* I looked up and saw tears in my brother's eyes. I was surprised at this.
>
> I am in camp, running up a hill. The scene of my brother pulls me forward. The sun is shining, but shadows are keeping me cool. As I run, my feet start to slip. When I look up, my brother is on the top of the hill. He opens his arms. I am happy and a smile spreads across my face. Tears almost pour out, but I control myself.
> "Time to go." *[Actions]* The car pulls away.

FIG. 16–1 Adam's draft with annotations

My brother (Jon) walked outside (with a suitcase to the car) where my mom and I were standing. (He turned around.) Our eyes met. Sadness seemed to flow straight into me just like the sound of Jon's bassoon when he practices. I ran to my brother. He embraced me in his tight hug. I pulled him closer. (Reword it. Too fast.)

It was already happening. My eyes stung. I tried to blink back tears, but they were inevitable. Tears started pouring out over my eyes. (List) I looked up and saw tears in my brother's eyes. I was surprised at this.

I am in camp, running up a hill. The scene of my brother pulls me forward. The sun is shining but shadows are keeping me cool. As I run my feet push the rocks aside, as I run faster my feet start to slip. When I look up my brother is on the top of the hill. He opens his arms. I am happy and a smile spreads across my face. Tears almost pour out but I control myself.

"Time to go." (ACTIONS) The car pulls away.

"This was Adam's next version." (See Figure 16–2.)

My brother came outside with one last suitcase in his hand. He crammed it into the back of my mom's car with all the others. Then Jon slammed the back of my mom's car shut.

Our eyes met when he turned around. Sadness flew straight into me as clear as the mournful sound of Jon's bassoon. My brother hugged me. I pulled him closer. "I'm going to miss you badly," he said. "I will too," I managed to squeak out. My voice was hoarse. It was already happening; my eyes brimmed, I tried to blink back tears, they wouldn't stop. Tears started pouring from my eyes. It reminded me of when I was playing basketball and I fell, pain throbbed through my arm. Jon came and took me to the hospital. With Jon there, I'd felt safer, calmer, less scared. It reminded me of when I was in camp and I hadn't gotten a letter for days, and loneliness was starting to haunt me. Jon's letter came and filled me with laughs and warmth and a feeling that it was good to have a big brother. I looked up and saw one tear roll down my brother's cheek. He brushed it away, but I remembered it.

"Turn and talk," I said. "What revision work do you notice Adam has done as a result of his careful reading?"

> My brother came outside with one last suitcase in his hand. He crammed it into the back of my mom's car with all the others. Then Jon slammed the back of my mom's car shut.
>
> Our eyes met when he turned around. Sadness flew straight into me as clear as the mournful sound of Jon's bassoon. My brother hugged me. I pulled him closer. "I'm going to miss you badly," he said.
>
> "I will, too," I managed to squeak out. My voice was hoarse. It was already happening; my eyes brimmed, I tried to blink back tears, they wouldn't stop. Tears started pouring from my eyes. It reminded me of when I was playing basketball and I fell, pain throbbed through my arm. Jon came and took me to the hospital. With Jon there, I'd felt safer, calmer, less scared. It reminded me of when I was in camp and I hadn't gotten a letter for days, and loneliness was starting to haunt me. Jon's letter came and filled me with laughs and warmth and a feeling that it was good to have a big brother.
>
> I looked up and saw one tear roll down my brother's cheek. He brushed it away, but I remembered it.

FIG. 16–2 Adam's revised draft

This bit of active engagement is tucked here, in the teaching component of the minilesson, and gives students an extra, more guided opportunity to practice this strategy. Next, during the proper active engagement, I will ask them to turn this work to their own writing.

ACTIVE ENGAGEMENT

Ask children to read the first section of their own draft as an especially responsive reader, noticing when the draft's potential deserves to be developed.

"Right now, would you bring out your draft?" I waited for them to do this. "Would you read just the first section of this draft, reading it as a bighearted, responsive, involved listener? Be blown away by parts of the writing. Find a bit of it that you can point to and say, 'This is just so important. There's more here!' Then jot in the margins, something like 'Say more' or 'List more examples' or 'Tell with tinier details.'"

Ask children to read the first narrative section of the same draft differently, this time trying to translate the words into a mental movie. Are the actions explicit and clear?

After the children read and annotated for a few minutes, I said, "I know you could work a lot longer on this, but you can go back to that. For now let me ask you to shift and be a different kind of reader. This time, read a passage that is a narrative, and read it as a stranger might. You don't know more than is on the page. Try to make a movie in your mind from the words, translating each sentence into the next bit of the mental movie so that you can be sure the words are conveying exactly, precisely what is happening. When you aren't exactly, precisely clear, mark your draft so that you can rework it."

LINK

Remind writers that when they see the end in sight and their energy flags, this is a time for fresh resolve.

"Dag Hammarskjöld, the famous Secretary General of the United Nations, once said, 'When the morning freshness has been replaced by the weariness of midday, when the leg muscles quiver under the strain, the climb seems endless, and suddenly, nothing will go quite as you wish—it is then that you must not hesitate.'"

"This is a good time for you to dig into your reserves of energy and to find new energy for writing. Remember that writers go to their writing desks not because of self-discipline, but because of love for the particular bit of writing. Trust that your piece can become so much better—as we saw with Adam's writing—if you allow yourself to shift from writer to reader and to let the page teach you how you can write even better than you've written so far!"

CONFERRING AND SMALL-GROUP WORK

Memoir is Writing about Yourself

WHILE EMILY REREAD HER DRAFT, trying to see a section with enormous potential, I sat beside her and did the same thing. The draft had originally been an entry in which Emily wrote off from Jacquelyn Woodson's collection of images in "Alone." In a similar fashion, Emily had accumulated images about her topic, growing up. The draft began with this list of images and thoughts about growing up, written by this young girl at the brink of adolescence.

> Whenever I wonder about my childhood, the first thing I think about is when is it over? You don't stop skipping down the street because you're old; you're old because you stop skipping down the street. I'm not exactly old and I'm not exactly young.
>
> Childhood is me. No one ever talked about when it's over. When I play the game of life, I like to think how I'd end up in twenty-three years. A successful business woman or a cashier at MacDonald's, living with three children happily or still living in my parents' house.
>
> The trampoline sits alone during the winter but in the spring, I'm all over it. I go on it a lot. When I did, Mama was right there with me. Jumping and laughing. Having fun. My mom is a grown up and still jumps around like me.
>
> When I try to act old trying so I can go on a roller coaster too old for me, I start dancing like a five-year-old. "Lala, la la, la, la, la . . ." I sing while I dance.
>
> "Stop, Em, everybody's watching," my embarrassed sister says. I ignore her.
>
> One, two, one, two, I say to the beat of my step. And I notice I'm not acting very old.

MID-WORKSHOP TEACHING — Persistence Matters

> Freeze exactly where you are. Writers, this room feels more like a farmer's market on a busy weekend than like a writing workshop. Look around the room. Notice what each person seems to be in the midst of doing. Notice how few of you were actually in the midst of writing!
>
> Writing well takes attentiveness. It takes putting one's butt on the chair and staying there. It takes getting to hard parts and pushing past them, instead of using the hard parts as an invitation to wander around hoping someone is going to deliver a magic solution.
>
> So, writers, sit back down. Reread your writing. If you have a problem, find tools that can help you solve your own problem. Max has his memoir checklist out next to his draft. Sonja is relying on one of our charts. You might do the same. But for now—silence. Back to work.

At some point in the entry, Emily stopped gathering associated images reflecting her relationship with growing up and instead wrote one longer narrative about a time when her sister put makeup on her and dressed her in her mother's fur coat (see Figure 16–3). This section of Emily's entry would end up becoming an exquisite memoir, but of course I did not know this at the time.

> After my sister graduated elementary school, something changed. The shine in her eye was gone, her smile wasn't bright. She wasn't bright. She wasn't the sister who dressed me up in grown up clothes. "Come on my bed," Jenn said, patting the bed next to her. "Now stay still," Jenn took a suitcase that looked heavy. My eyes

watched the suitcase, wondering what was in there. She opened it and told me to close my eyes. "Don't move," she whispered while putting something on my eyes. It felt cold. "Okay, open," then she put pink powder on my nose.

"That tickles," I said giggling. Then she put goop on my lips.

"Ptth," I spit the yuck stuff off. And wiped the remaining off with my sleeve. But she put more on again. This time I didn't budge.

"Voila. Done." But I'm guessing she wasn't because she turned me around and messed my hair. "Come here." She went around the house gathering clothes.

"Wear this and this."

I looked at what she was holding. A furry coat that was my mom's. I listened to her orders and when I came out of the bathroom door, Click. She took a picture I'll remember my whole life.

What I like to do, being a child, are very weird things. Reading instructions on a shampoo bottle, reading nutrition facts, and spinning on my mom's "merry-go-round chair," the twirly chair.

FIG. 16–3 Emily's entry with narrative

As soon as Emily finished reading the end of the draft, she pointed to the final half of it, and said, "I think this is the best part." I agreed with her, and for a moment we looked at the way Adam, like Emily, had begun trying to write all about his Life Topic, his brother, by creating an anthology of vignettes. Emily saw, too, that Adam had more recently decided to focus on just the story of Jon's departure and that he was trying to embed much of what he wanted to say into that narrative.

"Maybe I could try a new draft and just write about that final section where my sister dresses me up," Emily suggested. I nodded and added, "And try writing it as if the story of your sister dressing you up will be your whole entire memoir. It might turn out to just be part of the memoir, but try taking it so seriously that it could be the whole memoir."

When I returned, Emily had written this new draft (see Figure 16–4).

Before my sister went to middle school, after she graduated elementary school, and when the shine in her eyes was still there, matching her bright smile, she used to play with me. Once she called me to her room.

"Come on my bed," Jenn said, patting the bed next to her. "Now stay still." She took out a suitcase that looked heavy. My eyes watched the suitcase, wondering what was in there. She opened it and told me to close my eyes. "Don't move," she whispered while putting something on my eyes. It felt cold. "Okay, open," then she put pink powder on my cheeks and nose.

"That tickles," I said, giggling. Then she put goop on my lips.

"Pthh!" I spit the yuck stuff off. And wiped the remaining off with my sleeve. But she puts more on again.

"Voila. Done." But I'm guessing she wasn't because she turned me around and messed with my hair.

"Come here," she went around the house gathering clothes. "Wear this and this." I looked at what she was holding. A furry coat. I went into the bathroom and put it on. I'm finally old. I've always wanted to be. I looked in the mirror. I looked like one of the actresses with big fur coats, curly hair, walking down the red carpet in the old days. I scrunch up my hair. "Omigod!" I said to myself, trying to be like my sister. I point to the tub. "Omigod, it is so blue," I walk over to the toilet. "Omigod, that's gross!" I walk over to the mirror. "Omi–" I stop. Something is wrong. This isn't me! I'm not the thirteen-year-old I'm trying to be. Is this me? Is this who I really am? I stare at the girl who isn't me. I am a child. I won't grow up!

Emily wasn't pleased with one section of this, the lead that described her sister, so she worked on it and before long, it read:

After my sister graduated elementary school, something changed. The shine in her eye was gone, her smile wasn't as bright. She wasn't the sister who dressed me up in grown up clothes. "Come on my bed," Jenn said, patting the bed next to her. "Now stay still." She took a suitcase that looked heavy. My eyes watched the suitcase, wondering what was in there. She opened it and told me to close my eyes. "Don't move," she whispered while putting something on my eyes. It felt cold. "Okay open," then she put pink powder on my nose.

"That tickles," I said giggling.

"Emily," I said, "I absolutely love the fact that you are the kind of writer who rereads your own writing and finds parts that aren't the best you can do, and then you make them better. You are going about this like a professional." Then I nudged her to ask, "What other sections of my draft could take work?" She wasn't sure, so I taught her that often writers look for sections of our writing that we like a lot (not just those we don't like), and we think, "How can I build this up even more?" With that impetus, she set out to add details onto and to expand the section showing her sister rounding up things for her to wear.

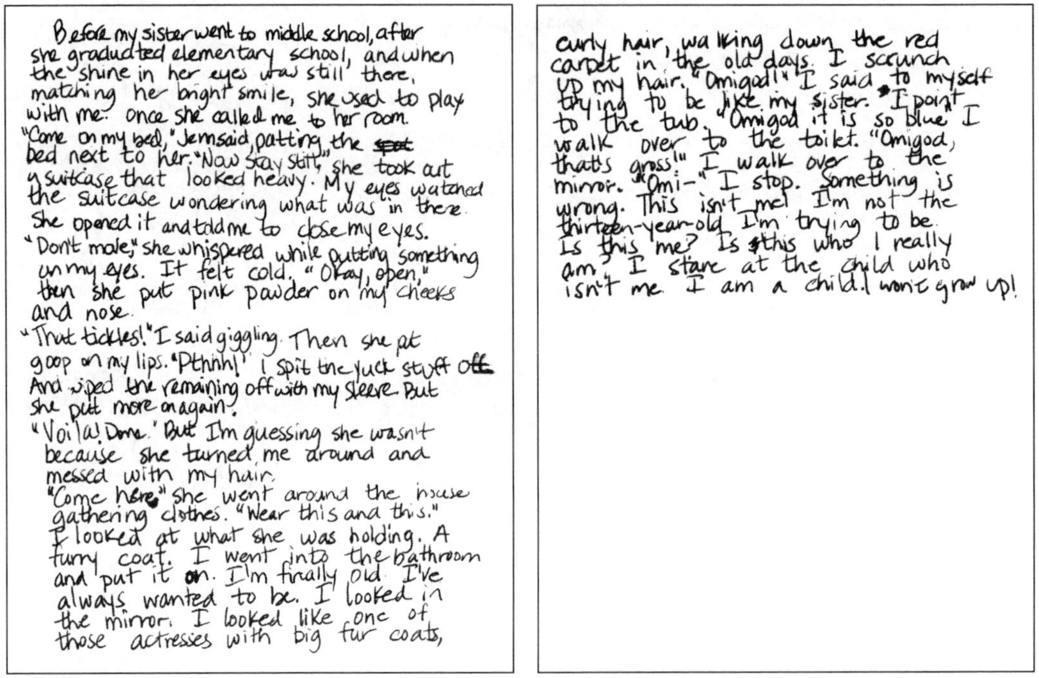

FIG. 16–4 Emily's new draft

At this point, I made notes to myself on a variety of things I could eventually teach Emily, though I would not do it now. First, I was quite clear that I'd want to tell Emily—and others, for she was not alone in this—that she needs to remember that when we write memoir, we are writing about ourselves. So, in the end, I would tell Emily she would need to focus less on her sister and more on herself. Then, too, I'd want to teach Emily ways to expand particular scenes to reveal more about *herself* and her life. Then, too, I'd want to teach her ways to think about the internal timeline of her pieces, as Tyler did with his roller coaster story.

In the end, Emily decided to show that at the start of the episode, she was happy to be dressing herself up to look older. She stretched out the dressing-up part of her piece, adding actions, dialogue, and images that show us how special she felt, at first, wearing makeup and her mom's fur coat. Emily also decided to show that her response changed. She described a turning point of looking in the mirror and seeing how wrong grown-up looks on her. Emily wrote, "I stare at the girl who isn't me. I am a child. I won't grow up." And we readers understand that the longing for and imagination about being grown up is just that. She isn't ready and she doesn't recognize herself as a grown-up. But this work is still just a glint in her eye for now.

SHARE

Looking for, and Revising for, Structure

Tell children that writers read their own drafts, noting the component sections, asking, "How is this draft almost but not quite structured?" Then they make revisions to bring forth and complete the nascent structures.

"Writers, earlier in this unit you read published memoir as if you were flying above them, trying to see their overall layout. You noticed memoir comes in different structures," and I gestured to our memoir structure chart. "Today I want to remind you that writers do not merely *plan* the structure of their writing; they also reread their writing to bring out that structure. Sometimes a text is almost, but not quite, structured in a specific way, and the writer revises to bring out the shape that is just under the surface of a text. Right now, reread your writing. Ask yourself, 'What structure is sort of, but not quite, evident? How could I clean up my writing so that this structure is more clear? Do this quietly, making notes."

We often ask children to study memoir texts at the start of a unit. Now, as children round the last bend of the unit, they can return to these texts, this time viewing them with new eyes.

Channel students to study a text structured like the text the writer hopes to write. Ask children to assign themselves some next steps based on this.

"When you are pretty sure of how you will be structuring your final piece, could you select a short text from the folders I'm putting at the middle of each table? Select a short text that you already know and that you like a lot. Select a text that is structured similarly to the way you want your writing to be structured. Then read it over to find ways it can help your writing." I gave children time to do this. "Writers, give yourself a self-assignment for this evening's work." I gave them time to jot assignment boxes then asked students to tell each other their plans.

Ways to Structure a Memoir...

- Write in a list-like structure, like beads on a string. The beads can be Small Moment stories that are linked (example: times when a writer was shy, or scenes from my childhood alongside the creek). Each memory can be as short as a sentence or two or as long as a page or two.

- A hybrid text that is a mixture of idea-based writing and a story or vignette.

- An essay in which the writer makes a claim and supports it with reasons.

FIG. 16–5

Figure 16–6 shows an excerpt from Joseph's memoir, which he realized had taken on an essay-like structure.

> After spending many times with my grandfather, I have learned that grandfathers are a wealth of knowledge. They love to tell stories, they are tons of fun and they can teach you things. But hanging out with my grandfather is the definition of having fun. He is the most important part of my life.
>
> Grandfathers love to tell stories and my grandfather is no exception to the rule. Last summer, I had a chance to coax my grandfather into telling me a story about World War II, and as he told me his stories, I could picture him in my mind. He was in a back-up unit, searching for the enemy after fighting took place. He was an American soldier, with his gun and his pack, cautiously looking for the enemy. I felt like I was right there in the forest with him!
>
> Grandfathers can teach you interesting things. One afternoon, my grandfather called me into his office and he took out a brown box from his closet; inside were old pictures. We shuffled through them and my grandfather showed me a picture of my mother in the 80's. "Where are the disco balls or the floors that light up?" I asked him. "Please don't tell me there is no John Travolta!" This box that I was looking through was like a time capsule filled with different generations, and my grandfather taught me a lot about my mother's family.

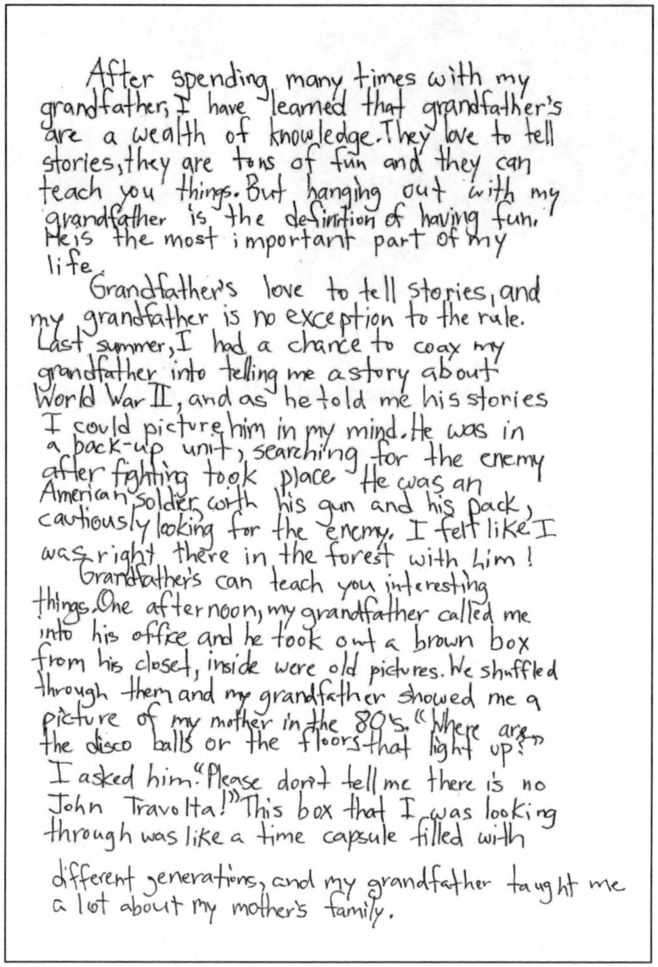
After spending many times with my grandfather, I have learned that grandfather's are a wealth of knowledge. They love to tell stories, they are tons of fun and they can teach you things. But hanging out with my grandfather is the definition of having fun. He is the most important part of my life.
Grandfather's love to tell stories, and my grandfather is no exception to the rule. Last summer, I had a chance to coax my grandfather into telling me a story about World War II, and as he told me his stories I could picture him in my mind. He was in a back-up unit, searching for the enemy after fighting took place. He was an American soldier, with his gun and his pack, cautiously looking for the enemy. I felt like I was right there in the forest with him!
Grandfather's can teach you interesting things. One afternoon, my grandfather called me into his office and he took out a brown box from his closet, inside were old pictures. We shuffled through them and my grandfather showed me a picture of my mother in the 80's. "Where are the disco balls or the floors that light up?" I asked him. "Please don't tell me there is no John Travolta!" This box that I was looking through was like a time capsule filled with different generations, and my grandfather taught me a lot about my mother's family.

FIG. 16–6 Joseph decides that to bring out the essay structure to his memoir, he will add transition words into the topic sentence of his second body paragraph.

Session 17

Metaphors Can Convey Big Ideas

JEROME BRUNER, the great developmental psychologist, has asked, should we not celebrate the day the child begins using combinational grammar? Isn't that the day, he asks, that marks a child's "entry into the human race"? At first, the toddler uses single words to represent things. But, one day, the child will, out of the clear blue sky, say, "Doggy bye-bye." A two-word sentence! And then, Bruner says, this new language work will lay down new mental tracks. Suddenly the child makes himself understood in terms of things and actions. Bring out the trumpets and the confetti! As writers grow, they make many breakthroughs in language that, like the one Bruner celebrates, lift the level of that child's thinking.

When you teach writing, you teach thinking. You help children lay down new mental tracks. Fifth graders come to you already speaking in sentences. But there are still important language lessons to learn, which can give your students whole new layers of understanding. One of the gigantic lessons that you can teach during this unit of study is the power of metaphor.

Metaphor is a way to grasp big ideas and capture meanings that are hard to pin down. My brother Geoff wants to thank our mother, and he knows that it won't work to say, "I am thankful for the Whole Works. It's all been great." So he finds one shining moment—the times, when he was a little boy with leukemia, when Mum would help to pass those long hours in the hospital by taking off her shoe, pushing it into the middle of the room, and taking turns with her son, pitching a penny into that shoe. Years later, when my brother wrote the story of the penny pitching, he wasn't thinking about forming a simile using *like* or *as*; instead, he was thinking, "How can I take this gigantic feeling of gratitude that wells inside me and somehow put it onto the page?"

Your children, too, will be holding insights, feelings, ideas that are too pure and deep for ordinary words. It is time to teach the power of metaphor. If they really learn what metaphor can be, then bring out the trumpets and the confetti, because they'll be laying down new mental tracks, thinking in entirely new ways!

IN THIS SESSION, you'll teach students that writers take a tiny detail from their lives—often something that could be very ordinary—and let that one detail represent the whole big message of their writing.

GETTING READY

✔ Excerpt of writing that uses powerful metaphors, such as *What You Know First* by Patricia MacLachlan (see Teaching)

✔ Story of a student's process of using metaphor in his writing with examples (see Active Engagement)

✔ Story of a student's process of searching for an object to use as a metaphor (see Share)

COMMON CORE STATE STANDARDS: W.5.3, W.6.3.d, RL.5.2, RL.5.4, SL.5.1, L.5.1, L.5.2, L.5.3, L.5.5.a

MINILESSON

Metaphors Can Convey Big Ideas

CONNECTION

Tell children a story that leads you to talk about the times when you—or any writer—wanted to capture something in print that felt too big for words.

"One of my favorite movies is *The Sound of Music*. At the start of the movie, Maria is preparing to become a nun and always gets in trouble because she'd rather be playing in the mountains than sitting solemnly in prayer sessions. At one point, some of the nuns gather and, trying to find the words to describe spirited Maria, they sing, 'How do you hold a moonbeam in your hand?'

"When I write, I often have the same trouble. The meanings that I want to convey sometimes well up inside me, and the more important those meanings are, the harder it is to find the words for them. Like moonlight, they are hard to pin down.

"I think you have all probably struggled with this. How does Joseph find the words to describe the important role his grandfather has played in his life? How will Judah find the words to capture the feelings that well up in her for home, Missouri?"

❖ **Name your teaching point.**

"Today, I want to teach you that writers often take a tiny detail from their lives—often something that could be very ordinary—and let that one detail represent the whole big message."

TEACHING

Remind children of a story they've learned about an author who wants to convey a big idea and does so by embedding that big idea into an object, a metaphor.

"Earlier, I told you that Patricia MacLachlan once said that every book she writes is in some way about a child's longing for home. One day, just after she'd moved into a new home, when she was having a lot of trouble writing, Patti visited a school and told the children there that she thought she was having a hard time writing because she missed the old

◆ COACHING

If you think about it, right here in the minilesson, I am using a metaphor to teach children about writing. I quote those nuns at the start of The Sound of Music, *talking about Maria, asking, "How do you hold a moonbeam in your hand?" This vignette is my way to talk about the challenge every writer faces when they try to capture something fleeting, multilayered, and nuanced, into little black letters on the page.*

Sometimes when our goal is to teach artistry, when we want to convey a quality of good writing that is very special, it helps a lot to refer to published writing. There are lots of advantages. First, you and I can't hold a candle to Patricia MacLachlan's abilities, so leaning on her brings extraordinary power into our minilesson. But also, if MacLachlan serves as the writer in the minilesson, then we are freed up to model learning from the writer, which after all is what we hope our children will be able to do.

house, with its snakes in the basement and mice everywhere. She told the children that she always carried a bag of prairie dirt with her to remind her of her childhood home. Patti then said, 'Maybe I should take this bag of prairie dirt and toss it into my new yard. The two places could mix together that way!' 'No!' cried a boy who was listening in. 'Maybe the prairie dirt will blow away!' And then a little girl said, 'I think you should put that prairie dirt in a glass bowl in your window so that when you write, you can see it all the time. So you can always remember what you knew first.'

"When Patti MacLachlan went to write her memoir, she had a feeling of homesickness for her childhood home well up inside of her. She had ideas about people's longing for home—ideas that didn't fit easily into ordinary words. Then, she remembered that little girl who'd suggested she put her prairie dirt in a glass bowl in her window so that when she wrote she could look at the bowl and remember what she knew first. Patti named her memoir *What You Know First*, after that little girl's advice. "The final page of the memoir tells about a girl bracing herself for leaving her home on the prairie. She considers staying, letting the family go on without her."

Mama says the baby would miss me

If I stay

My Mama says how will he know about the way the

Cottonwood leaves rattle when it's dry,

If I don't tell him.

And how will he know Uncle Bly's songs,

If I don't sing them.

What you know first stays with you, my Papa says.

But just in case I forget

I will take a twig of the cottonwood tree

I will take a little bag of prairie dirt

I cannot take the sky

Debrief, explaining that the author, in the example above, created a metaphor to say something too big for words.

"Did you see what Patricia MacLachlan did? It is something writers do often. She has found one very specific object, and one line of dialogue, too, and used those two things to represent ideas that are too big for ordinary words."

Throughout this unit I support reading-writing connections. In this instance, students reach toward the Common Core State Standards for both reading and writing, wherein students are asked to analyze, interpret and implement figurative language.

ACTIVE ENGAGEMENT

Suggest that children bring out the metaphoric aspects of their writing more, and ask them to help one child do so.

"When you write memoir, each one of you is creating a metaphor for your life. You are taking particular bits of your life and saying, 'Look closely at this bit of my life, because this one bit of my life stands for who I am as a person.' Or you are saying, 'Listen to this story of my father and me, because this story stands for my relationship with my dad.'

"Some of you will want to bring out that metaphor a little more explicitly. Let me tell you about and read you Justin's memoir. Will you think whether you can help Justin bring out the metaphor that is right beneath the surface, ready to be highlighted? Think, 'How might this story represent something huge about Justin and his life?' It won't be easy, so listen really hard," I said. Then I paraphrased part of his memoir and read other sections of it aloud.

"Justin opens his memoir by telling the story of a time in second grade when another classmate, a struggling student, read aloud. Justin has written about this one turning-point moment. His story starts, 'Hearing him read was the funniest thing in the world to me,' and then he continues, telling about how after Daniel stuttered his way through the text, other boys sat around at snack time, impersonating Daniel. 'I . . . want . . . ttto . . . ' After snack, the children reconvened, and this time a girl named Natalie read aloud beautifully. Justin wrote, 'I felt as if I was in the ocean and all the waves were rocking me to sleep.' Soon it was Justin's turn to read, and he was gripped by fear. He wrote":

> "Justin, your turn," Mrs. S. said. I stepped up and walked to the brown chair. I sat down. Chills scattered through my bones as I cradled the book in my hands like a feather floating down the water. My stomach was tossed around. I opened my mouth . . . nothing came out. I tried again as if every word on page 106, chapter 8 would come stumbling out. Still nothing.
>
> I tried one last time. Only a squeak came out. I wish all my troubles disappeared like a popped bubble. They started laughing, then, "Stop! You can't laugh at someone if they did not laugh at you!" I could not believe it. Thanks, Danny.
>
> He stood up for me after he had no reason. The teacher lost her temper and ended reading short. I got up and walked over to my locker.

"Justin," I said. "What do you want to say about you and Danny? What do you want your readers to know at the end of this story?" Justin thought and then said, "That we started to be friends?"

I nodded, and said, "So class, what action might Justin have himself do, or have Danny do, that can be the ending action of this story and can also be a metaphor, conveying the idea he wants to convey? What could one of them do or say that would show that they became friends? Turn and talk."

I selected Justin's draft because he is not a child who finds writing easy, and yet he has done a very significant piece of work. I suspected that he'd benefit a lot from children's help because with their input, he could take his drafts to a whole new level. Meanwhile, it is great for Justin to have the entire class learning to do something very advanced and challenging by standing on his shoulders.

Notice the way Justin reaches for the precise words that capture what fear felt like for him. Notice, too, that this boy, on the cusp of adolescence, trusts his classmates enough to write this beautiful piece.

Soon children were making suggestions to each other. I gathered a list from what I overheard. "I heard some of you suggest that Justin could pull some food out of his locker and offer it to Danny, or that he could look at something Danny owns—his coat, maybe, and say, 'Nice.' Or that Justin could say, 'You want to come over later?' Those are all good ideas. And each of you, in a similar fashion, may find that you can bring objects or actions into your story that carry the deeper meanings you want to convey. You can do this with memoir—and you can do this anytime that you want to write a really significant text."

Before the day was over, Justin had added an ending to his memoir (see Figure 17–1).

> I shut my locker and walked down the hall with Danny
> talking. "So <u>friend</u>, what's new?"

"Justin, your turn," Mrs. S. said. I stepped up and walked to the brown chair. I sat down. Chills scattered through my bones as I cradled the book in my hands like a feather floating down the water. My stomach was tossed around. I opened my mouth…nothing came out. I tried again as if every word on page 106, chapter 8 would come tumbling out. Still nothing.

I tried one last time. Only a squeak came out. I wish all my troubles disappeared like a popped bubble. They started laughing, then, "Stop! You can't laugh at someone if they did not laugh at you!" I could not believe it. Thanks Danny.

He stood up for me after he had no reason. The teacher lost her temper and ended reading short. I got up and walked over to my locker.

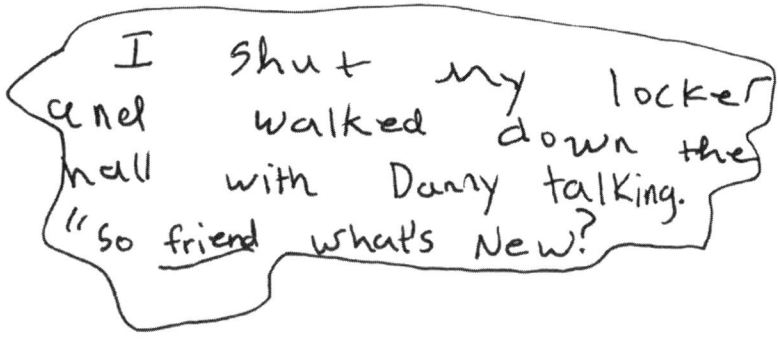

FIG. 17–1 Justin's ending.

CONFERRING AND SMALL-GROUP WORK

Letting the Metaphor Emerge

TAKUMA SAT AT HIS TABLE WRITING, rereading, and then erasing frantically. I approached him, sat down, and asked, "Takuma, how can I help you with your writing today?" He cleaned the eraser bits from the page with the back of his hand and said, "I've been trying to find a way to end my memoir, and after today's minilesson I thought that ending with a metaphor would really help me. But I can't seem to find one that really fits."

I wondered how Takuma was going about trying to find a metaphor. Was he rereading his writing to see the possibilities that already existed? Or was he trying to create a new metaphor? Takuma immediately explained, "I was trying to think of a metaphor that fits my relationship with my dad. I'm writing about how he always helps me and makes me feel safe. So I was thinking that my dad is like a security blanket. Then, I was thinking that I could say that my dad's a night light, but that sounded weird too."

I understood why Takuma was having difficulty. He was trying to think of a metaphor that was not emerging from his memoir. How smart he was to see that this was making his writing inauthentic. I explained to Takuma that he was onto something big. I decided to help him see that, if he thought through the writing he had already done, he would probably find that a metaphor already existed in the text and that it just needed to be given a spotlight. Takuma's job would be to recognize that metaphor and make it stand out. I asked Takuma to explain a bit more about how his writing went.

"Well, for this part of my memoir, I'm trying to show how my dad makes me feel safe. So I wrote a story about when I was on the beach with my dad. We had built a tunnel deep in the sand. I started to go through the tunnel, but as soon as my dad let go of me, I panicked because everything was dark. Then, he lifted me out of the tunnel, and I wasn't scared anymore."

I pointed out to Takuma that he already had the beginnings of metaphor in his writing. "When you are very frightened, Takuma, there is darkness all around you, right? Well, that's a metaphor. You are trying to show something about how you are feeling by using

> **MID-WORKSHOP TEACHING** **Using Refrains**
>
> "Writers, as I walk the room reading your drafts and conferring with you, I can see how you've focused on crafting powerful lines as you compose—lines that hold meaning that is enormous to your writing. Writers often search their writing for lines such as these, looking for ways to highlight them, because highlighting a particularly strong line can also highlight a particularly strong idea. One way to make a powerful line stand out is by repeating it here and there across a piece of writing.
>
> "In 'Eleven,' Sandra Cisneros repeats the line 'Mama is making a cake for me for tonight, and when Papa comes home everybody will sing Happy birthday, happy birthday to you.' Each time I read that line I get goose bumps, because I understand that there is an enormous idea behind it. Sandra might be trying to show through this line that birthdays are supposed to be wonderful occasions that celebrate the beauty of growing up.
>
> She repeats this line across her writing somewhere near the beginning and then again toward the ending. Sandra wants us to pay attention to this idea across the entire piece, so she repeats it to help us say, 'Yes, I see what you're trying to say!' So writers, take a moment to reread your writing for lines that could be highlighted. When you find one, think about where else you might try writing it so that it helps your ideas really stand out."

an image. In this case the image is darkness. Then at the end, you want to show that you come out of the tunnel and your dad is there. So if darkness and fear goes with your dad *not* being with you, what will the world be like when your dad lifts you out of the tunnel?"

Takuma smiled. "I got it," he said. "The beach will be filled with sunlight."

"Takuma, that metaphor is perfect! You've taken the image of darkness that you had already put into your story and you just pop it out, and use it to show your idea. Whenever you want a metaphor, try to do as you've done and find one in your existing draft.

SHARE

Finding an Object to Act as a Metaphor

Tell about one child who wanted to find a significant ending and therefore searched for an object that could stand for something big. Highlight that writers can make actions happen on the page that didn't happen in real life.

"Adam needed to find an ending for his story and decided that maybe he could find a way to use part of his writing as a metaphor. So today he reread his draft looking for some very specific details that he used early in the story, which he could revisit in a way that made those items or those actions represent the huge big feeling that he had, the feeling that is hard to put into words.

"Adam realized that he'd made references to the mournful sound of Jon's bassoon. But there was another object that represented his brother, too, and it wasn't in the early sections of the memoir—yet. So Adam did something very smart: he added that object—his brother's hat—into an early section of the draft. Now when Jon goes to climb into the car, he puts his Penn cap on backward, like always.

"Listen to the ending Adam has written for his piece."

> Jon rolled his window down and motioned me over. I walked up to the car, not sure what to say or do. He gave me a little punch, this time I didn't mind. "I'll miss you," he said.
>
> "Yeah, me too," I said. He handed me his hat.
>
> The car pulled down the driveway. I knew my childhood with my brother was ending this very moment. My brother opened the sunroof and waved his hand. I waved back even though he probably couldn't see me. The car made a left and climbed the hill til it was out of sight. I walked to the end of the driveway to see if I could get one last glimpse of the car. I knew Jon was moving on. It will only be a matter of time before he has graduated from college, gets married and has kids.
>
> I stood there for a moment, then slowly made my way back up the driveway. I remembered I was holding Jon's Penn hat, and put it on backwards just as he always did. I walked to his room and sat down on his bed. I squeezed his pillow and looked for any sign that Jon was once there. I picked up Jon's bassoon and put each piece together the way Jon had taught me. I went over to

This is a beautiful example of a student finding a metaphor within the details of a life story. You can help one of your students find a metaphor too, and use your students' work as an example. The writer must first think, "What should the message be at the end of the piece?" Once the writer knows what she wants to say at the end of the piece, then she needs to ask, "What action could the character do that would convey that?" The writer can brainstorm possibilities. The narrator who remembers a lost grandparent could place a photograph beside his bed, add a photo into his wallet, whisper a message to the missing person at a key moment, imagine an upcoming event and know that the grandparent won't—yet will—be there. Try helping a child imagine possibilities in doing this.

the chair Jon always sat in when he played, and I played the deep mournful sound I had heard coming from his room so many times.

Extrapolate from the example lessons that every child can learn, reminding them of the step-by-step process a writer can go through to create a metaphor. Set children up to help each other.

"So, writers, many of you may want to learn from what Adam has done. If you want to use a metaphor, think about what message you want to convey. Do you want to say you are filled with hope for tomorrow? Then look across your lawn and see the sun rising, its rays turning the world golden. Do you want to say you'd ended one chapter in your life? Then say that you said good-bye, turned to walk away, and didn't look back. You—every one of you—can make metaphor! Turn and help each other."

SESSION 17 HOMEWORK

DESCRIBING OUR WRITING PROCESSES

Our unit of study will soon end, and you'll move on to a final unit of study. Before this unit is over, will you once again take some time to think about what you have learned about the writing process? Earlier this year, I taught you that writers first live like writers, collecting lots of entries. Then we choose one entry to become our seed idea. Then we make a timeline or some other plan for our writing and read other texts like those we want to write. Then after we plan, we write, rewrite, and edit. By now, you have come to realize that the writing process is more complicated than that. Every day for the last week you've been shifting between writing, rewriting, planning, and writing some more. So, tonight I want you to think about how you might describe your own writing process right now. Then, write a bit about it.

Session 18

Editing to Match Sound to Meaning

IN THIS SESSION, you'll build on the work you began in Session 11, teaching students that editing involves, among other things, listening to the sound of writing and refining the text so that it sounds right. Too often, when our students edit, they think only about putting each period, comma, and capital letter into place. They check their spelling and their paragraphs, but they do not check their rhythm or tone. Their eagerness to correct errors is important, but before the year is over, it is also important for students to grasp that editing entails more than correcting.

When writers edit their writing, they read it out loud to hear the sound of each word, to hear the rhythm of their sentences. Truman Capote wrote, "To me, the greatest pleasure of writing is the inner music the words make." The sound of our words is powerful. It's an important part of what communicates our ideas to others. Writers choose words to communicate the mood, the tone, the feelings that they want to convey.

We can help children think about the power of punctuation if we ask them to consider how a passage might sound different (and mean something different) if the punctuation were different. "Why do you suppose this author made such a long sentence, with all these commas?" we can ask, "instead of writing several shorter sentences?"

In this session, you will help students learn that to edit their writing, writers pay attention to the sound of each word, reading the draft aloud over and over. You'll teach children to reconsider their word choices and sentence constructions as well as their punctuation decisions. They will begin an inquiry, studying the editing moves that published writers make to learn techniques that they too can use to strengthen their writing.

IN THIS SESSION, you'll teach students to listen to their writing carefully, then to choose words, structures, and punctuation that help them to convey the content, mood, tone, and feelings of the piece.

GETTING READY

✔ Two samples of writing to edit for sound (you might use your own writing or student writing) (see Teaching and Active Engagement)

✔ "Communicating Ideas through the Sound of Our Sentences" chart (see Active Engagement)

✔ Example of writing that uses punctuation to create sound, such as *Night in the Country* by Cynthia Rylant (see Mid-Workshop Teaching)

COMMON CORE STATE STANDARDS: W.5.5, RFS.5.4, SL.5.1, L.5.1, L.5.2, L.5.3

MINILESSON

Editing to Match Sound to Meaning

CONNECTION

Acknowledge that children already know that writers edit to correct errors.

"Writers, you know that it is important to edit to check for misspellings and to indent your paragraphs. You know that to be taken seriously as a writer, it is important to scrutinize your drafts, reading your writing over and over so that you can find and mend places where your ideas tumble onto each other or where your thoughts hang awkwardly in midair."

❖ **Name your teaching point.**

"But today what I want to emphasize is that when you, as writers, edit your writing, you can also read it out loud to hear the sound of each word, to hear the rhythm of your sentences. Truman Capote wrote, 'To me, the greatest pleasure of writing is the inner music the words make.' The sound of our words is powerful. Writers communicate with readers by choosing words that convey not only the content but also the mood, the tone, and the feelings that they want to convey."

TEACHING

Show students how reading writing aloud can help them to edit for sound. Demonstrate using your own writing or the writing of a student.

"Let's look at a draft of the memoir that Julia has been writing. Julia will read it aloud, and as she does, will you really listen to its sound? Julia will pause from time to time to tell us the images, feelings, and ideas that she wants to convey, and together we'll help her see if the sound of her writing communicates this. Listen to Julia's draft, and then we'll talk about what we notice." Julia read this.

> I stood on the platform. I watched the swimmers speed across the water. I looked down at my dad. I reached to him. I let his hands carry me into the water. "Don't let go!" I cried out. I clung to my dad's neck with both hands.

◆ COACHING

There are several options for how the teaching portion of this lesson might go. I have chosen to model using the work of one student, Julia, who I knew would be comfortable thinking through her writing in front of her classmates. Alternatively, you might choose to model using a small portion of your own memoir, thinking aloud about the ways you might match sound to meaning.

Turning to the children, I said to them, "Did you hear that Julia starts many of her sentences in a similar fashion? 'I stood,' 'I watched,' 'I looked,' 'I reached.' See how those are all so similar? Let's have Julia reread so we can listen for the way the sentences sound similar." I suggested Julia reread, and this time they concurred.

Julia quickly chimed in. "I never saw that before! Every sentence starts the same way! Except for the dialogue."

Highlight that writers decide how to punctuate once the writer knows what she wants to communicate.

Turning to Julia, I said, "This isn't necessarily a bad thing, Julia." Then I added, "The important thing for Julia to decide, class, is whether she wants those parts of her draft to sound the same. That depends on what she is trying to say, doesn't it? What do you want to show in this part of the piece? What feelings were you having?" I asked Julia.

She replied, "I want my reader to understand that there's lots of movement going on around me and that the pool can be overwhelming for me," Julia said. "But I'm also really focused on my dad, and that made me feel like I could go in the pool even though I was scared." Then, looking at her draft, Julia added, "Oh! I know! I need to rewrite this bit about swimming to show that more things were happening. Instead of writing, 'I watched the swimmers speed back and forth across the water,' maybe I should stuff more things into a sentence so the sentence sounds fuller and crazier, like the pool." For a second Julia closed her eyes, imagining the scene, and then she said, "Maybe . . ."

> Swimmers sped into and out of the water making quiet splashes with each stroke and creating short, rough waves.

"Writers," I said. "Did you see that when Julia first read her writing, her words and sentences lacked variety? Then, she edited this one part of her draft—and did so by first deciding to write a long sentence and then by thinking hard about what she wanted to communicate. The sound of her writing has changed, and she has also made her image clearer, hasn't she? "So, writers," I said, jotting on some chart paper, "it seems like we've uncovered two ways we can match meaning to the sound of our sentences. We can vary the way we begin sentences *and* we can vary the length of sentences."

Communicating Ideas through the Sound of Our Sentences

- Vary the way we begin our sentences.
- Vary the length of sentences.

My goal is to help children begin to hear the rhythm that their words and sentences create. I want them to see that if they vary their words and reconstruct their sentences, they can give their writing a new sound and, as a result, create clearer images.

If you choose to use a student to model this work, you might meet with that child the day before to practice. Teach him or her a few strategies to match sound to meaning. For instance, you might introduce the child to the notion of sentence length—namely, that we can make sentences longer or shorter to create a certain mood. You might also teach the student to tell, rather than read, a story, listening for places where she is naturally apt to string words and clauses together. Verbal rehearsal allows children the freedom to convey mood without worries about punctuation—something that can become stymied when they put pen to paper.

ACTIVE ENGAGEMENT

Set students up to examine their own writing for sentence beginning and length variety, and to rewrite any sentences whose structure doesn't convey the intended meaning.

"This is subtle, sophisticated work, but I know you're up for it. Remember a while back in this unit, when I taught you that writers can edit to bring out voice? You learned how to recognize when you were writing in ways that show 'you' on the page. This work is similar. Only now you're going to be listening for the way in which the rhythm of your sentences does or does not convey your intended meaning.

"So right now, pull out your current draft and take a minute to review it, looking at it the way we just looked at Julia's piece. When you notice parts where the sentence structure gets in the way of showing your meaning, think about how you might edit that part—could you vary your sentence length, or alter the ways in which the sentences begin? You might even notice a new editing move that will remedy the problem. Once you have an idea, share it with your partner."

FIG. 18–1   Sirah's scene

As children turned to their own writing, I circled the room, listening in to partnerships. Then I reconvened the group.

"Thumbs up if you noticed a part of your writing that could use a little more variety."

Share out one student's work and solicit students' help in naming how the edits clarify meaning.

"There's so much to see once we start looking closely isn't there? Let me share what Sirah just noticed in her writing. She had written a scene in which she notices that her sister is still on the train . . . *after* Sirah has already gotten off. This was a scary moment for Sirah. Sirah, will you read us your first version? Writers, as she reads, listen to the rhythm of her words, thinking, 'Does the sound of Sirah's words match the content of it?'" Sirah read aloud (see Figure 18–1).

> The doors of the train shut. I saw my sister concealed behind them. She was alone. I didn't know what to do. I just stood there. I watched the train pull away.

"This is a beautiful bit of writing, but it sounds a little robotic—a bit like recording the facts. When she reread it, Sirah realized that each sentence is short and none of them accurately conveys just how terrified she was in this moment. So here's what she did. She rewrote this scene, adding in longer sentences. She did something else, too. See if you spot it." I gestured for Sirah to read aloud her second version.

> Slam! The train doors shut behind me as I stepped from the train onto the platform. My sister wasn't next to me where she had been a moment ago! When I turned to find her, the subway started with her in it. All I could see was . . .

"What do you notice, writers? Try to incorporate today's teaching into your comments." "It's a lot more exciting," Jill said. "I think the longer sentences make you build up to what's coming next."

"Yeah, and I can tell Sirah is scared cause she added 'Slam!' It's like you can see and feel that door shutting."

"Great observations, writers. This new version works so much better to bring out Sirah's fear. A lot of this has to do with how Sirah varied her sentence lengths. She even included a one-word sentence with an exclamation mark. You're right, Jill; that sentence sort of punches us in the face. I bet that's how Sirah felt, when she saw the door shut and realized her sister was on the other side. She also begins her sentences in a variety of ways; this no longer reads, 'I, I, I . . .' It's more interesting, isn't it?"

"Writers, this is just one of many editing and revision techniques you have under your belts, now, but it's a powerful one. As you write today, you might try out this technique if you see a place in your writing where the meaning could be clarified with this sort of editing move."

LINK

Remind writers that today and every day, they can edit their writing to make sure it sounds just right so it communicates their ideas as best it can.

"So, writers, as you make editing decisions today, and on other days throughout your life, remember, it's not enough to make sure each word and sentence looks right. It's not enough to say, 'Oh, I've used capital letters and I've made sure to use punctuation.' We also need to make sure our writing sounds the way we want it to. We need to make sure the sound communicates our ideas."

CONFERRING AND SMALL-GROUP WORK

Using Sentence Structure to Vary the Sound

WILLIAM WAS READING HIS WRITING ALOUD TO HIMSELF. Every now and then he stopped and wrote a note down on his draft. I walked over to listen as he read, and this is what I heard.

> I walked into the bathroom. I turned on the water. I poured bubble bath into the tub. I tested the water with my toe.

I could see that William was trying to write this moment bit by bit, but I noticed that he read right past these lines and didn't seem to pay attention to how this paragraph sounded. So I asked him, "William, can I act as your writing partner? Will you reread this part of your writing to me so that together we can listen to its sound?"

William picked up his draft and read the first paragraph aloud. He stopped, looked, and waited for me to comment. "I like the way you've slowed down this part by using a series of small actions." I paused and let William take in the compliment. "But as you read it aloud, I noticed that each sentence seemed to have the same beat." I showed him what I meant by reading the paragraph aloud and hitting my thigh with my hand so that he could hear the rhythm of my words.

"Oh, I get what you mean. Yeah, I can hear that. Each sentence sounds so much the same." William looked down at his paper and reread that part. He nodded his head and looked up. I asked William if he was game for learning a new strategy that would help him to vary the rhythm of his sentences.

I could have taught William a way to combine sentences like these, using commas to set off each action. That would improve his writing now and in the future. But I decided that William also needed to stretch himself by using something other than a series of actions to tell his story; he needed to use all that he'd learned this year to lift up his ideas and improve the craft of his writing.

MID-WORKSHOP TEACHING
Using Punctuation to Create Sound

"Writers, can I have your eyes and your attention? As I walk around the room, I can hear your memoirs. I can see you editing them and listening to them again to hear how your changes sound. Many of you are reading your writing to your partners, asking them to listen and give you feedback. That's a great idea: sometimes we have a hard time hearing the sound of our own words because we've heard them so many times.

"You're working on varying your word choice and sentence lengths as well as rewording your sentences to add variety to your writing. But there's another choice that writers make that affects the sound, and therefore the meaning, of their writing: punctuation choices. I've put an excerpt up here from *Night in the Country* by Cynthia Rylant. There are three lines in particular that go":

> And, if you lie very still, you may hear an apple fall from the tree in the back yard.
>
> Listen:
>
> Pump!

"That last line is what really brings out the tone and mood. She uses a colon after 'Listen' to set up the sound that the apple makes as it falls. Then she adds an exclamation point after 'Pump' to make that single sound—one that would normally be so quiet—ring out.

"You can play with punctuation as you write so that you can bring out the tone of your writing. Right now, take a minute to reread your writing to see how the punctuation choices you've made help to bring out the tone in your writing. If you don't find that they do, find a spot you might rewrite. From now on, remember that using punctuation is another to way make your writing sound the way you intend!"

"When narrative writers craft their writing, they vary the kinds of details they use. They might include some small actions, but in between, they add details about the time or about the place or about the thoughts they're having—all to bring forth the meaning of the story. Let's look again at your paragraph and try this." William and I read the paragraph silently. Then I read aloud the first line and said, "So let's see how we might add some details about the time and place and the thoughts you had after the first action." I read the sentence aloud. "You're getting ready to run a bath for yourself so that you can relax, right? That's what you are trying to convey?" William nodded. "How about if we add details like this?"

> I walked into the bathroom. The tiles were cold under my feet, but the shag bath mat warmed me up. All my favorite bubble baths lined the rim of the bath tub, leaving me too many choices.

"What do you think?"

"That makes it different! It gives more information about what's going on." "Okay then, William. Try the next line." I pointed to the page. "Remember, you want to add in details other than actions."

William read the line over several times and then said, "Maybe I could write":

> I turned on the water. Steam started to fill the bathroom and fog up the mirror. It was toasty and the temperature was perfect for taking a bath.

"That makes me feel relaxed even reading it! Let's try to put all of that together."

> I walked into the bathroom. The tiles were cold under my feet, but the shag bath mat warmed me up. All my favorite bubble baths lined the rim of the bath tub, leaving me too many choices. I turned on the water. Steam started to fill the bathroom and fog up the mirror. It was toasty and the temperature was perfect for taking a bath.

"Wow! Now the sentences no longer sound the same, and these new details make this scene feel how you intended it to feel! Remember, William, when you are reading your writing aloud to see how it sounds, listen for sentences that sound too similar to each other. Then ask yourself, 'Where can I add in a new and different kind of detail that helps convey my meaning?' Do you know what your work can be right now?"

"Yes, I'm going to try that some more in this paragraph, and then I'm going to see if I've done that in any other places."

SHARE

Editing for Simplicity

Remind writers of the importance of writing with clarity. Ask them to find new partners and together read their writing to be sure every bit rings with clarity.

"All year we have stressed the importance of writing with clarity. You know that adding in lots of lush language can sometimes throw dust in your readers' eyes—keeping them from seeing clearly the worlds that you've created. One of the greatest rules of editing is this: simplify. As E. B. White and his writing partner, William Strunk, wrote in a book about writing, 'A sentence should contain no unnecessary words, a paragraph no unnecessary sentences for the same reason that a drawing should have no unnecessary lines and a machine no unnecessary parts.'

"So, today would you meet with someone other than your partner who can help you edit? Put one person's writing between the two of you, and read it through, inch by inch, asking whether each sentence creates a clearer image and moves the idea along."

SESSION 18 HOMEWORK

USING THE SOUND OF LANGUAGE TO CONVEY MEANING

Today's workshop focused new attention on the sound of our writing and how word and sentence and punctuation choices affect that sound. Being able to listen closely is a tremendously important part of being a writer. The way your writing sounds on the page helps you to convey meaning. Tonight I'd like you to read your writing aloud, just as you did earlier in the unit, and think about how your writing sounds. Ask yourself, "Does my word choice (and sentence structure and punctuation) convey what I'm trying to say?" Underline places where your writing has a strong sound—lonely or confused or elated. Then ask yourself, "Is this the feeling that I want my reader to have?"

Session 19

An Author's Final Celebration
Placing Our Writing in the Company of Others

YOU WILL APPROACH THIS CELEBRATION with poignant feelings. You will be sad because another unit is coming to an end and it won't be long before these children walk right out of your life. You'll look at them, each so quirky and so intense and so very much himself or herself. But, of course, there will be new beginnings around the bend. Author celebrations help us not only look backward, but also forward. We celebrate to name, plan, resolve, and remake ourselves.

In this celebration, family members gather. That alone can be momentous. The *Art of Teaching Writing* (1994) was released for publication just before a large conference at Teachers College. I knew my colleagues had planned a small get-together at the end of the day to toast the book's arrival. I keynoted that conference, as was typical for me. But this time, as I started speaking, I caught sight of a white-haired man in the back of the auditorium. I continued speaking, and as I did, it dawned on me that I was looking at my father.

IN THIS SESSION, students will read aloud their memoir to their friends and family.

GETTING READY

✔ Introduction to the celebration

✔ Preassigned readers for the whole group and for the small groups

"Author celebrations help us not only look backward, but also forward."

Then beside him, I saw Mum. "How could they be here? They live in Buffalo," I thought as I continued, somehow, giving my keynote. As I spoke about writing, I watched each of my words reaching my mum and my dad, and it was as if each word meant something more because it was said in their presence. My talk about writing became also a talk about growing up and families and childhood and values. It was as if I'd written this keynote just for them, as if I'd waited all my life to say these things to them. They sat there, listening

COMMON CORE STATE STANDARDS: W.5.3, W.5.6, RFS.5.4, SL.5.1, SL.5.4, SL.5.6, L.5.3

to my talk and through my talk, to me. It is eighteen years later, but I still have a lump in my throat as I recall what it meant that they were there for me that day. Your children will be reading texts that say, "This is my life." It will be intense for them to read these aloud in the presence of their families.

CELEBRATION

Welcome everyone and set the tone for the ceremony with an introduction or a story.

"When I was a child, I went to Camp Aloha. Each summer would end with all of us campers gathering on the shores of Lake Wannabee. Just as the sun was setting, we'd convene, as all of us are convening now, only at Camp Aloha, each one of us held a handmade wooden boat. It was just a block of wood, really, with a hole drilled in the center so the boat could hold a candle. Standing on the shores of Lake Wannabee, for that final ritual, we'd light the candles on our boats and sing, 'This little light of mine, I'm gonna let it shine, let it shine, let it shine, all the time.' Then as we sang, one camper, and another, would approach the lake, crouch down by the water's edge, and cast our boats off. Then we'd step back into the group and, linking arms, we'd watch the little flames of light bob across the lake, into the dark corners, and we'd sing. 'This little light of mine, I'm gonna let it shine. Hide it under a bushel? No. I'm gonna let it shine. Don't you try to blow it out! I'm gonna let it shine, let it shine, let it shine, all the time.'

"I say this to you now, because in a sense, each of the children here is holding his or her own little flame of light, and today these children will send their light into the world. Their ideas, their stories, their voices.

"And our message to these children of ours is 'This little light of yours, you've got to let it shine, let it shine, let it shine, all the time.'"

Explain the way the ceremony will go. In this case, explain that a few children will share with the whole group, then the group will divide, and the rest of the children will share with one of the two smaller groups.

"We'll begin with a few writers sharing their memoirs with all of us, and then we'll disperse into just two groups. These are larger groups than usual, but I know on this occasion that you'll want the chance to hear more, and I know all of the children here are eager for the larger audience."

Saying Good-Bye
By Adam

My brother came outside with one last suitcase in his hand. He crammed it into the back of my mom's car with all the others. Then Jon slammed the back of my mom's car shut. Through the tinted glass I could see the soccer ball that we would shoot into our goal on hot summer evenings. Our eyes met when he turned around. Sadness flew straight into me as clear as the mournful sound of Jon's bassoon. My brother hugged me. I pulled him closer. "I'm going to miss you badly," he said.

"I will, too," I managed to squeak out, my voice hoarse. It was already happening: my eyes brimmed. I tried to blink back tears, but they wouldn't stop. Tears started pouring out over my eyes. It reminded me of when I was playing basketball and I fell. Pain throbbed through my arm. Jon came to take me to the hospital. With Jon there, I felt safer, calmer, less scared. It reminded me of when I was in camp and I hadn't gotten a letter for days, and loneliness was starting to haunt me. Jon's letter came and filled me with laughs and warmth and a feel that it was good to have a big brother.

I looked up and saw one tear roll down my brother's cheek. He brushed it away, but I remembered it.

My dad appeared from the house, carrying an old picture of my brother close to his chest like it was a billion dollars. My brother's face was fat and round in the picture. Hair was starting to grow in on the top of his head as if it were a flower, sprouting. I looked up at my dad and he was wiping his eyes with the back of his hand. My dad sat down on the hood of the car and studied the picture like a textbook. He couldn't stop looking at it.

"It's time to go," said my dad "Say your good-byes now." Wearing his Penn hat backwards, Jon walked over to the passenger seat of the car, climbed in, and closed the door. He rolled the window down and motioned me over. I walked up to the car, not sure what to say or do. He gave me a little punch. This time I didn't mind. "I'll miss you," he said.

"Yeah, me too," I said. As I walked away, he handed me his hat.

The car pulled down the driveway. I knew my childhood with my brother was ending this very moment. My brother opened the sunroof and waved his hand. I waved back even though he probably couldn't see me. The car made a left and climbed the hill till it was out of sight. I walked to the end of the driveway, to see if I could get a last glimpse of the car.

I knew Jon was moving on. It will only be a matter of time before he has graduated college, and gets married, and has kids.

I stood there for a minute, then slowly made my way back up the driveway. I remembered I was holding Jon's Penn hat and I put it on backwards, just as he always did. I walked into his room and sat on his bed. I squeezed his pillow and looked for any sign that Jon was once there.

I picked up Jon's bassoon and put each piece together, the way Jon taught me. I went over to the chair Jon always sat on when he played, and I played the deep mournful sound I had heard coming from his room so many times.

FIG. 19–1 Adam's final draft

Writing by Emily

Before my sister went to middle school, when the shine in her eyes was still there, matching her bright smile, she used to play with me. We used to play merry-go-round-chair on my mom's spinning chair, but all that changed when she went to middle school.

One afternoon she called me to her room. "Come on my bed," Jen said, patting the spot beside her. "Now stay still." She took out a suitcase from under her bed and put it beside us. She opened it and told me to close my eyes. "Don't move," she whispered while putting powder on my eyes. She spread it around and around with a brush. It felt cold. "Okay, open," she said. She moved back to get a far view of me.

Then she dabbed pink powder on my cheeks and nose. Her brush swept up and down. "That tickles!" I said, giggling. Soon Jen was putting goop on my lips. She spread it around with a lip-gloss wand. "Pthhhh!" I spit the yucky stuff off, and wiped the remaining goo. Jen put an extra dab of blush on my cheeks and finished.

"Voilà. Done." But then she changed her mind and started putting curlers in my hair. "While we wait, come here," she said. I followed her around the house as she gathered clothes. "Wear this and this." I looked at what she was holding; my mom's furry shawl.

I went into the bathroom and wrapped it on. I stared at myself in the mirror. I took the curlers off and fluffed my hair. I looked great! I was finally old; I'd always wanted to be. I looked like one of those old Hollywood actresses with big fur coats and curly hair, walking down the red carpet. I scrunched my hair. "Omigod!" I said to myself, trying to be like my sister. I pointed to the tub. "Omigod! It's so round!" I walked over to the toilet "Omigod! That's so gross!"

To the mirror, I said, Omi-" I stopped. Something was wrong. "This isn't me!" I thought, "I'm not the thirteen-year-old I am trying to be." I splashed water on my face, scrubbing the teenager away. I combed water through my hair and the curls unraveled.

Being a child means jumping on the bed, having laughing contests, making funny faces. I don't want to lose that. When guests come over and look at my baby pictures, or if they haven't seen me in a long time, they say, "Awwww, you've grown so much!"

I have grown taller, but inside I'm still the little girl who plays with Barbies, and the one who's still afraid of lightning. I am the little girl who needs my mom right by my side me. I don't want to grow up! Not yet.

But I did look pretty good in that shawl.

FIG. 19–2 Emily's final draft

Henry's final draft

I've had fun times, and have gone many places. In order to have this much fun I've realized you have to take the chance of always living life to the fullest when you can. When you live life to the fullest it can take away your fears, living life to the fullest can also push your motivation to try new things, and living life to the fullest can help you appreciate what life offers.

When you life life to the fullest it can help take away your fears. I always try to do what I can in the mindset of "now" is your only chance. One example is that when I go to camp every year, I can hear the excitement roaring about what I think is the best amusement park—Dorney Park. 'Hang Time'—one of those loop-de-loop-de-flip rides was blurting fun and fright straight at me. Approaching the ride I could feel butterflies in my stomach. "I have to go on this ride," I thought to myself. I mean, really, who could lose an opportunity like this. But I still had "the feeling" inside me. I begged my friends to do it with me so I wouldn't be so scared.

"Lauren, Frankel" I hollered as they walked toward me.

"That" I said, as I pointed at 'Hang Time.' Their eyes popped with excitement and fright. We pushed aside the heavy metal entrance, and we were in. . . . I had the time of my life! When you live life to the fullest you can ignore your fears.

When you live life to the fullest it can push your motivation to try new things. Even if you end up hating your experience, nothing will ever hurt to try. One time I remember going to Steamboat, Colorado with my dad and brother. I walked with the desire to have fun and try something new. The loud music struck me as I scanned the beverage menu.

"An ice cream float? What in the world is that?" I asked in confusion.

"Try it!" answered my dad. The waitress arrived at the table in her all black attire. "I'll take an ice cream float" I said anxiously. This WAS my only chance to try one. When I spotted the shiny glass filled with pure paradise I was so excited. I placed my lips against the straw and took a sip . . . it was amazing! Trust me—I had many ice cream floats after that!

When you live life to the fullest it helps you appreciate what life offers. When you have a privilege you have a right to use it—that's when you really appreciate what life offers. For example, every year I'm fortunate enough to travel to several places like Colorado and Utah, Israel, and the Dominican Republic. Traveling to these places lets me see, taste and fully experience new traditions and culture, but most of all—just pure vacation! I'm really appreciative to be able to travel this much and see those special traditions and customs. Another example is being <u>very</u> appreciative for all my friends and family members, who I care for a lot. I'm very lucky to have people who I trust, care for, and definitely live life the fullest with! All those special moments, parties, inside jokes and a lot of courage to stick together. Being with people you trust can be one of the best things life has to offer.

From airplanes flying to new places, rustling rollercoasters, fabulous foods and more—living life to the fullest always serves me good. Living life to the fullest has helped me take away my fears, push my motivation to try new things, and last but not least, appreciate what life offers. Overall, I hope I always try to live life to the fullest so I can keep having chances to have amazing moments.

FIG. 19–3   Henry's final draft

My Grandmother
By Tyler

Have you ever made someone go on something you hated? Did you ever say, you don't have to go on? Or let's not do this? Well, that is the part of you that is eleven years old. Or when you say, please can you go on? That is the part of you that is four. And when you don't let her get off, that is the part of you that is two. Well, this happened to me once.

I stood at the line to get on the roller coaster, next to my grandmother. I was amazed at the roller coaster. My eyes followed it as if it were the strongest magnet in the world, and every second I got closer, closer and closer. The sun beat down on my grandmother and me. Nothing could stop me from getting on. And before I knew it, the roller coaster zoomed right next to me as it almost knocked me off my feet. Impatiently I waited to get on. I jumped up and down like a kangaroo. My hands shook from side to side, not wanting to wait any longer.

I saw five people get off and I heard, "That was awesome, let's do that again." That only got me wanting to go on even more. I heard the cranking of the roller coaster as it went up and up. And then it stopped for a half a second and I dropped like a cannonball getting shot out of a cannon. I heard a scream as the roller coaster hovered over my head. But in a theme park with a lot of roller coasters, you shouldn't be so surprised when you hear screams from a roller coaster.

Then it swooped up to the left, then another drop and another scream. "Out of the corner of my eye, I spied my grandma sighing with a scared face. The ride tracks made a sharp left and the people were tugged to the left, then up. I heard nothing else, noticed nothing else. There was only the roller coaster. A drop, and a thunder scream, then it tugged to the right and suddenly stopped! And then they got off. I saw the big sign that read THE INTIMIDATOR. I waited impatiently, wanting to block everyone off from moving and just cut the whole line. I could not pay attention to anyone or anything else.

Suddenly I noticed my grandma was acting strange. She stared wide-eyed, like it was some kind of monster. She shouldn't be going on this ride, I said to myself, feeling sick inside.

FIG. 19–4   Tyler's final draft

"Grandma, if you don't want to go on you don't have to. It is a pretty big ride."

"Tyler, I want to do this. If I don't go on this is roller coaster, I will be afraid of roller coasters for the rest of my life," she announced to me.

"This is our last chance; do you want to get off?" I said to her.

"No, Tyler. I want to stay." She said this, but anybody could know that she was lying.

We stepped into the roller coaster and sat down. As we sat, we pulled the handlebar against our stomachs. I heard a click, click as it locked. And I realized my grandma was trapped into her worst fear. Like when you have the scariest nightmare and you just can't wake up and it feels like forever.

We were cranked up like a huge fish. We moved up and up and up and her hand tightened, harder and harder on mine. At the top we stopped and, just before we began to fly down, I heard a scream so loud it felt like my ears drums had exploded. I pulled my hand away from her and tried to close my ears as hard as I could.

As I covered my ears I said to myself, why would I make my grandma go on a scary roller coaster? Who else can I blame but myself? I knew she would scream like a crazy person from the beginning to the end. She wouldn't do it for anybody but me. I turned my head and saw her face. She was still screaming and so scared.

As we got off the ride, she said, "I am sorry for ruining your ride, Tyler. I kind of overdid it on the screaming."

"You made it better by going on with me. And if you didn't go on I would forget it after a while. That was a ride I will never forget," I said, my ears still hurting.

"That is the last ride in my life. I will never go on that again—or any other ride," Grandma panted.

"Until tomorrow. Then we will go on a bigger ride," I replied with a smile.

FIG. 19–4 (continued)

When You Stay
By Ali

Some people think being brave is jumping off a cliff, running into a burning building and saving a person, diving in front of a bullet. Well, I think being brave is also telling off a bully, not running away from something you're scared of, waiting. And at first you may feel like you let someone important in your life down, that you weren't as brave as you wanted to be. It could be you don't hardly see your braveness. That is what I think being brave is.

I stood in the dark hallway in front of my parents' bedroom door, which led to the bed where my dad was lying. I pushed open the door. It swung all the way back to the wall and made a little clicking sound when it hit. I saw my dad, a pile of pillows and blankets all around him. I didn't go in, not yet. I am going to go in there and act normal, as if nothing is wrong. I will tell him about my almost goal and my 95% in spelling. This time he will say, "Good!" to me.

I walked in, then started to turn around. I stopped mid-turn. "No, Ali, stay," I told myself. I took a deep breath. I began to walk toward the bed again. I crawled up onto the bed, being very quiet, trying not to wake him if he was asleep. He wasn't.

"Today at soccer I was running down the field. I wound up for a big shot, kicked it . . . ! It stopped about two feet from the goal. We can work on my shooting together," I said.

No reply.

Does he not care? Is he in too much pain? That was it, that was the whole reason he was in bed. Too much pain! The pain had not only taken over my dad's life, it had taken over mine.

I stared at him with tough eyes. I wanted him to know that I was upset with him. He had caused me a lot of pain. He didn't get to see my almost-goal and he didn't get to help me study for my spelling test.

He looked back at me with sad puppy eyes. He was sorry.

I don't know if I wanted to forgive him. Giving me a little twitch of his eye, a little brush of his hand against the blanket. That wasn't normal for him. It amazed me. He was such a full guy. His movements were always full, not half.

I had to forgive him, though. He needed me and I needed him. I stayed, waiting for him. I sat next to him, holding his hand, watching the clock tick by . . . 3:33 . . . 3:34 . . . 3:35 . . .

I gently let go of his hand and placed it by his side. I got up and walked back to the doorway. I stood leaning against the wall, looking at him. I stood there, waiting. Expecting him to talk to me, expecting him to push his pain behind him. If I stood there long enough, he would come, get up, and practice my shot with me.

No, he couldn't. I knew that. So I guess I was just going to have to wait awhile. So I stayed.

When you're done falling off a cliff, when you're out of surgery to check for infections from when you were shot with a bullet, people clap and cheer for you and on your return home, news cameras are waiting to interview you. Those people's signs of bravery are on the outside. But when you walk away from a bully that you left behind wide-eyed, or when you stand close to the thing you were once scared of, those people's signs of bravery are the feeling of proudness, the feeling of people clapping that is on the inside of you. My sign was little sparkles, like a fairy sparking her golden dust over me.

FIG. 19–5 Ali's final draft